MW00633686

BEATEN, BATTERED
AND DAMNED

THE DRANO MURDER TRIAL

Robert B. French, Jr., BS, LLB, JD

Publisher-The Blackstone Company
308 Alabama Avenue Southwest
Fort Payne, Alabama 35967
ISBN: 978-1-54395-342-8

Also by Robert B. French, Jr.:

AN ADVENTURE WITH JOHN
THE LAWyer

Dedicated to Criminal Defense Lawyers who represent shockingly evil clients.

INDEX

PREFACE

I am fast approaching the age of 84. My children are educated and doing well. My grandchildren are the apple of my eye. My darling wife of 46+ years, Celeste, has been gone some 15 years. I still live in the home Celeste and I built on the west brow of Lookout Mountain 730 feet above Fort Payne, Alabama. There are 5 bedrooms, 4 baths and so on. It takes me two days to clean it every two weeks. I live alone with Red, a Standard Poodle. So, although you may see me suffering and plodding along deep in the Neelley case, you will never see me giving up nor whining. Tough as it was, I lived through it; and I have had a wonderful life.

I began this book as trial notes and diaries of the events when they were happening. I delayed reducing it to final form until I felt it was time to share my experiences of these horrible rapes, murders, thefts, and so on. To take you inside the trial of Judith Ann Neelley and how we defended her, I have quoted from the testimony in court, from my diary, and from other public records, such as motions, briefs, and court orders. Just skip the parts you find boring.

Being a trial lawyer, I am a storyteller. From time to time I will digress and tell you what may seem like a totally unrelated story; however, my purpose here is to allow you to experience one of the worst crime sprees in American history. This story includes horribly explicit sadism, torture, rape, kidnaping, murder, attempted murder, arson, theft, robbery, burglary, embezzlement, and forgery, among other crimes. And just when you think it can't get any worse, it does get worse.

It has taken me almost 33 years to be able to face this case again, and tell you my story. It was the darkest time of my life; rumor; the financial strain; the accusation from 'friends,' the community; and even some church members because I was defending Judith Ann Neelley.

Most of the public thought I was defending Neelley voluntarily. People didn't realize that when the court tells a lawyer to do something, it must be done. Even today, older people still associate me with this case with great disdain. Weekly, since I was threatened with a court order to take the case, I receive inquiries about the case. Book companies, television shows, movie producers, prospective authors, students, actors and distant lawyers want information about the Judith Ann Neelley Case. Sometimes I say into the inquirer on the telephone, "Well, this week is your week to mention Judith Ann Neelley."

The folks calling about the case never realize that I have lived and breathed it for years; that it is a hard story to tell; that it brings up so many dark memories; and that it is difficult to find the good that comes out of everything if one looks hard enough.

I have condensed the facts involved in my life during the Neelley representation, and I have written them as I would write a letter to you explaining what happened. I hope that you may experience the facts, the investigation, the preparation, trial, and final outcome with me.

As the events unfold along comes the wife beating that we now call domestic abuse. This was not a common term in 1982. The case added a new legal defense for women who kill - "The Battered Woman Syndrome." You will find it difficult to believe the horrors Alvin Howard Neelley visited upon his wives. In the end, you will be called upon to decide, was Judith Neelley guilty or not guilty.

I want this book to be interesting as well as a learning experience for the reader. Always remember as you read: this is not fiction;

these things really happened; and the horror and sickness of it is something that is next to impossible to forget

CHAPTER ONE

IT BEGINS

———◆———

September 28,1982, 9:30 a.m., it was Tuesday. The girl stood in the wind two feet from the edge of the canyon. She looked down and saw Little River 430 feet below her. She could see the tops of pine trees as they clung tenaciously to any spot of available dirt on the ledges stair-stepping the shear rock walls.

The autumn sky was clear blue. Lisa had just passed 13. She had blonde, almost brown hair, blue eyes, and a cute streak of freckles across her nose. She was very pretty, a well developed girl for her age, as she had been the victim of rape by her father.

Now she stood in jeans, with a loose shirt, the one she had worn when she ran away from the orphanage in Rome, Georgia two nights ago. She didn't know why she did it. Her medical examination said that she was a compulsive run-away. She must have been one, because she took a ride from the Riverbend Mall, orphanage sponsored shopping trip, with the booger woman.

She remembered that her mother had always warned her, "Never get in the car with a strange woman. She will kidnap you, her man will rape you, and she will kill you. She's the booger woman." Lisa wished she had listened.

The wind blew a little stronger. Lisa shivered. It wasn't that cold. It must have been the drain cleaner that the woman had injected into her body. Judith Ann Neelley, doing what her husband told her to do, had handcuffed Lisa to a tree. There she had injected her with Drano, through her clothes, four times. When nothing happened, the man told the woman to inject Lisa in the neck. She did, twice. The places where the needle stuck were stinging bad.

"Can I have another shirt to put on? I'm cold."

"Can she have another shirt?

From the trees, "No, the shots will take effect soon."

Lisa hoped the couple would let her go. She wouldn't tell anyone that the fat guy had raped her for two nights running, or that the woman had hit her over the head with a black jack. If only they would let her go she would never run away again. Her head still hurt.

"I'm cold. Can I please have another shirt to put on?"

"It won't be long, Judith said. "These shots will take effect soon. Just a while longer and it'll all be okay."

THE PLACE

Little River Canyon is one of the most beautiful places in the world. A wild river, gushing springs, creeks, waterfalls, and other scenic wonders may be found in its 34 miles of the 83 miles that make up Lookout Mountain. Little River Canyon is the most spectacular gorge east of the Mississippi River; only the Grand Canyon overshadows it in size. Little River Canyon is colorful and rock-faced with sandstone bluffs that change personalities with the season. Little River is one of three wild rivers left in the United States.

There are Indian carved multi-room homes in the sheer rock walls. Experts cannot explain who carved out these dwellings some 300 feet above the river.

It is nigh impossible to hike the canyon as it is some of the most inhospitable country in the world. The rocks are larger than automobiles and there are places the hiker must climb the canyon walls to circumnavigate where the river fills the gorge completely.

Night comes early and the temperature drops drastically. People report seeing wolves, wild dogs, mountain lions, and bears from the rim of the canyon.

A FAMILY OUTING

A casual observer coming across the husband and wife, teenager, and twins that morning in September might think they were just a family out enjoying the view, the weather - maybe even having a picnic. But what was happening was no picnic. It was murder, cold-blooded sadistic murder.

Earlier that morning Judith and Alvin had left the Five Points Motel in Scottsboro, Alabama bound for a location that Alvin had located during his first marriage. He was driving his clean red Ford Granada with Judith, her two year old twins, and Lisa Millican, following in her dirty brown Dodge. They communicated by CB radios--Nightrider and Lady Sundown--looking for the 'perfect' spot. Alvin liked the canyon overlook near a grove of trees with a concrete picnic table with benches.

Seventeen-year-old Judith had never given anyone a shot in her life, but Al had meticulously shown her how to load the syringe, and then inject the needle.

Alvin, hidden from view in a grove of trees, stood with hands on hips watching and listening to everything going on between Lisa and Judith. He thought that he had it all figured out; but, as usual with Judith, it wasn't working as he had planned.

"Give her another shot, you worthless slut. Can't you do anything right?" It had been more than two years since Alvin had called her by her name. He always called her "slut," "whore," "bitch," or worse. In public, he might call her "you."

"I'm really cold and I'm sleepy too." Lisa was now crying.

"Al, can I get her a sweater or something?"

"No, you dumb bitch. You're just like your mother, nothing but a nigger fucker. If you don't hurry up and do this right, I'm going to kill you."

The Drano wasn't working. Alvin had been told in prison that if a person was injected with Drano, the person would die of an untraceable heart attack, but when he sent Judith into the store to buy the necessary ingredients, she bought Liquid-Plumr, and insulin needles. She took a beating for that.

"I've got to go to the bathroom. Can I please go to the bathroom?"

"Let the bitch go to the bathroom but hurry up."

Judith knew she was going to get another beating because it was taking so long for Lisa to die. She looked back at the car to see what the twins were doing. They were a week away from being two-years-old and they wanted to get out of the car and run and play in the 'park.' Alvin was angry with them because they kept throwing things out of the car and making noise.

Al didn't come out from his hiding in the trees. He just yelled out instructions.

When she finished urinating, Al instructed, "Make her walk around some. Maybe that will get the Drano to flowing through her body."

Judith walked Lisa around for about five minutes but she still wouldn't die. She just seemed a little groggy, and was whimpering and begging to go back to the Home.

"I'm tired of waiting - here!" Alvin handed Judith a .38 Special loaded with wad cutter bullets. "Take her close to the edge, turn her facing the canyon, and shoot her in the back. Her body will fall over into the canyon and we'll be done. And, do it right, goddamn it!"

Back on the canyon rim, Lisa was begging. "Can I please just go back to the Harpist Home? I miss my mama. I want my mama. I promise I'll never tell anybody." She was whimpering quietly now, and she was shivering from the cool mountain air as the effects of Drano were coursing through her small frail body.

4

Everything the Neelleys had done to Lisa - rape, torture, Drano, canyon, all of it was done in front of the twins.

KIDNAP AND RAPE

On the night Lisa Ann Millican was picked up, the Neelleys had driven around all day looking for girls. They had arrived at Riverbend Mall around midday. Alvin and Judith were wearing T-shirts with rebel flags on the front of them. Alvin decided to play video games while he sent Judith out into the mall to look for women. Alvin became angry with Judith for failing to pick up an 11 or 12-year-old girl in the video arcade.

In Alvin Neelley's mind, while his wife had been in the reform school, she had been sexually abused, raped repeatedly and brain washed. He was determined to get even. His efforts against the perpetrators of his imagined sexual violations of his wife had been unsuccessful. He decided to embarrass the authorities by kidnapping women, raping them and having his wife murder them. It was an insane plan, but one that Alvin Howard Neelley Junior was determined to carry out.

While Judith had attempted to persuade girls to "go for a ride," Alvin concealed himself while he played Frogger. As the Neelleys were leaving the mall, Alvin spotted Lisa Ann Millican standing in front of the mall looking around as if she had lost her ride. Alvin told Judith to talk to her, and offer to take her wherever she needed to go. If she got in the car, Judith was to drive towards Cedartown and keep driving. Alvin would talk with her on the CB, and they would meet somewhere.

Judith went down the front of the mall, introduced herself to Lisa, and asked her if she needed a ride. Lisa said she was there in a van with some friends, but she couldn't find them. Some men had been bothering her, and she was scared. Judith offered to take her wherever she wanted to go.

Lisa said that she really had no place to go. Judith drove around the mall so Alvin could see them before heading toward Cedartown. It was then that Lisa told Judith that she was from the Harpist Home, and she really didn't want to go back there. Judith told Lisa that she had been in a Youth Detention Center (YDC) before, and she knew what it was like in a place like that. Al had Judith convinced that the YDC played mind games with the inmates, that they practiced sexual abuse on the girls, and that there was hatred in those places. Lisa agreed with Judith.

Soon Judith started talking with Alvin on the CB radio telling Lisa that Alvin was her boyfriend who lived in Rome, and was very kind to her. She told Lisa that Alvin had bought the car for her. Continuing to make small conversation, Judith told her that she had a set of twins who were staying with her mother-in-law. This was the story Alvin had given Judith, and he had rehearsed it with her warning her not to mess it up.

They stopped their cars, and Lisa and Judith walked to Alvin's car which was now stopped behind them. Judith introduced Lisa to Alvin. They decided to drive on to Franklin, Georgia where they stopped for the night at the Chattahoochee Motel.

After dinner, Alvin told Judith to tell Lisa he wanted sex with her. Lisa refused. Alvin told Judith to hit Lisa over the head with a slapjack that he had, and tell her that she was going to hurt her if she didn't have sex with him.

Judith took Lisa in the bathroom and begged her to have sex with Alvin. Lisa refused. Judith hit her in the head with the slapjack, and threatened her. Dazed, Lisa reluctantly agreed. The slapjack had hurt. Alvin took a chain, handcuffs, and chained Judith to the bed. She was forced to sleep on the floor and relieve herself in a pot used to warm baby bottles. The twins slept on a pallet.

COLD BLOODED MURDER

Now in the trees, the girl didn't know what the Neelleys were going to do to her. She knew what they had done, and so she cried.

With the pistol behind her back, Judith marched Lisa back up to the canyon rim.

"Lisa, you'll be better off this way. That home is evil and they're not going to let you go back to your mama. Remember, they took you away from her. You'll be much better off where you're going than back in that home."

Lisa heard the fat man holler in an ugly voice, "Get it over with, Bitch! You can't do nothing right. Do it! Goddamned you, you nigger fucking slut!"

Al was getting more and more angry, so without any hesitation, in near robotic-like motions, Judith pulled the trigger one time and the bullet hit Lisa squarely in the back. She was dead before she hit the ground.

The report of the .38 special died slowly as it echoed through the canyon walls in the crisp air, and after a few brief seconds, the canyon was beautifully quiet once more. However, no birds were singing, no sound from any of the 145 species that are indigenous to that area; no scurrying noises from the animals out scouting for a morsel of food; even the fish seemed to stop breaking the surface of the water below for just a moment in time. For in that one instant, the explosion had been deafening.

Lisa didn't fall over in the canyon like Al had said she would. Instead she just crumpled to the ground settling quietly on the earth right in front of Judith.

Through swollen parched lips, Judith broke the silence dutifully reporting, "She didn't fall in the canyon, Al."

"Now you've got to throw her over the edge, you stupid bitch. Can't you do anything right? Just push her over the edge, slut."

Judith knelt down, and with her right knee, pushed thirteen-year-old Lisa Millican over the edge of Little River Canyon. Her body tumbled and bounced as it folded when it landed on a ledge. Her arms were draped around a pine tree stump as if she was trying to stop herself. It was a burned tree trunk sticking out of a sharp incline of the canyon wall. Many bones in her small body were broken.

When Judith stood up she noticed Lisa's blood on her jeans. "I got her blood on me," she wailed in panic. "What am I gonna do?

"Take off the goddammed jeans, fool, and throw them and the other stuff over in the canyon. And hurry the fuck up."

Judith threw her jeans, along with a hand towel from the motel, hypodermic syringes, and a plunger over the rim of the canyon. They scattered near Lisa's body.

Eighteen-year-old Judith Ann Neelley stood now in her panties and shirt visibly pregnant. With pistol in hand, she walked from the canyon rim to her car, opened the trunk, piled with mixed rumpled up dirty, and clean clothes. She fumbled around until she found a pair of jeans. Without dressing, she walked through the trees and handed Alvin the pistol.

"Get dressed, goddamn it! We need to get out of here. That damned shot probably rang out for miles in this fucking canyon."

With a dazed expression on her face, Judith Ann Neelley put on her clean pair of wrinkled jeans. She pulled them up as far as she could. She tucked in her shirt, fought the zipper, checked on the twins, and got behind the wheel.

Before they left Little River Canyon, Al went and looked over the edge of the cliff and when he saw Lisa's dead body all broken up resting on the tree limb, he smiled. Then Judith heard him making guttural groans and grunts as he quickly masturbated while peering down at little Lisa's lifeless body on the narrow ledge some 50 feet below.

Leaving the canyon, as was their custom, Alvin pulled out first and she pulled in close behind him. He turned right on the Canyon Parkway, drove two miles to Alabama Highway 35, and turning right again, headed toward Rome, Georgia.

"Lady Sundown, this is Nightrider here. I sure did like that. We're going to go out later tonight and you're going to pick me up another girl. I'm sick of you, you slut. I want some young virgin pussy."

And so occurred the horrific event in DeKalb County, Alabama that changed my life forever.

CHAPTER TWO

TWISTS AND TURNS

———◆———

October 15, 1982, 3:47 p.m., the phone rang. "Mr. French, Judge Cole is on line one for you."

Having been in industry, I knew that nothing good comes from the boss calling an underling. There was nothing good that could come from the telephone call. I pushed line one and said, "Yes sir, Judge."

"Bob, I'm going to have to ask you to do something I really hate to ask you to do."

"What's that, Judge?" I didn't like the setup, but I was completely innocent of whatever he wanted.

I'm going to have to ask you to undertake the defense of that young girl they caught yesterday."

"What young girl?"

"Oh, you know the one - the girl from Murfreesboro, Tennessee, who is accused of kidnaping that young orphan at the Riverbend Mall in Rome, Georgia, while the child was on a field trip from the orphanage? In a span of a very few days they say she took the child to Little River Canyon, shot her in the back with a .38, and pushed her over the rim of the canyon. She may be accused of injecting the child with some caustic substance in an effort to kill her to make it appear to have been a heart attack. This case is going to attract considerable publicity, and you can not only give her a fair trial, you can handle the press."

"Hang on, Judge. No –hang on a minute! Are you talking about that woman from Georgia who injected the little girl with Drano, shot her in the back, and pushed her body over the edge?" I interrupted.

"I believe that is the accusation, yes. I'm afraid so, that's the one," the judge responded in his most judicial tone.

"Judge, I'm still working on the Hippie Murder Case. It's on appeal. That's the last double murder in this county tried without a lawyer fee. Surely, I have paid my dues."

"I know you worked hard on that case," the judge consoled.

"That case almost broke me. I must insist you find another lawyer to represent that woman." I wanted to sound businesslike with a slight whine imploring sympathy.

"Well, Bob, that's just not too easy," the judge sounded pensive. "I understand the State is going to ask for the death penalty in this case. I'm required to appoint the member of the Bar most qualified to handle such a case. In a way, the appointment is a compliment. On the other hand, it is a tremendous responsibility. I think you're the man for the job."

Thinking quickly, I said, "Okay, Judge, let me tell you this: I'm prejudiced against that woman. My farm practically joins the place where she killed the little girl."

"My wife said she could just imagine that child being marched up to the edge of the canyon, with that wind whipping through there, and being shot in the back. Celeste thought the wind would have swept her off the edge. That's about a 500-foot drop there."

"Well, the entire community has been concerned about this case," the judge agreed.

"Furthermore, I understand the little girl was injected with Drano six times before she was shot. And. didn't she kill another woman over in Georgia?"

"I believe that will be part of the State's case," the judge said, listening as I tried to avoid the case.

I thought the judge liked my wife. I didn't believe he ever cared much for me, but his wife and Celeste were friends. So I played the wife part as much as I could.

TRYING TO AVIOD THE CASE

"Celeste has been praying that woman would be caught. She said that she was the booger woman - the woman your mother warned you to never get in a car with. And I told some friends that I would pull the switch to electrocute her. I mean, this is just too much to ask. We raised our children on that canyon. I was chairman of the Tourist Association. The twins, Celeste, and I panned for gold out there after Michelle went off to college. I have close ties with that place. I don't want to defend someone involved in a murder case right in my back yard."

"I understand all that, Bob. Still --"

I interrupted again, "Judge, Celeste has been going around town looking for people who looked like the composite of the woman that appeared in the paper. I can't give her a fair trial."

"Well, I think you can put all that out of your mind and represent a client," the judge responded.

"I'm telling you, I can't." I thought that my argument sounded good. It would be hard for the judge to crawl around attorney prejudice.

The judge was firm. "I'm going to call one other lawyer, David Wear, and see how he feels about trying the case. If he doesn't think he is capable, I'm going to have to insist that you undertake the defense. I'm sorry for the problems the matter will cause you, but I feel I do not have a choice in the case. I'll call you back after I make the call and let you know the results. If you can't agree to take the case, I may have to order you to take it."

12

Then I knew what was happening. Wear was a property closing lawyer who had never tried a murder case in his life. This was a cruel joke the judge was playing on me to force me to take the case. I knew it, and he knew it. The political shots never quit coming my way.

I caved in. "Look Judge, no lawyer in his right mind is going to accept this appointment. Save your dialing finger. I don't see anything I can do other than take the case. I don't want to be the subject of a court order."

"That's probably a fair assessment of the situation," the judge replied.

As had happened 16 times in the past, I knew when I had had the lick. Now, another murder defense at my own expense.

THE POLITICS OF THE APPOINTMENT

Since DeKalb County, did not have a public defender, by tradition and rules, lawyers, as officers of the court, were required to come to the aid of the Court in order that the Court might dispense justice. The State of Alabama was supposed to pay the lawyer $500 for a murder case. Neelley would be my 17th appointment and I was paid $500 once. I had always believed that I was given the real bad "freebies" because I was the only Republican going all the way back to law school.

Democrat judges, looked my way for the most heinous cases. One judge called me to the courtroom to defend the man accused of raping the virgin daughter of the President of Auburn University. His lawyer resigned when the case was called for trial. Instead of forcing the prominent democrat lawyer, who had been partially paid, to remain in the case, the judge gave me 20 minutes to prepare the defense for a man I had never seen nor heard of. The rapist got 10 years from the jury. I had to appeal the case at my expense. The Court of Criminal Appeals, and eventually the Alabama Supreme Court, ruled that the accused had adequate representation, and I was qualified to try the case on such short notice. I would never have been involved if I had been a Democrat.

I was in the Alabama Supreme Court on a divorce appeal where physical cruelty was required. My client had sat next to his cheating wife and said, "Look at me when I'm talking to you."

Chief Justice Livingston was coming down the hall to the courtroom He was old and hard of hearing. Sitting at the appellant's table, I heard him clearly shout to Justice Bloodworth, "Come on, Jimmy. We've got to go save Bill Beck from that damned Republican, Bob French."

I warned the Court that if they found my client's conduct cruelty, or even the apprehension of cruelty, the Legislature would pass no-fault divorce within 6 months of their ruling. I was wrong. We got incompatibility as a ground for divorce within 30 days of the decision.

Judge Ruben Wright forced me to take two capital cases less than 6 months into my practice in 1963. He practically said it was politics during the settlement conference. Five Ku Kluxers had raped a black woman in the presence of her family. It was such an explosive case in Tuscaloosa in 1963 that the judge said it had to be settled. He became angry with me when I would not settle my client's case for more time than a prominent democrat, representing another Klansman, was going to settle for.

Alabama has never cared much for criminals, and the fact that lawyers had to "give something back to the profession" was fine with the citizenry. Judges called upon lawyers in open court, by name, and assigned cases. The attorney acted as if he was just waiting for the case. Since the appointments were distasteful, a lawyer who acted as though he did not want the case, lost points with the court.

Being the only Republican in Law School, I knew that I had no points with any Democrat Judge. After 53 years, I can count on my fingers the discretionary rulings I have been granted in Alabama. In any other state, foreign country, or federal court, I stand a chance. But in Alabama, where politics are hard ball, the discretion was always used against me. I have had judges suggest to the other lawyer what he had to do to get that discretion.

My path through law has not been easy - - reported to the Bar Association for discipline several times for nothing, and never rated above average by my fellow lawyers in legal publications. I knew the score. I just kept winning the big money cases before juries.

So, I became counsel for Judith Ann Neelley, one of the most hated notorious murderers in Alabama history. It was my second free high profile double murder defense in 22 months. Talk about paying a price for my politics....

THE HIPPIE MURDER CASE

The Whisenant murder case had been called the "Hippie Murder Case" because Joe came in from California wearing a wig, dressed like a flower child, and driving an old beat up VW hippie painted van. He pulled into Whisenant's Garage at Ider, Alabama, and asked to have his motor checked. His father didn't recognize him.

After a father-son reunion and laugh about Joe's joke, the pair went to the father's home for dinner. Joe ran through the shower while his stepmother washed and dried his clothes and placed them in a neat pile on a counter between the kitchen and dining area.

Later, after dinner, while the stepmother was canning beans, the father took a shower. He came out in a bathrobe and kidded Joe about staying away so long and looking so bad. While they were talking, Joe pulled his .357 Magnum out of his stack of laundry and killed them both.

I was threatened with an order if I didn't represent this miscreant. The trial played to a packed house. Whisenant was convicted after a week-long trial and given a life sentence. Then, jurors fixed the sentence. That law changed before Neelley.

Eddie Brown, our investigator, sat with me while the jury deliberated. Very seriously, Eddie said, "If they free that bastard, I'm going to kill him myself." It was bad.

I had to appeal the case at no charge. While the appeal was in progress, I was forced to take Neelley. I told Celeste that it was like being ridden out of town on a rail, "If it weren't for the honor of the occasion, I had just as soon not go."

BECOMING INVOLVED

"What's her name, where's she from, and has she given a confession?" I was defeated.

The judge generously gave me the information I wanted. "Her name is Judith Ann Neelley. That's Neelley, with two e's and two l's. She is 17 years old; from Murfreesboro, Tennessee; visibly pregnant; and, yes I do think she has made a statement."

"Thanks, Judge."

"I'm sorry Bob. But, I know you'll give it your best." The judge was happy that one was over.

I would have never been forced into the case if not for my politics, and name recognition. I had paid my dues, it was some other lawyer's time for a horrible freebie.

Later, I learned that the D.A.'s investigator had finished interrogating Neelley at approximately 3:30 p.m., and took her before the judge for the appointment of a lawyer. The judge inquired as to her ability to hire a lawyer. This matter was concluded by 3:45; and at 3:47, the judge had called me. So in 17 minutes that woman had signed a confession, and I had been threatened with an order to represent her at my own expense.

Short of a something as serious as a severe heart attack, this was the worst thing that could have happened to me.

I quickly read the account in the newspaper. Then, I walked into the hallway and yelled so everyone could hear me, "This firm now represents the bride of Frankenstein!"

Heads popped out of almost every doorway. "The what?" Steve Bussman, asked.

"You mean that woman who killed the little girl out on the canyon?" a secretary asked.

"You got it," I continued my announcement. "I'm on my way to the jail to visit with Halloween's newest ghoul. Look out Jason Bates, you can't hold a candle to this one."

CHAPTER THREE

DEFENDING THE BOOGER WOMAN

———◆———

"Do you want me to go over to the jail with you?" Steve asked.

"No. Call Judge Cole and ask him to appoint you as co-counsel to help with this case. If he'll do that, we can pick up a grand for a born loser. That's more important than meeting this witch. I believe it's going to be more than bad." I went out the front door.

Charles Houston, the DeKalb County Jailer, was skin and bones; but he was facetiously called "Muscles." I descended the steps to the courthouse basement, and approached the steel jail door. I pecked on the metal door and someone looked back at me through the small wire mesh window.

While never moving from his show on TV, Muscles said, "Somebody let Mr. Bob in."

A trustee turned the large key in the cumbersome lock, the steel door creaked open, and I entered the jail.

"Mus, I need to see your most famous guest in the DeKalb Hilton." I was smiling, as I genuinely liked our jailer.

"Oh, you must mean our new girl, Miss Judy. Henry, turn that new girl out so Mr. Bob can see her." Looking back at me, Muscles said, "You're going to have to see her in the laundry room. Some of these bastards took some mattresses and scorched the visiting room real bad. You mind the laundry room?"

"Nah, it's probably the cleanest place down here."

"It'd better be," an inmate charged with rape stated emphatically. "I sleep in there."

MEETING THE DEFENDANT

"Thanks. That'll be fine," I responded, as I caught my first glimpse of my client coming into the jail dayroom. She was wearing a dirty T-shirt that had enscribed across her extra large breasts, "Eat Your Heart Out, I'm Married."

She was tall and seemed to have a fairly decent figure, but her face was in bad shape. Her eyes were dark and swollen. She had big, protruding teeth, with one front tooth broken giving her mouth an even worse appearance. She had pimples all over her face. It was apparent she did not bathe regularly.

Her lips were what some folks would call "busted," as she appeared to have been beaten around her mouth. Dry flaky skin was beginning to form over some of her lip ulcers and lacerations. She had large purple bruises on her naked arms and shoulders. Her long brown hair was oily and stringy. She couldn't zip her jeans due to her pregnancy. Seeing her cotton panties through her open fly made her look all the more the part of the booger woman who would kill an orphan child and later murder a totally innocent woman.

"Mrs. Neelley, I'm Bob French, your lawyer. Let's go into the laundry room and talk."

Through her dry, swollen, obviously beaten mouth, she said, "I'm Judy Neelley. Can you arrange for me to see my husband?"

As I closed the door to the laundry room, I said, "I'm here to talk about you. I'm not interested in that robbing, raping, murdering bastard." I took out my legal pad, and sat down on the bunk bed.

She leaned against the door jamb talking with her eyes glazed over, and reciting some pre-programmed instructions as to what she was to say.

"My husband did not rape, kidnap, or murder anyone," she mumbled through her swollen mouth. "I did it. I need to get a note to my husband, Can you help me?"

I looked in her eyes. There was nobody home. She had no affect - no facial expression on her face; and she seemed to be in a trance -- like a fictitious zombie.

I despised this woman and felt animosity toward her.

Some jailhouse talk might give me better luck with this monster. " That son-of-a-bitch husband is snitching you out, and you're wanting to send him a letter? On second thought, give it here. I'll take care of it."

Alvin Howard Neelley, Jr. was in the Floyd County Jail in Rome, Georgia telling authorities that she had kidnapped the women, shot Lisa Ann Millican, John Hancock, and that she had killed Janice Chapman. She had raised the amounts on money orders, burglarized post office boxes, stolen money from convenience stores, robbed a woman at gunpoint, and had sex with Lisa Millican and Janice Chapman before she killed them in a fit of rage. He couldn't quite explain the semen in each of the female victims.

I had no intention of mailing the letter to Alvin. I thought it might give me a window into the case.

"You promise he will get it?"

"I'll promise you that it will get into the proper hands."

"I assume you will deliver it to Al."

"I'll deliver it in the appropriate manner."

"Okay," handing me the letter, "just see that my husband, Al Neelley, gets it."

"Tell me a little about yourself, your husband, and how you became involved in two murders."

"First, you must know that my husband is innocent. He is innocent at all costs. He did nothing. He hardly knows anything about what I've been doing. He wasn't with me on the days of the murders. Please make sure the authorities know this. I don't care what they do to me. He just must go free. They can put me in the electric chair, but he needs to be out of jail. He has a bad leg."

Stunned at her lack of grasp on what was going on, I tried to interrupt her. She was talking at a staccato rate. I had never seen this type of behavior before.

"What did you say your name was?"

"Judy," she said through the swollen lips, attempting to focus the sunken eyes on me.

"Fuck you, Judy!" I looked her dead in those eyes. She shrunk back as if she had never heard such words before.

"What do you mean? I can't believe a lawyer would talk that way to me." She was still talking fast.

"This one will because you are lying, and trying to sell me a load of bullshit. I'll be back when you have marinated a little in jail. You might be willing to come closer to the truth then."

As I passed her at the doorway, I noticed that she was tall, at least 5'9." I looked into her eyes again and shivered – it was like looking into nothingness.

"You don't like me, do you?" she mumbled.

"Lady, I don't like you, I don't like what you have done, I don't like being here, I don't like your husband, and I don't like your lies. I have a living to make. The next time I see you I will have my associate Steve Bussman with me. Be prepared to give us an in-depth interview. And I don't want to her any more lies, get me?"

"You promised you would give my letter to my husband, please. Even if you don't like me, you are the only person who can get that letter to Al so he will know that I'm doing what I'm supposed to be doing."

"We'll see," I said without looking back as I walked away.

I heard Judith Neelley say under her breath, "Well, I sure as hell don't like you, either."

EXPLAINING TO CELESTE

Celeste was placing food on the table as I arrived home. "I've already heard what happened today. Wasn't that pretty rotten of Randall Cole? Did he make you take that case because you're a Republican?"

"I don't want to think so. But I'm tired of being the only lawyer at this bar who gets the free double-murder appointments."

"Why didn't you tell him that you were sorry, but you were not going to take the case?"

"Don't you think I did? I used every argument I knew. He didn't buy a one."

"You could have just said, no, you weren't going to do it."

"Yeah, and I'd probably be before the Bar Association again. Do you remember how much trouble we got into when Fay Freeman satisfied that mortgage on our railroad property that we had paid off, and Wisner wouldn't satisfy the mortgage? They called me to testify in an unrelated case, put me on the stand, and I didn't know what they were talking about.

But Cole reported me to the Bar Association. Remember the trips to Montgomery, the expenses involved, and the humiliation of it all? I had no knowledge of what happened. I was totally innocent. No one lost a penny; yet when a lawyer is reported by a circuit judge, he has trouble."

"Yeah, we don't ever want to go through that again," she said, remembering a bad situation.

"Then you know why I am now representing our own private ghoul.

CHAPTER FOUR

ALVIN HOWARD NEELLEY, JR.
AND
JUDITH ANN NEELLEY

———————◆———————

Our later investigation showed that she was born Judith Ann Adams in Murfreesboro, Tennessee, on June 7,1964. Growing up in a dysfunctional home, she was nine-years-old when her father, all boozed up, decided to go for a ride. He lost control of his motorcycle and wrapped it around a pole. Barbara Adams was left with five children and no income.

For entertainment, Judith and her younger brothers nailed a barrel hoop to a tree and played with an old basketball that their uncle had given them for Christmas. Sometimes they would stretch a rope between two trees and play volleyball. Their home was a rusty old doublewide on eight acres of land their father had bought during his better days. Their dogs and cats ripped the insulation out from under the mobile home resulting in it being cold in the winter and hot in the summer.

The Adams' children did not eat breakfast as their mother didn't get up to get them off to school. Usually there was nothing in the house to eat. They left home hungry in hand-me-down clothes. Despite her difficult home life, Judith Adams was a happy child who made straight "A's" in school.

Only once she had a friend over to spend the night. The smell and the nastiness offended her friend. She told the kids at school about her experience, and Judith never had anyone else over – nor did she ever visit anyone.

Her house had other visitors – plenty of them – men who made nightly visits to see the Indian Princess, Barbara's CB handle.

Judith's room was separated from her mother's bedroom by a bed sheet that allowed the youngster to hear the near nightly sexual adventures of her mother. Judith begged her mother to stop drinking, but her mother refused. Men with whiskey on their breath would come into Judith's room after her mother had passed out, but she never allowed any of them to violate her.

She had a crush on a 16-year-old boy who came over to sleep one night because he was too high on marijuana to go home. He went to bed with her mother, and that was the end of that crush.

On June 10th, three days after Judith's 15th birthday, Dan Hartley, a plumber whose CB handle was Ape-Man, came to the double-wide with Alvin Howard Neelley, Jr., "Box Car," a 26-year-old ex-felon. The adults sat at the kitchen table all night drinking and talking. Judith listened for a while. Alvin Neelley was married with three children. Dan Hartley was married with four children. Hartley never left, and moved in.While Judy's older brother and sister drifted in and out of trouble, Judith became the caretaker of her younger brother and sister. When she passed from the 9th to the 10th grade, it should have been the happiest time of her life. She was a cheerleader, she was being noticed by boys, and she had made good grades in school.

The day Dan Hartley moved in, Alvin Neelley returned all dressed up bent on courting Judith. Knowing nothing about him, Judith thought he was a gentleman.

MEET ALVIN HOWARD NEELEY, JR.

From Cleveland, Tennessee, Alvin was also the product of a dysfunctional home. A slow learner in public schools, he was often in trouble and went to prison before he was 17-years-old. Although he was large for his age, he had a withered leg which prevented him from being able to use his size to his advantage when confronted by several men bent on raping the young boy. Alvin came out of prison with a twisted view of reality.

He moved to Dalton, Georgia, to work in the carpet mills where he met his future wife, Jo Ann. They never formerly married, but they lived common law for a number of years. Jo Ann had a child by a former marriage, and the Neelleys had two children of their own.

Alvin began to work in convenience stores as a cashier. He became a wife beater and liked it. He terrorized Jo Ann. When she finally escaped from him, Alvin returned a week or so later and shot her in the back while she was working in Calfee's Market in Dalton.

Early that summer Alvin Neelley, had left his children with his mother in Cleveland, and moved Jo Ann to Murfreesboro. They lived in cheap apartments while working in convenience stores.

After visiting the Adams, Alvin openly courted Judy. He took her to the store where Jo Ann was working, and smooched her in the automobile where Jo Ann could see them. Judy did not know it, but Jo Ann was praying Alvin would devote his attention to the young girl so that she could somehow escape from him. After a date with Judy, Alvin would go home and beat Jo Ann. Once Judy discovered bloody bras and panties in Alvin's possession. He admitted they were Jo Ann's.

Eventually, Alvin convinced Judy to leave her mother a hateful note that he had dictated, run away from home and marry him. The night she disappeared, he took her to Cleveland and on to Georgia.

He and Jo Ann had left their children with his mother. When she met Judy, she claimed Jo Ann had abandoned her two children, and the court allowed her daughter to adopt them. When Jo Ann came for her children, Mrs. Neelley would only allow her to take Michelle, the child that was not Alvin's. It was a horrible way for Jo Ann to lose her family, but she was dealing with Neelleys.

After the birth of twins, Alvin married Judith. During the year leading up to the marriage, he forced 15-year-old Judith to steal, break into post office boxes, and prepare false documents. He also began beating her.

Alvin weighed more than 350 lbs. He easily handled the pregnant girl. He beat her mercilessly. In anger he raped her with a baseball bat, hit her with a saw blade, left the scar of every tooth in his head in her forearm, and shot at her at close range. Alvin had made cruelty an art form.

Judith had saved $3.76 toward a bus ticket away from Alvin. He discovered this secret fund and blacked both of her eyes. He attempted to force her into a miscarriage of the twins by beating her stomach . After this, and other beatings over the course of her first year with Alvin, Judith lost her own sense of self and her will to live. At age 16, out of contact with her family, without funds, and without hope, Judith Ann Neelley became the slave of Alvin Howard Neelley, Jr.

JUVENILE DELINQUENT

July 5, 1980, Judith Ann Neelley was arrested for Theft by Taking. She was found to be a juvenile delinquent in Daugherty County, Georgia. Alvin had stolen money from the store and said Judith did it. Alvin was arrested on other warrants outstanding. When Judith was released from the detention home, Alvin forced her to come to Rome, exonerate him.

August 24, 1980, Judith Ann Neelley was once more declared to be a juvenile delinquent and sent to the Youth Detention Center in Macon. Because she could not gain his release, Alvin blamed Judith for his incarceration.

After they got out of confinement, in the fall of 1980, the two lived in an automobile. Alvin nicknamed them, "Boney and Claude," after the notorious criminals who lived in their automobile, Bonnie and Clyde Barrow.

November 11, 1980, while she was 8 1/2 months pregnant, Alvin forced her to rob a woman at Riverbend Mall in Rome. Seven days later, Judith was arrested for armed robbery and forging checks in the victim's name. Five days after that, she delivered twins.

The robbery had netted $10.00 in cash and a checkbook. Newspapers played the story as, "The Pregnant Robber." Judith was charged with 15 counts of forgery and sent off to the Georgia girl's reform school, i.e., the Georgia Youth Detention Center.

July 12, 1982, after almost two years, Judith was released from YDC. Alvin was waiting outside. Judith now had two children born while she was in custody. Soon, she would have three.

Judith purchased money orders from convenience stores. Alvin had taught her to increase the amounts of the money orders. She would buy a $5.00 money order and raise it to $50.00. Judy worked the money order scam on convenience stores across Northwest Georgia.

ALVIN'S TWISTED MIND

Alvin convinced himself that his wife had been sexually violated while in the YDC. She was a passionate teenager before she had been sent off for almost almost two years. His wife had been abused and prostituted by the system. He decided to get even.

Judy was forced to attempt to lure staff members of the Macon YDC to a local motel. There the victim would be held at gunpoint and injected with drain cleaner. Each of the staff members found some reason to decline Judy's invitation.

Failing in Macon, Alvin took Judy to Rome to attack the YDC there. She was forced to firebomb the front yard of one staff member, and to shoot a .22 bullet into the home of another. To Alvin's dismay, neither plan resulted in death.

He was furious. Something had caused Judy to lose interest in sex, and it had to be the fault of the YDC. He never considered it might have been the beatings he was giving her daily.

Unable to take his revenge as planned, Alvin decided to embarrass law enforcement by having the 17-year-old Judy murder other women, and tell the authorities by phone. It was an insane plan concocted by a maniac.

He chose the Riverbend Mall in Rome, Georgia, as the target of his frustrations

CHAPTER FIVE

A LAWYER'S TALE

April 10, 1944, I was eleven years old, and I stood quietly frightened before the huge double brown oak doors of the gothic red brick building, "Joe Wheeler Grammar School." It was located on 9th Avenue West, Decatur, Alabama. I was a fresh boy transferring in from the 5th grade at Red Bank Grammar School in the suburbs of Chattanooga, Tennessee.

I had to enter that strange "new boy" territory accompanied by the principal. My father, a "railroad man, had transferred to the Decatur Southern Railroad Yard. My three younger sisters and I entered the school year interrupted. Our mother had walked with us from our newly rented "defense" home on 6th Avenue to the school.

Miss. Eleanor Harvey welcomed me to her 4th and 5th grade classes of about 40 children.

"Boys and girls, this is Robert French. He has just moved to Decatur from Chattanooga. Robert is a fine person, with a good school record, so please make him welcome."

The boys and girls looked up from their work expressionless as Mrs. Harvey guided me to one of the old fashioned desks in front of Barbara Hurst. She then told the 5th graders to turn to their workbooks and complete an assignment in Chapter 7. Meanwhile, she taught the 4th graders arithmetic. I went to work in my 8 X 12 pulp-paged book – "Penmanship."

During recess I noticed one girl who had red hair – Bobbie Mae Mooney. She was tall, pretty, and in the 4th grade. Little could either of us known then what fate awaited us 55 years later.

HIGH SCHOOL

When I reached the 9th grade, I asked my mother to let me quit school. We were dirt poor due to my father having been injured in an on-the-job accident. We lived out in the country, without running water, or many other conveniences.

My mother said, "Young man, you will not quit school. Education is all we have. I went to college, your father went to college, and we read. Remember that. We are not trash because we read books. Now get back to your schoolwork."

Although I remembered the incident all my life, I'd show my mother by failing the 9th grade. I was put back, and Bobbie Mae Mooney was a classmate of mine. We graduated from Decatur High School in 1952. I went off to the University of North Alabama and, after two semesters, into the Korean Conflict. She went off to Auburn, and I lost track of the redheaded girl – for a while.

BUYING THE FARM

June 16,1965, was a very hot day as I stood on a hill overlooking 15 acres of cleared land down a gentle slope to a paved road. Beside me was Grady Price, a dandy of a man, with a Clark Gable moustache.

"See how it slopes down to Little River Canyon? This is the first individually owned canyon property this side of Highway 35.

There are 55 acres here; and you will own 2,300 feet of the canyon, subject to the Alabama Highway Department's right-of-way. We had to give them that to get them to pave the road. Plus, you have this old log cabin that's falling in, and this good barn. What do you think?" Grady was pushing the sale.

I countered, "Well, that settler's cabin is worthless. About the only thing of value in that is the stone in the fireplace. It has three rooms of rotted floors. It never did have windowpanes. The doors are falling off. The barn is another matter. It is in good shape, but it is not closed in on all sides."

Grady interrupted, "I built that barn. See those creosoted posts? That barn will be here after we are both gone. You can have all that hay in there if you want to run cows on the place."

"Well, I don't want to run cows. Say it goes to that creek over there that empties into the canyon?"

"Yeah, not only that, there is an island in Little River about a hundred yards long. You own to the middle of it. The Cherokee County line goes down the middle of the canyon - what we used to call May's Gulf - so you only own this wall and half the canyon. What'd you think? $4,500, and I'll finance it for you at 6% interest and you pay me however you want to."

"I'll give you $4,000 and pay you within two years."

Grady smiled. "You lawyers drive a hard bargain, but being a good Republican, and all, I'll do it."

We rode back around the property in Grady's pickup truck. I would soon own a canyon overlook - "Eagle Point."Later, I told Celeste, "I bought that farm we looked at. Let's ride out and see our place."

Being a Midtown Manhattan girl, Celeste liked the idea of owning a farm. She, our daughter Michelle, and I walked over the property. We went to the edge of the canyon and looked down at our island in Little River. We explored the cabin, the rock spring nearby, and the creek. We immediately fell in love with the place.

For the next several years, our Sundays, after church, were spent walking over the farm. Each Christmas, we had the family

fight over which tree to take home. I could not convince Celeste or
Michelle that the tree they were selecting was too large to go into the
house. When we would get home, I would dutifully cut it down to fit,
and we wouldn't fight again until next year.

ALABAMA'S FIRST TOURIST WELCOME CENTER

On November 10, 1965, without being a member of the DeKalb
County Tourist Association, I was elected Chairman of the Board. I
still have a list of the members present that night.

In those days lawyers couldn't advertise. We had to "get our
name out there" through the church, politics, or civic work. Lawyers
competed for civic responsibilities, so I didn't turn down the job.

I told the board members that with the recent opening of
Interstate 59, DeKalb County needed a tourist welcome center.
Motorists had to come off the freeway if our tourist industry was
going to survive.

One member asked, "How are we ever going to do that? We
have no money, no land, and no hope."

"Just keep the faith," I positively responded. "Who knows
someone who owns a good log cabin?"

I knew politics and civic work were better than a license to
steal; they were a license to beg.

Dr. George Weatherly said, "Dude Burton at Henagar bought
that old Thornberry cabin. It is still in good shape and some of the
descendants are still around. Pearl Thornberry works at the hospital.
She'll help out, but I doubt Dude will sell it."

"I'm not interested in buying, I'm interested in borrowing.
What about some property on the south interchange? Who knows
the Dewyers? There is still one vacant corner on the southwest side.
Who can talk to Mr. Dewyer, or his two sisters, about allowing us to
use that corner for a tourist center until they sell or lease it?"

Betty Noel spoke up. "I went to school to both of the Dewyer sisters; Ms. Sarah Dewyer is very civic minded. The trouble will be with their brother, but Ms. Sarah can move him. I'll go see her."

"Okay. I'll go see Dude Burton. Remember, all we want to do is save our tourist trade now that the interstate is bypassing town. We don't want title to anything. We just want to borrow. See you next Tuesday." I knew that Burton was a good Republican.

I drove out to Burton's Potato Shed. Dude was grading chip potatoes coming down the conveyor belt. I approached him about lending us the Thornberry cabin. We would move it down to the interstate and move it back to his farm and set it back up when we were finished with it. We would keep it insured for $50,000. Plus, we would put up a plaque that Dude Burton was the owner and furnishing it to the traveling public.

After hemming and hawing a bit, Dude agreed to allow us to use the cabin. Now all I had to do was find someone who would take it down, number the logs and boards, haul it to the interstate, and put it back together like a big jigsaw puzzle; that is, presuming we landed the Dewyer property.

When we met on Tuesday night, I announced that we had the cabin. Betty Noel announced that she had seen Sarah and Richard Dewyer, and we had the property.

"Now all we need is a construction crew and a hauler."

While we were meeting in my waiting room, Dude Burton called and said he and his crew would relocate the cabin.

The old pioneer cabin was about 75 feet long and 40 feet wide. It had the usual dogtrot, being about 12 feet wide. It had three rooms and a kitchen with stone fireplaces in each room.

One of the members said he would take his crew over the following day, and clean off the site, prepare the foundations, and build the fireplaces.

Within a matter of days the cabin was erected on the site, underpinned with mountain rock, landscaped, and open for tourists. Surprisingly, Pearl Thornberry and some of her relatives came down and dressed in pioneer garb to welcome tourists. Several people brought old family artifacts to furnish the cabin.

With generous loans, we were able to install three old wooden corn shuck beds; an old cooking pot; some hand hewn tables, chairs; and other antiques from the Pre-Civil War Days. Colorful quilts set off the old beds. Persons from Chicago, visiting our tourist center, would feel as though they had stepped back in time.

Eight weeks from the time I had been elected Chairman, Alabama had its first tourist welcome center. We printed full color brochures, handouts, tracts, and you-name-it. We were in business, and the traffic was unbelievable. I kept thinking, The Lord works in mysterious ways.

We maintained that welcome center until the State of Alabama built one on Interstate - 59 at the Alabama-Georgia line in 1969. Dude Burton took his cabin back to his farm and reassembled it. The Dewyers leased their site to the Hampton Inn.

While all the action was going on at the Tourist Association, I photographed DeSoto Falls. I was fortunate to get the cover of *Southern Progress* magazine.

SAVING THE FARMER'S PRODUCE MARKET

I was trying to practice law when, without my knowledge, I was elected President of the Northeast Alabama Farmer's Produce Market. Wendell West came to my office and announced that at a meeting of the stockholders the previous evening I had been elected president.

"I don't even know what they do, or where they are located. How can I possibly be president of such an organization?"

"Well, the community has seen how you took over the tourist problem, and I put your name in nomination. Milford Kuykendall made a campaign speech for you, and you were elected by acclamation.

We are a central gathering place for farmers' produce concentrating on cucumbers, watermelons, cantaloupes, squash, and other produce. We have grading machinery and buyers. Our problem is farmers can't seem to get used to it. They either grow the wrong kind of produce, not enough of it, or the brokers cheat them. Everything needs to change. We think you can change it."

"Well, I'm enough of a politician not to turn down an elective office."

"You shouldn't. We have almost 3,000 members, and they are potential clients for you."

"Do you have a Board of Directors?"

"They don't get along, somone, or some clique, stymies everything. This attitude goes back to the Civil War when most of Sand Mountain was pro Union. We have a $200,000 operation going to hell because of personalities."

I rode up to the site on 38th Street with Wendell. It was an imposing facility, 250 feet long and 80 feet wide, a steel-beamed shed with offices on the south end. Wendell said that Sand Mountain farmers were growing potatoes and abandoning produce that would readily grow and make money.

"Where is the most money to be made for the farmer?"

"Super select cucumbers. They are nothing to grow. They grow fast. The vines just keep producing. The leaves are so large they kill all the grass, and they sell for a lot of money."

"Who is our best cucumber grower?" I inquired.

"Well, there is a guy down at Crossville that probably does best with them. He's a Bruce, but I can't remember his first name. Fairly big- time farmer."

The next day I was in Crossville talking with Kenneth Bruce. He was familiar with the problems of the Farmer's Market, and I persuaded him to put in 20 acres of cucumbers.

"Do you have any idea how many cucumbers 20 acres will produce?"

"No, Tell me. Is it a lot?"

"Thousands - more than you can imagine. Probably more than 50 trailer truck loads. But I'll grow 'em if you can sell 'em."

I said, "I'll not only sell them. I can grow 15 acres of them on my farm on Little River Canyon if you will haul your equipment over there."

"I'll do it. You and I are about to get into the super select business in a big way."

GROWING CUCUMBERS ON THE CANYON FARM

I liked Kenneth Bruce, particularly when he agreed to go around the county with me persuading other farmers to put in 20 acres of super selects. It helped that he was a good Republican.

He and I went in halves on the seed and fertilizer. He planted the field, fertilized the crop, and later came back and cleared the rows of weeds. We then waited for cucumbers to grow.

Celeste and I would sleep with the windows open in our house on Lookout Mountain in order to feel like the cucumbers as they grew on our farm.

As it neared picking time, Kenneth told me that we needed to find some pickers, and I needed to find a broker who would be fair with the farmers, and pay market price, less commissions, at the shed.

Kenneth said he would get his 20 acres picked by Mexicans that came into DeKalb County to pick strawberries, produce, and potatoes every year. He knew a crew chief. He couldn't help me though, as he would be imposing on the crew chief just to get his done. "This is a big job. You'll see."

I located three brokers in Florida and recruited kids from the housing project, and all my friends to help pick the crop. I bought a heavy duty Dodge pickup truck with an oversized bed.

I contracted with the most honest-appearing broker I could locate - a guy named Jimmy Thomas. He had been a professional wrestler, and he knew the cucumber business inside and out.

All at once it was harvest time. I had never seen so many cucumbers in my life. I would go to the project at daylight, load up my pickers, and head to Little River Canyon. Celeste would be on the telephone calling all our friends to get them into the field. Yes, even Betty Noel, that wonderful civic Trojan, came to the farm and helped pick, as did her children.

We loaded that red Dodge so heavy the bed would be down on the axle and I would waddle off the mountain and down to the market. It seemed those super selects grew overnight. At evening time, they would be pickles. The next morning, they were super selects and had to come off the vines.

Harvest went on for three weeks. With Kenneth Bruce and other farmers we enticed to grow cucumbers, we influenced the U.S. market, and the price began to fall. When that happened, we quit. However, everyone had a profitable growing year. Jimmy was an honest broker, and married a local girl. He wanted to come back next year, and I wanted out of the produce business.

The Northeast Alabama Farmer's Produce Market had shown the most profitable year since its organization. The stockholder's meeting was a big party.

I refused to stand for reelection, and several farmers got into it, as usual. A school teacher-farmer from Fyffe, on Sand Mountain, was elected president, and I became a lawyer again.

I was a lawyer until the following year when the president of the market came to me and asked me to grow again. I couldn't say no. Kenneth Bruce said he didn't want to partner with me again because my soil grew too many cucumbers - too much Eastern sun. He did agree to come and plow my farm, plant the cucumbers, fertilize them – and that was it, no cleaning the middles. All I had to buy was the seed, fertilizer and pay him $300 to haul his equipment three times and operate it. I thought that was fair enough.

At harvest time, I once again became Farmer French, the Cucumber King, and went through the same problems as the year before. The kids loved it because they got to ride on the cucumbers down to the shed and watch the grading. Plus, they were paid well. Several cucumber patch romances blossomed for a time. Me? It was just another hassle I didn't need. I made a profit both years, but that was my last year to farm on the canyon.

CIVIC AWARDS AND POLITICS

The Man of the Year Award was held locally toward the end of 1966, the year of the tourist center and farmer's market. Morris Beck, our Democratic Legislator, who did nothing other than drive back and forth to Montgomery, was Man of the Year.

I didn't know that I had been nominated. I think out of guilt, the locals awarded me a cheap silver plated tray inscribed for "Civic Contributions." It was delivered to my office the day following the meeting. They weren't about to give Man of the Year Award to a Republican.

Later, I was selected as one of the Outstanding Young Men of America and one of Four Outstanding Young Men of Alabama. I was named the National Outstanding Young Republican State Chairman for the contributions I had made in changing the political landscape in Alabama. These were all great honors, and helped my practice.

A FUTURE FEDERAL JUDGE

The farm was an integral part of my life. My three children and I would go out and explore the woods, garden, even pan for gold in the creek. We imagined a little of everything. We loved drinking from the rock spring.

Ed Nelson, my law partner and later the US District Judge who designed the Federal Judicial Computer System, went to the farm on a regular basis. We would take along my children and pick muscadines, a wild, sweet fruit, that looks a big grape with a tough skin. Nelson and I made some great wine with them. When he was on leave from Viet Nam, Nelson's brother, Charlie, would go with us. Sadly, Charlie was killed right at the end of the Viet Nam War.

The family continued to go to the farm for the Christmas argument, and I continued to take friends out there, and hike down to my island in Little River. The farm was my security blanket. If worse came to worst, I could always grow enough out there to tide the family over until we could do something else. I had offers, but it was never for sale. It was a treasure to me. I loved the place.

RUNNING FOR LEIUTENANT GOVERNOR

It was 11:55 p.m. in the early fall of 1970. Dick Bennett, Chairman of the Alabama Republican Executive Committee, had flown his twin Comanche into Fort Payne to persuade me to sign papers to run for Lt. Governor against Jere Beasley, an old classmate from law school, who had been George C. Wallace's campaign manager.

The executive committee wanted to get enough votes to qualify the Republican Party of Alabama to hold primary elections to select the party's nominees. Alabamians did not understand the GOP convention system. The Democrats said that we nominated our candidates in a telephone booth. People laughed at us.

A sacrificial lamb was needed to make the race in 1970. I had the 11th best known name recognition in Alabama during the George C. Wallace years. If I could get 25% of the vote, the Republican Party could have a primary and grow as a political entity.

With Celeste and daughter Michelle, we reluctantly agreed to make the race for the party. The three of us went to Isbell Field, and I signed the qualifying papers on the wing of the airplane five minutes before the midnight deadline.

Later, I was told to go to Opelika and meet a fellow named Forest James who owned a company that made barbells out of plastic filled with sand. He began his company, Diversified Products, in his garage and grew it into a company employing more than 1,500 people and worth more than 1 billion dollars.

I met Mr. James and introduced myself. I told him that I understood he might help me financially with my campaign. After we toured his factory he gave me a check for $2,500. That was a lot of political money in 1970.

"We have a connection, you know. Maybe more than one," he said.

I asked him to explain.

"I went to Auburn, and played halfback. I married a friend of yours – our head cheerleader -- Bobbie Mae Mooney. She knew you were coming today and said to tell you hello. Further, she has qualified for the State Board of Education to try to get some of the Auburn vote for you guys in order to get the primary."

I was shocked but very pleased. I asked him to give my fondest regards to my old classmate.

Between the two of us we got more than 25% of the vote that year. The Republican Party became a political entity that would eventually take over the state.

Still, fate lay in wait for my classmate and me. We would cross paths again in an even more interesting way.

CHAPTER SIX

GETTING CHRANKED UP

————◆————

December 30, 1982, Steve said that Neelley was playing Pete and repeat with us. She was not going to give us enough facts to defend her against capital murder.

After another fruitless interview, we were crossing the courthouse lawn again. It was almost 11:00 p.m. I was frustrated.

"What do you think?" Steve asked me, the more experienced lawyer.

I began slowly as we walked through the dew that had settled on the dead lawn. "Richard Igou said that he will not take less than life without parole. A jury hasn't burned anyone in this county since 1934. So she is not going to get the death penalty. We have nothing to lose by trying the case. The worst a jury is going to do is life without."

"Would you be satisfied with that?"

"Let me tell you. I think we ought to try this case, get her out with life - - just life mind you - - and send her to Georgia and let them fry her until her eyeballs pop out for the Chapman murder. I've had all this woman I can stand."

Bussman stopped in the middle of the walkway leading to the west entrance of the courthouse. In the courthouse lights I could see that he was looking at me with total dismay.

"I don't believe you said that," as if he had just lost a hero. "I can't believe the strongest advocate I ever knew would say that."

I defended myself, "What's wrong with that? We have no defense. We have a non-cooperative client who is nutty as a fruit-cake, killed two women, guilty as sin, and we are about to get the crap kicked out of us."

"We ought to at least go down swinging," Bussman said. "You always said that if you can't represent a client with everything you have, you ought to send the client to someone who is used to losing."

The trial lawyer's soul, that lived deep within my being, responded to my own argument. "You're right - Bad as I hate to admit it - You're right. Let's go flat out on the blamed thing. Let's go for the win."

The case became the driving force in the lives of Steve Bussman and me. Still, I didn't know how to defend someone I despised and who would not cooperate nor tell us the truth.

FRIENDS AT JACKSON HOLE

The National College of Criminal Defense was conducting a three-day seminar in Jackson Hole, Wyoming. I thought I might get some help about how to handle Neelley. I had always admired Gerry Spence, who was going to be running it, more or less. Jessica Myers, the criminal psychologist from Washington, D.C., along with other distinguished faculty, were going to help out.

Eddie Brown, our investigator, had attended these events with me in the past. I told Steve to try to make some money. Eddie and I would fly out to Jackson Hole and see if we could get any help regarding Neelley.

My Beech Barron was a great twin-engine aircraft below 15,000 feet. I think we cleared the Continental Divide by maybe 500 feet. Looking out of the pilot's window, I could see footprints in the snow. Soon we landed at Jackson Hole and were on our way to our hotel.

The following morning with some 132 lawyers in attendance, Gerry Spence led off with a keynote address. As usual, he mesmerized the audience.

Spence said, "If you can't defend the most despicable person you have ever seen; if you can defend the most miserable wretch you can imagine; if you can't defend a 40-year-old repeat sex offender who has raped and slit the throat of an eight-year-old girl; then get the hell out of my profession!"

Eddie Brown nudged me with his elbow. We knew he was talking to me.

A lawyer from California raised his hand, and Spence hesitated. "How do you do that, Gerry? Some of the people I represent deserve to die."

"You can't make that judgment!" Spence shouted. You are not the judge of your client! You are not his jury! You are his goddamned defense lawyer. You are the only thing standing between him and execution or life without parole."

He dropped his voice into an instructional tone. "Now, I know what I'm telling you is tough. What you have to do is find something about your client to approve of. In other words, you need to learn to love the unlovable. Find something good about the person. Soon, you will notice other things about the person you can approve of. When that happens, you are beginning to love the unlovable."

He continued, "By 'love,' I do not mean romantic love -- God forbid -- don't ever get involved romantically with a client. I mean to give the accused attention juiced up with approval. That's what love is without emotional affection dialed in."

For two more days, inspirational attorney speakers held me spellbound. During quiet times and after dinner, I would corner Jessie Myers and explore her brain about Judith Ann Neelley. I asked her about the Stockholm Syndrome, and she went into great detail about the Patty Hearst case. She also mentioned a female lawyer whom she had heard of in Pennsylvania who had successfully represented women who had murdered their husbands. She didn't know her name, but she would send it to me. It turned out to be Barbara Hart.

As I pointed the nose of the Barron up, up, and away out of Jackson Hole, I felt like I had been to a religious revival. My world had changed.

The challenge became: What can I find in Judith Neelley to approve of? There was nothing about that woman that I liked. Having to pass the murder scene ruined my going out to my farm. The case and the characters involved were so despicable and confusing that I could not make heads or tails of it.

CHAPTER SEVEN

THE INVESTIGATION

———◆—◆———

I told Steve, "Let's start all over. Ignore Judith Neelley. Let's go to Murphreesboro and talk to people. Then, let's go to Cleveland, Tennessee, and find out all we can about Alvin Neelley."

We went to Murphreesboro, Cleveland, Rome, Dalton, and other points where the Neelleys had lived, worked, or traveled. We dug deeply into the facts.

We confirmed that she had survived a less than favorable childhood. She was ready for a way out when Alvin Neelley appeared. Barbara Adams was broken hearted when she found the note from her daughter, and searched for her for more than six months.

In Cleveland, Tennessee we did little more than confirm what we knew about Alvin.

In Dalton, Georgia, from court records we confirmed that when Jo Ann finally escaped from him, Alvin returned a week or so later and shot her. He was later arrested for attempted murder, jumped bond and moved on.

At the YDC, we learned that Judith Ann Neelley was a near perfect inmate. She participated in activities, was very pleasant, cooperative, and everyone liked her. She was a victim of domestic abuse. She was counseled to stay away from Alvin Neelley.

Steve and I confirmed the sordid details of the events near my farm on Little River Canyon.

Knowing of the other murder, Steve and I received cooperation from Georgia from the Catoosa County Sheriff's Office in Summerville, Georgia. Unfortunately, my hidden recorder, clicked off after an hour. Cooperation was over. We learned a lot during that hour.

Steve and I spent considerable time in Murphreesboro trying to locate Casey, the young lady who would have been the last victim, but she had used a fake name, and who that woman was, is still a mystery.

After about three weeks, we concluded our preliminary investigation, and the case didn't look good at all.

RAIDING ALVIN'S BEDROOM

We had to find Alvin's first wife and see what she could tell us. We had to get into Alvin's bedroom in Cleveland and see what we could find there.

The more people we interviewed, the less sense the case made.

Once more we confronted Judith Neelley. She would not give us the information we needed, but she did tell us Alvin's first wife was named Jo Ann, but she did not know her last name nor her whereabouts as she had married again.

Bussman moved the Court to declare Judith Ann Neelley a juvenile and try her as such. Denied.

Bussman moved to have Neelley declared insane. The Court ordered a mental evaluation and sent her to Bryce Hospital for the Insane in Tuscaloosa, Alabama. She was returned after a couple of weeks with a diagnosis that said she knew the nature and quality of the charges against her; she was not suffering from a clinically proven insane delusion; and she did not have a mental defect affecting in her capacity to distinguish between right and wrong.

"Those bastards would find Nero capable of standing trial," Bussman complained.

We worked, we investigated, we traveled, we researched, and we did everything in our power to find a defense for 18-year-old Judith Ann Neelley.

We went to Cleveland, and Mrs. Neelley allowed us to search the room where Judy and Alvin had lived after his release from prison.

Mrs. Neelley kept saying, "Junior wouldn't do anything like he is accused of. That girl did all that."

I was agreeing with her while Bussman loaded two large grocery bags full of evidence he found in the room.

He found Polaroid pictures, in color, of Judith Neelley having sexual intercourse with Alvin. Horrible black and blue bruises were all over her body. Letters from Alvin in prison clearly demonstrated his total dominance of Judy. A sawed-off rifle was found under the lavatory in the bathroom off the bedroom. Bussman was proud of finding that weapon. The FBI and several other law enforcement groups had searched the room and missed it.

Pulling out of Cleveland, I said, "Finally, Steve, we may have something to build on."

"Yeah," Bussman replied, driving my Porsche. "It ain't much, but we have a case that she didn't have the requisite intent to commit murder. Now, all you got to do is sell that to a jury."

"That's no hill for a climber. If we can keep her out of the chair, it's a win. If we beat life without, we've won the case," I said joyously, as I fumbled through the documents and pictures Bussman had lifted from the trailer.

"Pretty slick, huh?" Bussman grinned.

"Pretty slick," I grinned back. "Pretty slick, indeed. I kept the old hag occupied while you made a clean end run for a TD."

"Let's hope."

"Yeah, let's hope."

SOMETIMES A LITTLE MAGIC IS REQUIRED

The day after returning from Cleveland, I announced, "Today we are going to find Jo Ann."

"Bob, tell me how we are going to find this woman. We don't even know her name, no address - - nothing. We don't even know where to begin"

"Well, we're not going to find her in Fort Payne, Alabama. Let's go to Dalton, Georgia."

Arriving in the outskirts of Dalton, Steve said, "Now what?"

"See that guy walking along the road. Pull up beside him." I lowered my passenger side window.

"Hey, Mister. Can you tell me how to get to the housing projects here in Dalton?"

"Yeah. You ain't that far away. Go on up a couple of blocks and turn left on Underwood Street. Follow Underwood down, and it runs right in front of the largest housing project in Dalton."

"Thanks. I appreciate that." Then, turning to Steve behind the wheel, "You heard the man. Go to Underwood and take a left."

Soon the public housing facility appeared. "Now what?" Bussman asked.

"Circle the outside all the way around." I was intently looking at the apartments as we passed. "Stop!"

"We haven't gone all the way around yet."

"Don't worry. We're here. Stop the car. Let's go in."

Bussman looked at me like I was from another planet. "How do you plan to find Jo Ann here?"

"Elementary, my dear Bussman," I said, faking an English accent to parody Sherlock Holmes. "Jo Ann has several children. She and her husband both work. She has an aged mother to help her who qualifies to live in the projects. The mother watches the children. Old ladies like a little action. So they want to live on the outside of the projects where they can see the public and streets. No need of looking at apartments facing the playground or office. No automobile around. The curtains are old. Someone has lived here a long time. See those toys? See this worn grass? See that anywhere else? Yard apes. They're inside today because of the rain. I do believe we're here."

"Shall I keep the motor running?"

"Nah, we'll be here awhile."

We approached the front door, and I knocked. An attractive girl about 11 years old with long red hair appeared. The television was blaring cartoons.

"Yes sir?" She said with large blue eyes surrounded by freckles.

Using my most fatherly soothing voice, I said, "Hi, young lady. We're looking for Jo Ann."

At that point a voice of an older woman sounded from within the confines of the apartment. "Who is that at the door, Michelle?"

"It's two businessmen looking for Mama," the child responded innocently.

"Bingo!" I chortled to Bussman.

"I'll be damned," Bussman grinned. "Bingo it is!"

The older woman came to the door. "We don't know a Jo Ann. Are you insurance men?"

"No, Ma'am," I responded as smoothly as I could. "We're lawyers representing Alvin's second wife, Judith. We need to talk with your daughter, his first wife." Honey wouldn't melt in my mouth. We needed this interview.

"There's no one here by that name," the woman replied. "I don't know what you're talking about."

"Of course you do, Grandma," Michelle chimed innocently. "Alvin Neelley is my daddy, or at least he used to be before my mama got me back. Mama's gone, but she should be back any time."

I pushed my right foot into the doorjamb and addressed the elderly woman in the gingham dress. "Ma'am, can we come in and wait for her? It's uncomfortable out here." I was halfway in the doorway.

"Oh, I guess you might as well," Grandma said resignedly. "We wanted to stay out of this mess, but it seems you've found us. How on earth did you find us? Jo Ann does not have this apartment, I do. She's married to a Browning now, and no one is supposed to know that."

"Just the gift of God," I said, taking a seat in a stuffed leatherette chair with a torn seat, and removing a legal pad from under my arm. I began, "Tell me what you know about Alvin Neelley."

During the almost two and one-half hours before Jo Ann Browning and her husband returned to the apartment, Grandma and Michelle gave us an earful.

When Jo Ann realized that she would be forced to testify, she began to cooperate, and gave us an overview of her relationship with Alvin Howard Neelley. We would not hear her real story until she came to court, and testified under oath.

Jo Ann concluded by saying, "When Alvin brought the young girl to the store where I was working, and smooched with her in the car where I could see them, I wanted to run out and warn her away from him. But I saw in her my chance to escape that monster. If he would just become interested in her, I could get away from him!

"At home, I pretended to be jealous; and he beat me up, brought me to Dalton at 4:00 a.m. He pushed me out of the car into the middle of Main Street in a bloody pulp. He said that he never wanted to see me again. I had to crawl to a phone booth and call my sister. I was a mess -- clothes ripped off, a tooth missing, and filthy -- but I was away from Alvin Howard Neelley for the first time since I had met him. It was worth it all. I felt sorry for that young girl. Finally, thank God, I was away from Alvin Neelley!"

We had taken a lot of notes. "What do you think now, Steve?"

"It seems like this guy was some kind of Marquis de Sade -- a Svengali. He is one mean dude. At the same time, he is a coward. I just don't get it. How could he influence women the way he did?"

"Hearing what Jo Ann told us, has made me a little sorry for Judith Neelley. I guess I may be on my way to finding something to like about her. Maybe it's the wasted innocence of her youth."

We confronted Judith Neelley with the results of our month long investigation, and finding Jo Ann Browning. Realizing that she was not the only one Alvin had beaten, she began to open up a little - not much - - but a precious little.

January 3, 1983, Judy delivered Jason Alvin Neelley at DeKalb Medical Center.

DRAGGING ON

The case dragged on as cases do. I went back to Riverbend Mall, and the YDC. We explored the Stockholm Syndrome. We investigated each potential juror, all 120 of them. We met with Judith Ann Neelley trying to persuade her to tell us the truth. She was friendly enough, but she would not give us the honest story of her marriage to Alvin Neelley. She was hiding something. I couldn't figure out what.

March 3, 1983, we examined the evidence the district attorney intended to offer on trial. It was overwhelming: pictures, confessions, statements, tape recordings, hair samples, ballistics, blood samples, semen comparisons, witnesses, and expert testimony.

"What else do they need?" I asked Bussman as we left the grand jury room where the evidence had been laid out for us.

"I think they are lacking one essential ingredient," Bussman said, as we boarded the elevator. "The hydrogen bomb. They ain't got the H-bomb." He grinned.

"Well, they've got everything else, all the aces."

"What hand are we holding?" Bussman queried.

"We have a pair of queens against four aces," I responded.

"Four aces win."

"Yep," I agreed. "But it isn't how you play the game; it's whether you win or lose."

"Well, we better pull off our best bluff. We're betting the limit," Bussman said, with worry in his reply.

A REAL BIG MISTAKE

As the trial date was bearing down on us, the press reached a fever pitch. Early on, Steve had refused to answer any questions and referred the press to me. At least two, and usually three or four, television trucks were in the parking lot across from the office every work day.

I am thankful the 24 hour cable news cycle had not been developed at that time.

Being an old politician, I tried to be kind to the reporters. At some point, I would go out and give them something for their evening news.

Then I made the mistake of my life! I said something that would be misinterpreted.

A young reporter from a Huntsville television stations asked, "Mr. French, how can you represent someone as horrible as Judith Ann Neelley?"

I answered, "I didn't choose this client. I am not her judge nor jury. I take the facts the best I can and defend the citizen accused."

The young lady continued. "But, Mr. French, this woman killed an orphan and an innocent woman. She is horrible. Yet you find a way to defend her?"

And here it is: "When you are a criminal defense lawyer, you have to learn to love the unlovable." I quoted Gerry Spence.

"Do you mean you love Judy Neelley?"

"I am a Christian man. I teach Sunday School. I try to love everyone. That's what Jesus instructed. I do not love what Judy Neelley did, but I do try to love her soul, and pray for her forgiveness."

Bad mistake! The reporters only heard that I loved Judy Neelley, and they ran with that story. It probably would have died, but the County Democratic Executive Committee was meeting that night, and I was discussed. The beat committeemen went back to their neighborhoods and said that Bob French admitted to being in love with Judy Neelley. He is going to divorce his wife and marry her.

Plus, he is the father of her son that was born in January. The promoter of these lies was a public official who had known me almost 20 years. He knew it was all a lie. He saw a chance to strike a blow against the Republican Party, and he took it.

The following day, I was the talk of the area, and the rumors spread into three states.

Inmates in the county jail told people they saw me kissing Judith Neelley. Others said I came into the jail late at night and had sex with her. And on it went while I was still trying to love the unlovable.

The insanity was reaching a fever pitch, while I was quickly becoming a hated man. After all these years, the Democrats had what they wanted - - rid of Bob French.

INVESTIGATING THE JURY

March 6, 1983. "Let's go over that jury list one more time, Steve," I said, looking up from the documents spread over every flat surface in my office.

Bussman thumbed the 5x7 jury cards as he would a deck of playing cards. The cards were worn. Each juror had been reviewed and investigated. Neighbors had been asked about the juror's attitudes. What clubs did the juror attend? Where did the juror go to church? Friends, relatives, hobbies - - you name it, and we were interested in it.

Our *vior dire* examination touching on their attitudes and qualifications, had been written long in advance. A preferred juror profile had been agreed upon, and individual jurors had been compared to the profile.

"Here's a woman whose husband beats the shit out of her. I hope we can get her on the jury," Bussman said, looking at a card toward the end of the stack.

"Yeah. Here's an old devil we have to get off the panel if we have to shoot him off."

"Let's go see Judy one more time," Bussman said, as we finished reviewing the juror information for the last time.

Judy was nervous. We carefully explained to her exactly what would take place during the trial and what the State would be trying to do. I told her to sit with her head down, hands clasped in her lap, and never react to anything going on in the courtroom.

"If you smile, the jurors will say, 'Kill the bitch.' If you don't smile, they'll say, 'Look at that hard-hearted bitch.' So, you can't win if you do anything. Sit still, head down, just like we practiced, and don't look up. I don't care what happens, don't look up. You got it?"

"I got it."

"Do all the clothes fit?" Anita Fuller, a secretary from the firm, about her size, had provided dresses for Judy to wear at the trial. The baby, Jason, had been born January 3rd; and Judy had most of her figure back. She looked pretty good in the clothes.

"Oh, yeah, they're great. Thank Anita again for me."

"Just look good tomorrow morning. That's thanks enough for all of us," Bussman instructed.

As we locked the office door to leave for home at almost midnight, I said, "Have we forgotten anything?"

"I'm sure we have, but it's too late to worry about it now," Bussman said, twisting the key. "Tomorrow she flies or crashes and burns."

"That's a bad choice of words," I said, opening the door to the Porsche. "Let's take it to 'em!"

"All the way!" Bussman slammed the door to his car, and we drove into the night.

CHAPTER EIGHT

THE TRIAL

———◆———

March 7, 1983, about 8:50 a.m. Red Taylor, a state trooper friend of mine, caught up with me and said the sheriff wanted either Bussman, me, or both, to accompany Judith Neelley from the jail to the courtroom. "He doesn't want to be accused of any funny business." We struggled through television cameras and crews packing the hallways.

By 9:00 a.m. the courtroom was packed. Some members of the press could not find a seat. The atmosphere was electrifying. We walked through the door to the left of the judge's bench with Judith Ann Neelley dressed in a light blue dress with white collar, high heels, and a new hairdo. She looked like a school teacher. After a gasp at seeing her for the first time, a hush fell over the audience.

DeKalb County Sheriff Harold Richards, tall, gray-haired and dignified, walked through the door behind the Defense. He was wearing his full uniform as sheriff of the county.

The State, consisting of D.A. Richard Igou; his assistant, Mike O'Dell; and Danny Smith, D.A.'s Investigator from Cherokee County, was seated at its table. The Defense, consisting of myself; Steve Bussman; our investigator, Eddie Brown; and Judith Ann Neelley took seats at the table designated for the defense. Brown, as was his custom, sat in one of the chairs along the rail separating the pit from the audience.

"All rise." There was noise as the courtroom rose when Circuit Judge Randall Cole came through the door in his flowing black robe with a stack of papers and books. He hesitated momentarily while the sheriff called the Court to order.

"*Oyez, Oyez, Oyez,* the Circuit Court of DeKalb County, Alabama, is now open according to law. The Honorable Randall Cole presiding. Be seated." *Oyez* is an ancient word of a public crier demanding attention for a proclamation -- O yes!

The sheriff sat in his seat near the door to the left of the bench that led to the witness rooms. The opening and closing of court for the remainder of the trial would be done by Cecil Reed, Chief Deputy. Mrs. Martha McPherson, Judge Cole's bailiff, administered the courtroom. She had taught him English in high school. Now it became her duty to attend to the jury.

The Honorable Randall L. Cole peered over his half glasses at the packed courtroom. He made several preliminary remarks for about 30 minutes and then looked to the State and said, "Is the State ready?"

"We are. Your Honor," Igou responded, rising from his chair. His name is pronounced I-go. The u is silent.

"What says the Defense?" asked the Court.

We're ready," I said, already standing.

The Court methodically qualified the 120 potential jurors.

The Court denied the Defense motion for individual *voir dire*, i.e., questioning each juror separately. Instead, the judge ruled that the jurors would be questioned in panels of 12. The state and then the defense would be allowed to propound questions on *voir dire* to the panels.

Usually, potential jurors are questioned about their qualifications in one large group. The impaneling of 12 jurors did not give us what we wanted, but it did allow a more give and take with the potential jurors.

The State and Defense questioned panels of jurors for the remainder of the day.

Judith sat with her head down. Now and then she would become caught up in the colloquy between the lawyers and the jurors, and joined the audience in laughing or otherwise reacting to the questioning. I warned her to keep her head down. No reactions!

Each recess the television lights and cameras went to work. Thirteen television stations, countless reporters from newspapers, and radio stations jammed the hallways with spectators and pro-spective jurors.

March 8, 1983, the jury selection process continued.

Toward the end of the day, the Court said that it would take up certain motions at that time. The final jury selection would take place the following morning.

We had filed a motion in *limine* to prevent the State from referring to any statements or alleged confessions of Judith Neelley before hearing our motion to suppress her confessions. The District Attorney gave the Court assurances that he would not refer to any such matters until after the hearing of the motion. The Court denied the limiting motion, and recessed for the day.

March 9, 1983, after the jury was seated in the box and sworn, the State made its opening statement followed by our opening.

Judge Cole looked at Richard and said, "Call your first witness."

THE DISTRICT ATTORNEY

District Attorney Igou, the son of a local doctor,began his career as Assistant District Attorney to Jay Black, a great nephew of U.S. Supreme Court Justice Hugo Black. He attended the National College of District Attorneys at Bates Law School at the University of Houston. I had attached the national College of Criminal Defense at the same place. We had graduated from the University of Alabama School of Law 12 years apart. I was the senior alumnus.

Igou followed the recommendations of the national college. He never gilded the lily. The only time he would become emotionally involved in a case was during the final argument. He was a very skilled legal technician plying his craft. He never allowed the Defense to place him in a position critical of the state's case.

His favorite closing argument was, "Ladies and Gentlemen of the Jury, I work for you, the taxpayers of this county. I do not win nor lose cases. The State wins when justice is done. Dispensing justice is the job of the jury and the Court. As your district attorney, I bring the facts to you. The facts have been brought to you. Now, if you feel this person is not guilty, say so. But if you believe the State has met its burden of proof and convinced each of you beyond a reasonable doubt and to a moral certainty that this person is guilty as my office has charged this person, then convict by finding this defendant guilty as charged."

It was a tough argument to combat.

Richard Igou was not the kind of guy you would call Dick.

WITNESS TESTIMONY BEGINS

A trial is really a highly structured debate that can become boring with all the rules involved. I am going to summarize the testimony as briefly as I can from my notes. Other times, I will quote directly from the record. I am not going to describe the physical appearance of the witnesses.

Melda Davis, was a case worker with Walker County Family and Children's Services. She became acquainted with Lisa Ann Millican due to an abuse complaint filed for her sister Tina. There were three children in the home, Calvin, Tina and Lisa. Lisa was the oldest of an abusive alcoholic father.

Living in a trailer, in a very poor environment, the father often left home. Another child - Judy was born. On August 19, 1982, the department took temporary custody of all four children. The order confining Lisa, her brother and sisters was Exhibit No. 1. Lisa was placed in institutional foster care with the Ethel Harpst Home in Cedartown, Georgia, sponsored by the Methodist Church. It was an orphanage, not a detention home. Davis identified a picture of Lisa, which became State's Exhibit No. 2.

Lisa had been sexually abused by her father from the age of 11.

Gail Henderson, a 26-year-old relief house parent, relieved house parents on their days off. On September 25, 1982, she took six girls to the Riverbend Mall in Rome "window shopping." The group arrived at the mall at around 7:00 p.m. Ranging in age from 12 to 15, Henderson kept the 12 year old with her. From the wicker store, they paired off into two groups. Agreeing to meet back at the Radio Shack in one hour, the older five went off together.

In one hour, Lisa was at the Radio Shack, and did not know where the other girls were. She volunteered to help find them, and was to return within 15 minutes.

Henderson located all of the girls other than Lisa. This was the first time she had met Lisa Ann Millican.

After quickly searching the mall a security guard was alerted. Twenty minutes later, the Rome Police Department was called. The witness never saw Lisa Millican again.

I felt sorry for Henderson. She was a part time worker, attempting to do a good thing, and lost Lisa to a murder. Her memories must haunt her terribly.

Lieutenant Lonnie Adcock, a shift supervisor with the Rome Police Department, received a telephone call on Tuesday, September 28, 1982 around 1:00 p.m. A woman asked if they were looking for Lisa Ann Millican. He could find the body in Little River Canyon, "where I left her." This call was taped.

Sergeant Wallace Wilson, said that this call was taped at 12:26 p.m. It was then played for the jury, and admitted into evidence.

COPS AT THE CANYON

Gerald "Red" Taylor, a former State Trooper, was in the DeKalb County Sheriff's Office when a call came in that there might be a body in Little River Canyon. He and Deputy Eddie Wright went to the overlook, but did not see the body. They did not go to the edge of the canyon and look.

James Mays, Deputy Sheriff, said that on Wednesday, September 29, 1982, the day after Taylor and Wright had acted on the call, he received a call from a woman at 6:35 p.m. She gave directions to a body in the canyon. Mays went to the canyon with three officers. At the edge, they saw what they thought was a body. He called for lights and sealed the area. Members of the Fort Payne Fire Department repelled down, set up lights in the canyon, and secured that area. Eddie Wright took charge of the investigation while Mays stayed at the top until the next day.

The voice on the Rome tape and Fort Payne call was the same.

Eddie Freeman, a fireman, and Glenn Leath, another fireman, went to Rocky Glade Point on Little River Canyon somewhere around 7:21 p.m. on September 29, 1982, set up lights, and the body was located. He did not touch the body, but he did look at it closely and concluded it was female.

Dennis Weaver, a deputy, was called to the canyon at 9:15 p.m. to stay with the body the rest of the night. He was in contact with the rim by walkie-talkie. Although he did not touch anything, he saw various items in the canyon, and looked closely at the body. It was female. She had fingernail polish on some of her fingers.

Danny Smith arrived on the scene shortly after 7:00 a.m. on Thursday, September 30th. Smith took State's Exhibits No. 4 and 5 that were photographs of the area above where the body was recovered.

State's Exhibit No. 6 was a photograph at the edge of the canyon with the body down below on a ledge. Smith leaned over the edge to take this picture.

Exhibit No. 7 was taken from down in the canyon looking up at the rim to show the distance from the top to the body. Exhibit No. 8 was a picture on the ledge looking toward the body. Exhibit No. 9, a photograph showing the body lying on a steep incline with its arms draped over a burned pine tree trunk felled in a forest fire.

Other photographs were introduced and we objected to each offering on the grounds that each was cumulative, highly inflammatory, and prejudicial. Overruled and the pictures were admitted for the jury.

Smith helped place Lisa in a body bag and a Stokes basket (to lift her out of the canyon) for the Forensic Science agents who had now arrived on scene.

On top, the body bag was unzipped, the underclothing was pulled back, and Exhibit No. 13, a photograph, was taken to show the exit wound of the bullet in the left breast. This picture also showed the facial features of the victim.

We objected on the grounds that the picture was inflammatory - - taken for the purpose of inflaming the jury - - and the evidence had been tampered with, as her bra had been removed to show the bullet hole. "Overruled."

While on the ledge, Smith had recovered a pair of blue jeans hanging on a tree limb 8 feet above the ground and 56 feet down from the rim. State's Exhibit No. 14 was a picture of the blue jeans in the tree.

Exhibits No. 15 and 16 were pictures of the jeans with one showing the blood stained leg of the jeans where they were folded across a tree limb.

Forty feet northwest of the body, Smith photographed a white hand towel from the Five Points Motel on the ground. This was State's Exhibit No. 17. Approximately nine feet from the towel was a barrel of a hypodermic syringe and four feet away was the plunger for the syringe. A photograph of these items was admitted as State's Exhibit No. 18. Exhibit No. 19 depicted the towel after it was unfolded

How do you cross-examine a witness such as Smith? He was killing us. I had to do something. I decided to exploit Alvin directing everything going on while hiding in the trees like the coward he was. I had Smith make a drawing of the area. Smith admitted that had Alvin Neelley been standing in the trees directing the actions of Judith Neelley, and if she had normal hearing, she would have had no trouble hearing him.

SOME LADIES TESTIFY

Deborah Ann Madaris, Director of the Open Door Children's Home, said that Lisa Ann Millican had stayed in that home from July 13, 1982, through August 13, 1982. Madaris identified the body as Lisa Ann Millican. Lisa was a more physically developed than a normal 13-year-old girl and a little withdrawn. She had tried to run away once during her 30 days at Open Door.

Suzanne Clonts, 19 years old, from Rome, Georgia, was a part-time married student at Floyd Junior College. On Saturday, September 25, 1982, she was in the arcade in Riverbend Mall with her husband. At about 5:00 p.m., she was approached by a woman with long, dirty hair, dressed in a T-shirt, with no bra, jeans, and appeared to be unkempt. The conversation was odd as the woman would ask a question, and Clonts would ask her one. Clonts told the woman she lived in Armuchee, and the woman replied she lived there also, but when pressed, she could not say where she lived in Armuchee.

When told that she was there with her husband, the woman walked over to a large, heavy-set man. The woman she met that day was Judith Ann Neelley who had given her a false name.

On cross-examination, Clonts said the woman did not have makeup and appeared "she was from the other side of the tracks." Clonts had watched the couple earlier. The man was larger than a football player and played Frogger in a dark corner where she could not see his face. If he were hiding while appearing to play games, the best game to play would be Frogger. The woman reported to the man after the conversation.

Clonts thought the meeting with Judy Neelley strange as she walked up and rushed into a conversation without any preliminary pleasantry. The woman did not appear to be a healthy, average person.

AN ASIDE

Remember as you read the direct and cross-examination of these witnesses, they are under oath, and we have to get from them anything favorable that we can. I have established that Alvin could have hidden in the trees on the canyon, and given instructions to Judith. We have learned the appearance of Judith and Alvin. We have developed Judith's approach to strange females, and Alvin hiding out while Judith does his bidding. Clonts had been approached the day before they picked up Lisa. The next witness was approached after they had killed Lisa and Janice. It's not much, but we had to press on.

ANOTHER LADY

Diane Bobo, was 22 years old from Rome, and worked at Hardee's. She was married. The district attorney asked her if anything unusual happened to her on October 3, 1982.

We moved to approach the bench where we objected to the line of questioning because it was after the death of Lisa Millican, was remote, and was not part of the *res gestae* (a spontaneous happening or statement). The State responded that the witness would show identity, motive, pattern, and design. The Court asked what the witness was expected to testify to. The District Attorney summarized her testimony. We renewed our objection on the grounds that it was after the fact, and the testimony could not show design. The Court agreed with the district attorney that the evidence could come in to show motive, pattern, and design. "Objection, overruled."

Diane ran out of gas on Shorter Avenue on October 3, 1982 on her way to work. She had help pushing the car to a shopping center where she called her husband, and sat on a rock base to wait. Stores were closed because it was 5:00 p.m. on Sunday. A brown Dodge, with a white or cream stripe, with a CB antenna coming out of the middle of the trunk parked close by. A woman went to the newspaper vending machine.

She then walked to Bobo and asked, "Don't I know you from somewhere?" The witness replied, "No."

The woman wanted to know if she was Patricia Alexander. Again, Bobo denied she was. The woman then asked her to go riding with her, as she was just riding around and was lonely. The witness told her she was waiting for her husband. The woman offered to take her to work. Bobo refused, and the woman left.

After she identified the woman as Judith Neelley, she said that she had one small child in the car with her. Bobo did not see a red Ford with a CB antenna. The woman who had approached her had on wrinkled and worn clothing. Her T-shirt and jeans looked too big for her, and looked like they had been worn for several days. She did not look well kept. She looked like she had gone without taking a bath for several days.

The woman's persistence struck Bobo as odd. She was more than just helpful; she was anxious. She wanted to go riding "real bad."

Bobo wanted no part of the woman. She did not see any bruises or scratches on the woman, but her eyes were sunken in with dark circles like she had been awake quite awhile. She looked haggard. She made a lasting impression on Bobo by insisting that she go riding after she had repeatedly told her she did not know her and wouldn't go riding with her.

Bobo reported the incident to the police the following day. She helped draw the composite of Judith Neelley.

JOHN HANCOCK – SURVIVOR

The state then brought a witness whose testimony was so prejudicial to the Neelley defense that we believed that we had to keep it out or her fate was sealed.

John Hancock, a 26-year-old grave digger, worked for the City of Rome's cemetery department. He had lived with Janice Morrow Chapman, his common-law wife, two and one-half years.

The district attorney directed the witness' attention to October 3, 1982, the same day as the Bobo episode. The Defense asked to approach the bench where objection to testimony subsequent to the case on trial was made.

We objected on the grounds that the murder of Janice Chapman was a completely separate murder case than the one in Alabama. We pointed out that the defendant had been indicted for the murder of Chapman in Georgia. The murder of Janice Chapman was not part of the *res gestae* and could do nothing but prejudice the jury. This testimony required the Defense to defend a second murder case, while defending a first murder case. The defendant could not, under any circumstances, overcome the taint and prejudice of the Chapman murder testimony.

The State responded with its usual song and dance, that the evidence was offered to show identity, motive, pattern, and design. Richard then summarized what he expected the evidence to show.

We strongly argued that the Chapman murder testimony would be so prejudicial that there would be no way to overcome it in the minds of the jury. "Overruled."

HYPNOSIS

We then pointed out something that we had uncovered in our investigation; John Hancock had been placed under hypnosis to refresh his memory. Testimony subsequent to hypnosis is inadmissible as a denial of counsel's right to confront witnesses. The State assured the Court that it would not elicit any evidence which the witness had given as a result of being hypnotized.

Upon request, the Court allowed the Defense to take the witness on *voir dire* examination. The Defense requested a copy of the witness' statement to police. The Court excused the jury, and the State proceeded to examine the witness first.

Hancock said he made a statement to the police, which was tape-recorded. Three days later he was hypnotized. He did not know whether he was placed under hypnosis for the purpose of making a composite picture of the assailant.

We objected to the admissibility of any identification made subsequent to the hypnosis. Hancock was not sure how much he was able to recall under hypnosis, but it helped him recall the facial characteristics of his assailant.

The Court ruled that the witness could not testify to any matter he was able to recall as a result of the hypnosis. That precluded identity of the defendant. Hancock was taken down, but we had not seen the last of him.

Danny Smith said that he was present when John Hancock's statement was tape-recorded by Detective Kenneth Kines and Detective Bishop of the Rome Police Department. The tape-recorded Hancock statement was State's Exhibit No. 20.

MURDER AND SURVIVAL

John Hancock was recalled with the jury present. He and Janice Chapman were walking home down Shorter Avenue in Rome on October 3, 1982. He reached down to pick up some nuts and bolts off the sidewalk. When he looked up, his wife was talking to someone in a car.

The woman said she was lonely, from out of town, and wanted to ride around and talk for a while. He noticed a Tennessee tag on the car. He told the woman they were only a few blocks from home. She persisted, and John and Janice got into the brown Dodge automobile with her. John told her when she passed their street. She said she was going to her aunt's to get money for gas.

The woman picked up a Cobra CB radio and asked for a 10-36 - "What time is it?" A man answered and gave her the time. She asked him who he was, and he said, "Nightrider." She asked his location (10-20), and he said, "Dunkin' Donuts." The woman and man agreed to meet at the Coosa Post Office. As they approached the post office, the man told her where to turn off. The woman told Hancock and Chapman she wanted to go back and talk with the man and get to know him a little; she would be right back. Hancock told his wife he did not like this set-up. The woman came back to the car and said the Nightrider wanted to meet them. All four were CB'ers and met beside the Dodge. John introduced himself as Fortune Teller - Janice was Lady Rose. The man invited John to ride with him. The woman went to the man's car and took two children from the car. Janice Chapman rode with the woman and children. According to the man, they were going to get something to drink, and take John and Janice home. The man was driving a red Ford Granada.

The group went in the two cars to a beer joint on the Alabama line. It was closed. The man suggested a bootlegger at Summerville, Georgia. He said the bootlegger had a big red mailbox. They turned toward Summerville. After failing to locate the bootlegger, the man turned off a side road where they could "go to the bathroom." The man instructed the woman that whenever he pulled off, she should turn in behind him but turn her lights off so on one could see him and John going to the bathroom.

Both cars pulled off the road with lights off. The woman was talking to the man at the back of her car. When she walked back, she pulled a pistol, cocked it, and pointed it at John. She told John to walk down the road and not to pull anything funny. John tried to talk to the woman as he walked down the road. She told him to keep walking, and keep his back to her.

John told her there was water up ahead and, "surely she didn't want to walk in it and get wet."

She told him to turn left into the woods, toward some hedge.

The man hollered, "Hurry up and get it over with. We have to go."

She hollered back and said, "Okay. Just a minute."

John asked the woman if he could ask a question. She said, "Hell no. Just keep your back to me, and don't say anything." She told him not to worry about his girlfriend; she would take care of her, too.

The man hollered again for her to hurry.

She said, "Okay," and shot the witness in the back.

When Hancock was shot in the right shoulder blade, he fell on his face and lay on the ground. He heard her run back up the road, the car door shut, and both cars left. John Hancock never saw Janice Chapman again.

CROSSING JOHN

Where do you go with this cross-examination? I started again trying to put the blame on Alvin. The CB was on channel 40. When the woman asked for the time, the man answered as if he were waiting for the call. They appeared to be adequate on the CB radios. At the Coosa Post Office the man told the man told the woman to make a left-hand turn. Throughout the evening, the man directed the woman, and she did exactly what he told her to do.

The man was heavy built, dark-headed, not real tall, and well groomed. The woman did not match the appearance of the Nightrider. She had long, stringy hair and was wearing a jogging suit. His hair was neatly trimmed. When the woman went for the children, they acted as if they knew her. The man explained that the children were his brother's, and the woman looked like his brother's wife. The Ford was a better car and neater than the Dodge. The people matched their cars in their appearance.

I was digging for any little nugget I could get from Hancock. He had put the hat on Judith Ann Neelley. I had to get a little help from him.

The man drove away first, the woman followed, and did not let him get out of her headlights. The beer joint was about 10 miles from the Coosa Post Office. The man totally ignored Hancock and was not friendly.

Failing to find the bootlegger, they returned toward Rome. John told the man he had to go "piss." The man said he had to be excused also. He told the woman to follow him and turn off her lights so they could be excused. When they turned off on the dirt road, the man did not relieve himself. John did. The man got out and went back to her car. John heard him say, "If we're gonna do it, let's get it over with."

John never heard the woman's voice during the conversation at the rear of his car. At the end, she said, "Okay."

With John's help, I made a drawing of the area, and events taking place where the cars pulled off on the dirt road. Hancock drew the direction he walked with the woman behind him, how he turned off the road at an angle to the left, and then went back to the right, across a clearing, and into some bushes. He said they walked for several minutes.

Hancock heard the man yell, and she said, "Okay, just a minute."

"He yelled again, 'hurry up.' He told her exactly what to do."

She told John, "Don't worry about your girlfriend; we'll take care of her."

She yelled, "Okay," to the man, and pulled the trigger.

The man gave all the directions; he always led the way in his car, he decided where to pull off, and the woman did exactly as she was told. The man was in charge of that evening's transactions from the time the woman picked up the CB mike and asked, "What time is it?"

I had Hancock talk about citizen's band radios as the jury needed to know about them. Channel 40 was one of the weakest CB channels due to the shortness of the radio wave. Based on his experience, when the woman first asked for the time, the man was close.

That was about all I could get from Hancock that might help our case.

Realizing what I had been trying to do, show lack of intent on the part of Judith Ann Neelley, Richard directed Hancock to say that the woman did not appear to be afraid of the man. She was not upset, scared, or nervous. She was calm and aware. She gave John directions before she shot him.

He then took Hancock through a few negative-type questions, such as:

Q. John, did she ever tell you that she was awful sorry about having to shoot you?

Q. Did she ever tell you, John, that you could run away and she would just shoot up in the air?

We objected to each of these questions. "Overruled."

PILING ON

Deborah Smith was a 13 year old 8th grader dressed in her cheerleader uniform. On the 4th day of October 1982, she was walking home from school when a woman called her "Michelle" and tried to give her a ride. The woman was wearing a T-shirt and jeans. She was in a brown car with a child. "She looked like when you first get up out of bed."

The woman talked fast and a lot. She looked haggard, "She just wasn't fixed up." When Deborah would not go for a ride, the woman wanted to know if she had any friends who might like to go for a ride. This was hours after killing Janice Chapman.

Kenneth Kines, returned, testifying that Alvin Neelley had given him consent to search the red Ford Granada while in the

Rutherford County Jail. A copy of this consent form, was introduced as State's Exhibit No. 21.

Kines found an Alabama driver's license in the name of Benny Andrew Farrington with Alvin Neelley's picture. At our request, Kines produced pictures of the trunk and interior of the Granada. These photographs were marked Defendant's Exhibits No. 1 through No. 24 and were introduced by agreement.

I tried to lay the ground work for an argument about the violation of the defendant's constitutional rights that we would raise later in the proceedings. I had Kines testify that the search was made on October 14, 1982. He could identify 13 officers from outside Rutherford County, Tennessee, taking part in the investigation and interrogation at Murfreesboro on October 14, 1982.

When Kines interviewed Neelley, Alvin said that he was doing undercover work for GBI Agent House. He had testified in a case House was investigating. Kines questioned Alvin Neelley for three hours that evening.

Ernest Dorlina, a Special Agent with the United States Treasury Department, helped search the home of Barbara Adams after she had signed a consent to search, Exhibit No. 22.

The Court allowed me to conduct a *voir dire* examination of this witness. He stated that two Rutherford County deputies, and two other officers, Darrell Collins and David Burkhalter, accompanied him. Bill Burns, FBI Agent, was with them. He gave the defense an inventory of the items seized from the home.

David Burkhalter, an investigator with the Rome Police Department, took six wad cutter bullets from the home. These .38-caliber bullets were flat-nosed and used for target practice. The inventory was introduced as Exhibit No. 23 for the State.

He seized a pair of handcuffs from a little shelf in the living room. The inventory of the automobile was admitted as State's Exhibit No. 24. The witness found a Smith & Wesson Model 10, .38-caliber, blue steel pistol under the passenger seat of the Ford Granada. He found other .38-caliber wad cutter bullets in the car. He also located the brown Dodge. It had been sold by Alvin Neelley. Burkhalter took pictures of both automobiles. These pictures were introduced as State's Exhibit No. 25, No. 26, and No. 27.

False identification, checks, a stack of car titles, and a ball bat, along with other items, were taken from the Ford belonging to Alvin Neelley. There were directories of local police frequencies, CB equipment, a 30.06 rifle - a high-powered bolt-action rifle - and an RG .22-caliber rifle. He found tapes, ammunition, a roll of film, and a set of walkie-talkies along with blood in the right-hand door.

Burkhalter had helped us by finding blood in the door where Judth ould normally sit. He said that if he were to stop a parolee, with a gun, he would arrest him for violation of parole.

Barbara Lankford, I. D. Clerk with the Rome Police Department, received all the items confiscated at the Adams residence. We had no objection to the introduction of any of the items, other than the handcuffs, pending a Defense motion on lack of consent from Barbara Adams.

The Court reserved a ruling on the handcuffs. State's Exhibits Nos. 29 and 30 were admitted.

Alvin Neelley attacked his women's private parts with a baseball bat, and hit them in the head with the metal end of a holster. Sure enough, when I questioned Lankford, she had the black baseball bat, and a holster taken from the Ford. She said she would bring them to court for the defense.

Parsottam Patel, known as Pete, ran the Five Points motel in Scottsboro, Alabama. We objected as his testimony could only flow from the alleged confession of the defendant, which was contested at this time. The Court agreed, and the witness was excused.

Danny Smith took samples from the head hair of Judith Ann Neelley. He was present when a blood sample was taken from Alvin Neelley in Chattooga County Jail in Summerville, Georgia. All body fluids and samples were given to Darrell Collins.

Darrell Collins, investigator for the District Attorney's office, received all of the samples taken by Smith, including a saliva sample from Alvin Neelley. He delivered this evidence to the Alabama Department of Toxicology in Huntsville, Alabama.

Kelly Fike was a firearms examiner from the Georgia State Crime Laboratory in Atlanta. Barbara Lanford delivered a .38-caliber pistol to him on October 15, 1982. He produced State's Exhibit No. 31, the pistol. Mr. Fike looked at State's Exhibit No. 12, a photo depicting the shirt and bullet hole in the back of Lisa Ann Millican. He said the front of the bullet has "cookie cutter" characteristics resulting in a clean hole in whatever it strikes. He also took carpet samples from the red Ford, which he turned over to Bob Clemensen of the Georgia State Crime Laboratory.

Robert D. Clemensen, a micro analyst with the Georgia State Crime Laboratory, said that he received all the samples from Mr. Fike; and he passed them on to John Kilbourn. **Josefino C. Aguilar, MD**, a forensic pathologist, collects evidence from dead individuals, preserves it, submits it for proper analysis, and determines the cause and manner of death. He received the body of Lisa Ann Millican on September 30, 1982. He saved the clothing and other items removed from the body. Kilbourn, the trace evidence expert, helped him examine the evidence. He took pictures, took notes and made diagrams of the pathology he observed on the body.

He found three types of injuries to the body: blunt-force trauma, gunshot wound, and attack by ants. He observed blunt-force trauma all over the body, with multiple abrasions and contusions, which were all consistent with the body having gone over a cliff 40 or 50 feet high. There were numerous broken bones, including the spine, the right leg, and the left half of number nine backbone, secondary to being struck by a bullet.

After bringing in the ants, I wondered how much worse this case could get. I was about to find out.

Having entered the body through the mid part of the back, the bullet tracked through the left lung and exited the front of the chest. The chest cavity was filled with blood. State's Exhibit No. 32, a photograph of the entry to the back of Lisa Ann Millican, was offered into evidence.

We objected on the grounds that it was cumulative, served to excite the passions of the jury, inflamed them and prejudiced them against the defendant. "Overruled."

The gunshot wound was consistent with a .38-caliber pistol projectile. He took blood samples and gave them to Roger Morrison for serological analysis.

The victim was examined for sexual abuse and determined that she failed to show recent injury. Although the hymen was intact, it showed a notching, or discontinuity, indicating it was broken previously and was scarred. He took a vaginal swab and gave it to Morrison. It appeared she had recently had sexual intercourse.

The doctor found unusual injuries to the body, one to the left buttock and one in the left side of the neck. These lesions showed deliquiation of the fat giving it an anchovy-sauce appearance. These injuries were consistent with the fatty tissue coming into contact with a caustic substance. "Needle marks" on the body appeared to be ant bites. "Lisa Ann Millican died of a gunshot wound in her mid back, and death was almost instantaneous."

I looked up deliquiation and it is a rarely used word meaning to liquefy. That anchovy-sauce analogy made the jury look away sickeningly. In this case things just continued to get worse. Being in the courtroom was difficult, and playing a role in the proceedings was terrible.

CRIMINALISTS HAVE A FIELD DAY

John Kilbourn, a criminalist from Huntsville, identified State's Exhibit No. 36, human hair; Exhibit No. 37, microscopic slides of hairs removed from various pieces of evidence; Exhibit No. 38, a white hand towel; and Exhibit No. 39, mounting slides of hairs. Examination of the hairs removed from the white hand towel indicated that one of the head hairs was similar to the hair of Judith Ann Neelley, and two of the hairs were similar to the known hair of Lisa

Ann Millican. State's Exhibits Nos. 33, 36, 37, 38 and 39 were admitted into evidence.

As Steve said earlier, all the state lacked was the atomic bomb. By now they had us standing in a hole up to our eyeballs. The evidence was mounting; the press was in attack mode; and the jury was sick of Neelley and her lawyers.

These forensic witnesses just kill the defense as the jury likens them to television shows. Kilbourn identified State's Exhibit No. 40, the jeans found at the scene by Danny Smith, as well as Exhibit No. 41, the panties of the victim. State's Exhibit No. 42 was the carpet from the Dodge Dart, while Exhibit No. 43 was microscopic slides of fiber taken from the white towel, which were identical to the fibers of the Dodge carpet. Exhibits admitted. There was no powder residue or particles found on the shirt near the entrance wound. This indicated that the gun was discharged some distance from the shirt when fired.

State's Exhibit No. 44 was a syringe found near the towel. Exhibit No. 45 was a plunger found nine feet away. Exhibit No. 46 was the white towel with syringes wrapped inside. These were insulin syringes that were examined for drugs, and none were found. The syringes had contained a very alkaline entity with a high pH. Chemical analysis revealed the presence of sodium hydroxide and hypochlorite. Liquid Plumr is primarily sodium or potassium hydroxide or potassium hypochlorite. The primary constituent of Drano is sodium or potassium hydroxide. State's Exhibits Nos. 44, 45, and 46 were admitted.

Mr. Kilbourn didn't want the jury to mistake the caustic substance causing Lisa's "anchovy-sauce" flesh – it was Drano!

Roger Morrison, a criminalist whose specialty was forensic serology -- which is the identification of biological fluids in dried form or stain. State's Exhibit No. 47 was a vial holding a blood sample from Lisa Ann Millican. Exhibit No. 48 was a vial, which had contained Alvin Neelley's blood sample. Exhibit No. 49 contained a sample of Alvin Neelley's saliva. The witness' tests indicated the blood on the leg of the jeans was the same classification as the blood of the victim. Exhibits Nos. 40, 47, and 48 were admitted. Morrison then identified the vaginal swab from the victim. It was State's Exhibit No. 50. Human seminal fluid, including spermatozoa, was present in the vaginal swab, as well as on the panties of the victim. All tests indicated she had been involved in the sex act, and there were no inconsistencies with Alvin Neelley's blood test and saliva. State's Exhibits Nos. 41, 49, and 50 were admitted into evidence.

HERE COMES THE FBI

The Court excused the jury and began hearing the defendant's motion to suppress certain statements made by the defendant – mainly, her confessions.

Bill O. Burns, Special Agent, FBI, stationed in Rome, Georgia, went to Murfreesboro, Tennessee, on October 14, 1982, for the purpose of investigating the death of Lisa Ann Millican. He interviewed Judith Ann Neelley after she was told that anything she said could be used against her.

He took her to the interview room at the Rutherford County Jail. Lester Stuck, Investigator for the Gordon County, Georgia, Sheriff's Office, was present. Judith Neelley read the form and said she understood it, but she would not sign it. She was willing to talk without an attorney present. FBI form FD-395 was admitted into evidence

On cross-examination, I needed to establish that the constitutional rights of Judith Ann Neelley had been violated. She had been told that she could have a lawyer, but then was intentionally denied her duly retained attorney.

Here is the way it went - Burns admitted that he knew that Judith Neelley had retained an attorney by the name of Bill Burton who was waiting outside the door in the hallway. Everett Stewart, Special Agent of the FBI, called a US Attorney and was told that he did not have to allow the attorney to see his client, unless the client requested to see the attorney. Burns did not tell Neelley that her attorney was just outside the door wanting to see her, and took a confession from her.

Neelley told Burns that Bill Burton was her lawyer at the time he had her read her FD-295. He knew Neelley had a retained attorney before he asked her any questions. However, she was willing to talk without an attorney. When Agent Stewart came in and told Burns that the defendant's lawyer was outside wanting to see her, he did not stop the questioning, nor did he tell her what Stewart had told him.

The agent wrote ithe statement attributed to Judith Ann Neelley: "She stated that Bill Burton was her attorney, and that the reason she did not want to discuss this issue was because some people would think that a person who traveled around without having a steady job was not a good person." Later on in the evening the Judith Neelley confessed to murder.

During this part of my questioning, the audience laughed and clapped when the agent became sarcastic with me. I thought he was going to get a standing ovation for one smart remark. The Court called the audience down by saying, "All right. We'll have none of that, absolutely none of that."

Obviously, the crowd did not appreciate the difficult job that had been forced on Bussman and me. We were now as hated as much as Judith Ann Neelley.

Burns questioned Neelley about passing bad checks and forged money orders in an interview that began at 6:45 p.m., and lasted until 12:20 a.m. Danny Smith joined the interview at 9:10 p.m. She was never told that Burton was still in the hall waiting to see her.I told Bussman that had I been Burton, I would have yelled at the top of my lungs. "Bob French is here! Don't say a word!"

Burns talked to Neelley again on October 19, 1982, at the Dekalb County Sheriff's Office in the presence of Tony Gilliland, Ron Turner, Bob French, and Steve Bussman. The purpose of this interview was to discuss some incidents with the YDC of Georgia.

At some point in time, the agent was of the opinion that Judith Ann Neelley may have threatened him in a letter to her husband that had been given to me when we first met.

Agent Burns brought a search warrant to search my office and took possession of the letter. Four agents made this search at night, during the trial. They like to do things like that thinking it intimidates the defense lawyer. They wasted their time with me.

Burns interviewed Alvin Neelley several days after he interviewed Judith.

On re-direct, Richard's questions centered on Neelley not wanting an attorney or to stop talking. Burns read a paragraph of the statement: "She did state that she was willing to talk about any other matter. She was told at that time that if she wanted to terminate the interview that she could, and that she could return to her cell without further questioning. She insisted that she did not want to leave the interview and wanted to continue talking at that time."

The agent was questioning her about passing money orders in Alabama and Georgia. He agreed that Bill Burton was her attorney regarding the charges for checks and money orders in Tennessee, and he was not interrogating the defendant regarding those matters. According to Burns, Judith Ann Neelley did not have an attorney representing her in Georgia nor with regard to the Lisa Ann Millican murder in Alabama.

Burns was splitting hairs, and the courts allowed him to get away with it, all the way to the U.S. Supreme Court.

Burns asked if she wanted to stop the interview at 7:25 p.m. At 7:29 p.m. she said she wanted to continue the interview and that she did want to talk about other matters. At 8:42 p.m., she was offered the opportunity to terminate the interview. At the time Danny Smith came in, she said that she was sick of hearing that, and she wanted to keep talking. This process was repeated at 12:05 a.m., and she did not wish to return to her cell.

Burns' testimony was amazing. If Neelley said the things attributed to her, then the case made even less sense than we had grown accustomed to expect.

NEELLEY'S ATTORNEY KEPT OUT

Bill Burton, practicing law since 1968, was licensed to practice in the US District Court for Middle Tennessee, and all state courts. Ricahard agreed to his qualifications.

Burton regularly represents criminal clients and represented Judith Ann Neelley at her preliminary hearing in October of 1982. Aside from representing her relatives, that was his first contact with her. She was accused of altering money orders. The day following the preliminary hearing, he met with her about making bond. He was not aware of any other charges.

Burton reported to her that her grandmother was financially unable to make her bond. Jail officials had allowed him to accompany her while she made other phone calls to relatives.

On October 14, 1982, between 6:30 and 7:00 p.m., Alvin Neelley called Burton at home, after supper, and asked him to come to the jail. Officers from out of state wanted to talk to him and Judith. The attorney went to the jail immediately.

Burton asked the dispatcher if officers from Georgia were talking to Judith or Alvin Neelley. They were. The hallway was "just full of officers I had never seen before." He was allowed to talk with Alvin, but when he asked to talk with Judith, he was told, "We don't have to let you see her because she has to specifically request to see you."

Burton responded, "Well, you may mess up your case, or you may mess up your evidence if you don't let me see her."

An officer called some superior and came back and said, "We've checked, and we don't have to let you in. She has to specifically request you to come in and see her, but we don't have to let you in."

Burton considered himself Judith's attorney. He had been paid to represent her. He had not been hired for just one specific purpose. He had undertaken to represent a criminal client.

The attorney had represented Judith's father in a car wreck 10 years previously, and had represented her mother closing her father's estate. He had been hired to protect Judith Ann Neelley two days before. He went to the jail to prevent her from talking to the detectives. His fee had been paid by Alvin.

On cross-examination, Burton said that he represented Judith Neelley in a case involving forged money orders, and was not aware of any charges in Alabama or Georgia before going to the jail.

Whether he represented Neelley on the murder of Lisa Ann Millican, Burton said that he was summoned to the jail by her husband to protect her. The officers prevented him from talking to his client about the Millican murder case.

Burton was allowed to talk to Alvin Neelley because he had requested an attorney. Although he talked with Alvin, he did not consider himself representing Alvin in a murder case.

With Burton, I made a drawing of the layout of the Rutherford County Sheriff's Office, which was offered as Court's Exhibit B for the purposes of this hearing.

Burton could not say he represented Judith Ann Neelley on murder charges as he was prevented from discussing the matter with her.

Although I was aware that Miranda rights belong to the accused and no one else, I thought it was illegal that a retained attorney was forcibly prevented from seeing his client. This bordered on Gestapo tactics. They were playing fast and loose, and going to get away with it.

Danny Smith was called by the Defense. He left Fort Payne and went to Rome, Georgia, where he met with other officers. Four or five cars proceeded to Murphreesboro where interview rooms for both Alvin and Judith Ann Neelley were provided. The officers divided into teams and did interviews, searched the automobiles, and the home of Barbara Adams.

When Burton first arrived, he was shown to the room of Alvin Neelley. When Burton asked to see Judith, Smith denied him admittance to the room where she was being questioned.

Smith told Burton they were not questioning Neelley about the forgeries that he represented her on, they were looking into a homicide. Burton would not be allowed to speak to the defendant, unless she specifically asked for an attorney.

When Smith joined the interview, "Agent Burns ascertained from the defendant whether she would be intimidated or uncomfortable with three investigators in the room, and she said she would not."

Smith saw Burton within two or three feet of the door to the room where the Neelley was being questioned.

JUDITH NEELLEY'S FIRST TESTIMONY

Judith Ann Neelley, was called to testify for the limited purpose of this hearing. She was 18 years old. On the evening of October 14, 1982, shortly after dinner, an officer took her from her cell to an interview room where Burns and Stuck told her they would like to talk with her about some forged money orders in Alabama and in Georgia. Her rights were read to her. She refused to sign the form and asked for her attorney. The officers said they wanted to ask a few routine questions. She agreed to answer without her attorney present. At that time, she did not know her Attorney Bill Burton was in the hallway. Bill Burton, who represented her family was expected to be there that night to protect her. She never knew he was available to her that evening.

On cross-examination, she said that Burton had not represented her personally before October 10, 1982. At the time of her interrogation, Burton was representing her on bad check charges in Murfreesboro. "But if I had had a chance to ask him, I'm sure he would have represented me for this."

She understood what her rights were and was willing to make a statement and answer questions. "To a certain extent I told them I would answer questions about my background." She told the officers she did not want an attorney present. After talking about two hours, the officers mentioned the murder of Lisa Ann Millican.

She talked with agent Burns for over an hour about her background. "Then he started to get into the money orders, and I told him I didn't want to talk about that. I wasn't going to say anything about it without my lawyer present."

The subject of money orders was dropped, and the interrogators began to discuss the facts of the murder case. Later, the money orders were brought up again. Several times during the night the defendant was offered the opportunity to terminate the interview and return to her cell.

She asked to see her husband, and they told her they were trying to arrange that. She was trying to find out what the officers wanted, as they kept beating around the bush.

With this testimony, we concluded seeking to suppress the statement given by Judith Ann Neelley in Rutherford County, Tennessee.

The Court reserved a ruling on the motion until the next morning.

The State went forward with the other part of the motion to suppress - the statement taken from the defendant on October 15, 1982, in Fort Payne, Alabama.

Danny Smith, along with Pat Wetzel, ABI, and Investigator Darrell Collins, interviewed the defendant in the Grand Jury room of the DeKalb County Courthouse around 1:00 p.m. The Miranda warning was given to the defendant, and she said she understood her rights. She did not want an attorney. Her statement was made voluntarily.

On cross-examination, I maintained that the interrogation of October 15, 1982, was a continuation of the interrogation of October 14, 1982, with references such as, "... and, like I told you last night, we do not...," "... like I told you last night, we want to try to understand why...," "... last night that we do thank you for the information."

"I have explained to the district attorney that probably we would be able to, ah, talk to you and your attorney and maybe work out something that you've expressed to be with your husband in Georgia, okay?"

Other phrases concerning the prior investigation were: "... based on what he told us and based on what you said last night ..." and "... you had told me last night that, ah, you had met Lisa ..." The defendant did not ask Smith for an attorney on the 15th.

The Court reserved ruling on the motion to suppress until the following morning, the sixth day of the trial.

When court reconvened, the Court announced it's ruling – "Overruled." You may read the verbatim transcript of the ruling denying our motion as **Appendix 1**.

Had the judge suppressed either of the confessions, this would have changed the complexion of the case. Either would have been considered to be the fruit of the poisoned tree. All confessions would have been excluded.

The Court could have gone either way, as it was obvious the officers were playing fast and loose with the defendant's rights against self-incrimination. Certainly, she did not understand her rights nor was she aware her attorney was there to help her. She said she waned her attorney. Now without the Court suppressing any of her self-incriminating statements, we had to press on.

BACK TO THE FBI

Now, you are going to plod through the testimony that was actually heard by the jury. You know most of this due to prior proceedings. Now, you will get it directly from the witnesses. This is how trials work, so bear with it.

Bill O. Burns, now in the presence of the jury. After testifying as to the voluntariness of the statement, Burns stated that he showed the defendant a photograph of Lisa Ann Millican. She said she had met the girl at the mall in Rome, Georgia, approximately two months ago. She was shown a second photograph of the victim. Tape recordings of a female calling the Rome Police Department, talking about fire bombings, shootings, and the reporting of the location of the body of Lisa Ann Millican. She did not want to listen to either tape.

Her response to the playing of the second tape was, "Did you record the calls I made to Fort Payne, also?"

Judith Ann Neelley told Burns she had shot Lisa Ann Millican once in the back near the place where the body was found. She was driving a Dodge Dart automobile.

She had met Lisa Ann Millican at the mall on Friday or Saturday. Lisa did not want to go back to the Harpst Home. They drove around for a while and went to a motel near Cedartown. After leaving the motel, they drove to a town she did not know in central Alabama. They stayed in an L-shaped motel near a Dairy Queen-type restaurant. Alvin Neelley followed them to the motel near Cedartown in a Ford Granada.

She registered in her own name at the motel in central Alabama. They stayed in this motel until Tuesday when she told her husband she intended to get rid of Lisa. She took Lisa to Little River Canyon near some picnic tables and rocks and shot her in the back. Before shooting her, she injected Liquid-Plumr and Drano into the victim while she was handcuffed. Two shots were injected in the left side of Lisa Millican's neck, two shots into her hips through her blue jeans, and one shot in each arm. Lisa walked around slowly for about half an hour. She said she was cold. When the injections had no appreciable effect on the victim, the handcuffs were removed; and Lisa was told to walk to the edge of the canyon and turn her back to the defendant. After Lisa was shot in the back, Neelley pushed her body off the canyon rim with her knee. She got blood from the wound in Lisa's back on the right knee of her jeans. She took off the jeans and threw them in the canyon with the hypodermic needles and a white towel. She took another pair of jeans from the car and redressed. Defendant then went back to the motel where her husband had been staying.

The Neelleys drove to Rome, Georgia. Neelley said she killed Lisa so she would not have to return to the YDC. She would be better off dead. Defendant had purchased the Drano and Liquid-Plumr and hypodermic needles in Alabama about a month before because she wanted to see the effect it would have on the human body.

The agent showed defendant a photograph of Janice Chapman, and she denied knowing Chapman or John Hancock.

I objected to any further questions concerning Janice Chapman, since the statement given by defendant concerning Chapman had nothing to do with the present case and could only serve to inflame the prejudice and ill will of the jury toward the defendant. "Overruled."

Judith Ann Neelley then said that she had taken Janice Chapman to the Oak Hurst Motel in Rome, Georgia; spent the night with her; and killed her the next day by shooting her in the back. The defendant had met Chapman and Hancock on Shorter Avenue and took them for a ride. While driving out Highway 20, the defendant called her husband, known as the Nightrider, on the CB radio for a time check. She then met her husband, and drove to Summerville, Georgia, where they turned right toward Calhoun, Georgia. She told her husband to turn off a dirt road because she had something she wanted to do. She felt that John Hancock was a threat to her. So when they pulled off on the dirt road, defendant took a .38-caliber pistol and forced Hancock to walk into a wooded area where she shot him in the back. She returned to her car and told her husband they had to get out of there. They drove to the Oak Hurst Motel where they stayed that night with Janice Chapman. When she had returned to the car, she told Janice Chapman she had shot up in the air; and Chapman had nothing to worry about, so long as she did as she was told. The following day, defendant drove Janice Chapman to a remote area near the old Armuchee High School in Floyd County, Georgia. There she told Chapman she was going to be tied up loosely so she could get away. She walked Chapman into some bushes and told her to turn her back to her because she could not stand to look her in the face while she killed her. Defendant then shot Chapman in the back. Chapman was hollering loudly, and defendant was afraid someone would hear her.

At this point, Judith Neelley began to cry. The Court granted a defense request for a five-minute recess in order for the defendant to regain her composure.

Upon return of defendant and counsel, the direct examination of Burns continued. He stated that when Chapman began to holler, she shot her twice in the chest. Then she went back to the motel where her husband was. Defendant told the witness she had told Chapman about killing Lisa Ann Millican because she wanted her to fear her, since she enjoyed people fearing her instead of her fearing others. She did not call the police after this shooting, as she knew John Hancock was alive and could describe her and her husband.

She attempted to pick up a girl wearing a Hardee's uniform and one other girl in Rome. Had she picked them up, she would have killed them. During the relation of events, she did not show any emotion. She was perfectly calm and completely in control.

SOME FBI AGENTS WILL BELIEVE ANYTHING

It was a bizarre tale Neelley had told Burns in an attempt to clear Alvin Neelley. I cross-examined him as to his general knowledge of the facts when he went to see Judith Neelley. He felt the case was important enough to return from his annual leave and take part in the investigation. His testimony was substantially the same as it was during the motion to suppress hearing.

I forced the agent to agree that he spent 5 hours and 30 minutes interviewing Neelley. Four minutes of that time, he advised her of her rights and allowed her to read the FBI Waiver-of-Rights form. On the 302 form prepared by the witness, the defendant would not talk about money orders but was willing to talk about any other matter. According to Burns, after the assertion on his statement, Neelley began telling of passing money orders in her name after Alvin Neelley got out of prison. She had stolen the money orders from a Majik Market where her husband worked.

Alvin Neelley did not pass any of the money orders nor did he have the ability to raise them. Judith took all the blame for stealing, changing, and passing the money orders. She also told Burns about the sexual abuse of the inmates committed by employees of the Youth Detention Center in Rome and Macon, Georgia. Her husband reported it to Sam House of the GBI.

Were spouse beatings brought up? Burns said that Neelley told him that her husband had beaten her in the past, but she did not elaborate. At the time of the interview, she had a black eye. She told the agent of a miscarriage in 1980 in Albany, Georgia, after having carried the child for five months. She admitted firebombing the home of Ken Dooley and shooting up the residence of Linda Adair. She did not implicate Alvin Neelley in any of her acts. She used gas in a Coke bottle with a rag wick, known as a Molotov cocktail, to firebomb the Adair residence. After throwing the bomb, she ran back to the Dodge automobile and entered the car through the passenger door in order that witnesses might think there were two people in the car. She strongly denied that anyone accompanied her during the firebombing.

Defendant wanted the agent to clearly understand that she committed all the crimes alone. She did not implicate Alvin in any of these acts.

Neelley told Burns that she purchased the pistol she used to do the shooting in Phoenix City, Alabama. Ken Dooley had sex with her at the YDC in Rome, and in one of the cottages in the center in Macon. Her court-appointed attorney, Robert Kauphman, defending her for armed robbery, forced her to have sexual intercourse with him on the floor in the courthouse; and after he reached an orgasm, he forced her to have intercourse with a black officer guarding the door for them.

She called Ken Dooley's residence to find out where he lived. She told him she was a friend of his wife's and wanted to see her. She shot in his house four times. She knew where Adair lived from an outing earlier. She drove to the house and tried to throw the firebomb in the carport but did not have the strength to do so. She stated that she would have hurt Dooley and Adair badly if she had been able.

Defendant then told the agent that she bought hypodermic needles and a can of Drano in a store in Alabama to inject it in someone from the YDC to see what it would do to them. She told of trying to pick up other girls she would have killed. The agent understood the defendant enjoyed killing people. She explained her black eye by saying she ran into a girl from the 8th grade whom she did not like.

The agent understood there was a possibility that the defendant had been abused. The agent questioned Alvin Neelley about beating the defendant, and Alvin told him that the defendant beat him.

The agent believed Alvin's statement that the defendant beat him as it was consistent with what he already believed about the defendant. The agent considered her black eye to be the result of a long-standing argument defendant had with some girl named Kathy from the 8th grade at Oakland High School.

JURORS GET THE WEEKEND OFF

When the Court recessed for the noon break, Judge Cole discussed the possibility of allowing the jurors to visit with their families over the weekend. The Defense and the State agreed that this would be satisfactory.

BACK TO WORK ON MONDAY

My cross-examination of Burns continued. He said that the defendant told him that Alvin Neelley was there when she talked with Lisa Ann Millican. Burns could not remember questioning Alvin Neelley about this matter.

When he began to play the tape recordings, Judith Neelley did not want to hear them. When Neelley asked him if they recorded the calls she made to Fort Payne also, he knew he had a confession to murder.

Neelley told Burns that she had called the Rome Police Department, a Rome radio station, and the Fort Payne authorities to report the murder of Lisa Ann Millican. Incredibly, he did not consider this unusual.

Alvin Neelley, admitted that Judith, Lisa Ann Millican, and their two children had spent the night in a motel in Franklin, Georgia. He admitted to having sex with Lisa Ann Millican that night. The following night the group traveled to middle Alabama. That evening, Lisa came to him and told him she wanted to have sex with him because Judy had told her that if she didn't have sex with him, she would turn her back over to Georgia authorities. Alvin was just a passive party, and Lisa was frightened of Judy. Judy had threatened him many times, and he was afraid of her.

Burns formed the opinion Judith Ann Neelley enjoyed torturing people and killing them. He never explored why she was telling him the bizarre things she was saying.

I questioned the agent as to inconsistent statements made by Judith Ann Neelley during her interview. For example, she left a motel in Scottsboro to "get rid of Lisa Millican." Then she returned to the motel in Rome to tell her husband she had gotten rid of Lisa Millican.

She purchased Drano and Liquid-Plumr to administer it to the staff of the YDC. Later, she said that she purchased it to see what it would do to a human body. She could not tell the agent where she had spent the night before Lisa was killed. She could only say it was in middle Alabama – "L" shaped next to a Dairy Queen. The agent never considered this was the Five Points Motel in Scottsboro.

He did not find any of this inconsistent. He just accepted it as the truth. Bizarre!

Regarding Janice Chapman, Judith told him that, as the group drove back from Summerville, Georgia, she told Alvin to turn off the road, that she had something she wanted to do. Although he was riding in the car with Alvin Neelley, John Hancock was a threat to her. Judith told Burns that Alvin Neelley did not know what was happening. She simply walked John Hancock into the woods and shot him. Alvin did not know that she was going out to shoot Janice Chapman.

Alvin Neelley told Burns that he told Judith over the CB that he had to stop and go to the bathroom. When first questioned, Alvin Neelley said he did not get out of his car that night, nor did he hear a gunshot. Later, he admitted getting out of the car and that he did hear a gunshot. Alvin said that Judith came running back to the car and took her children from her car to his car. Judy was laughing and making fun of him because he was terrified about the incident.

The drawing and testimony of John Hancock were reviewed for the agent. He admitted that the story of Hancock and Alvin Neelley were two different stories.

Alvin Neelley had told him that Judith shot Hancock, the group went to the Oak Hurst Hotel, where they spent the night in the same room. While Judith had gone to get some food, he asked Janice Chapman if she wanted to fool around. Janice said she did. They were still engaged in the sex act when Judith returned. Judith took Janice Chapman out the next morning and killed her. Alvin Neelley learned the details of the crimes when he saw the newspapers later and read the articles about Hancock and Chapman.

I was amazed that the agent believed Alvin when he said that Janice Chapman wanted to have sex with him minutes after she thought Judith Neelley had killed her husband, and father of her children. If the jury was as naive as the agent, Judith Neelley was on her way to death row.

Judith Neelley told the agent that she told Alvin what she had done after he read the paper. According to Judith, Alvin did not have anything to do with the shootings. He did not know that she was going to shoot John Hancock or Janice Chapman.

When Burns and other agents searched the premises where Alvin and Judith Neelley lived in Alvin's mother's mobile home, they looked in areas Alvin pointed out to them. Alvin had been taken from the Chattooga County, Georgia, jail to accompany the officers to the area to be searched.

The officers did not find any letters from Alvin to Judith. Neither did they find any color Polaroid pictures of Judith Neelley. There were no weapons in the room. The officers took a box of letters from Judith to Alvin.

After a short re-direct examination, the witness was excused.

We asked that the state produce an 8" x 10" color photograph of Judith Neelley, taken on October 15th. The state produced the picture.

MOTEL OWNER DESCRIBES HIS GUESTS

Parsottam Patel was recalled to produce a registration card made out to Ben Farrington. The person signing in on the 26th day of September, 1982, indicated they had a Dodge automobile. A woman registered for four persons. The woman asked for a room for herself, a girlfriend, and two children. The motel is 30 miles from Fort Payne. The people stayed in room No. 12 for 2 nights. He saw a second car at the room. This car was red. There is a Dairy Bar nearby. State's Exhibit No. 52 was the motel registration card. He saw the children but did not see a man with the party. He could not identify the woman.

March 14, 1983, the seventh day of the trial resumed. The Court opened stating that there would be no comments or whispering to anyone while court was in session.

DANNY SMITH IS BACK

Danny Smith, testified that Judith Neelley had told him about meeting Lisa Ann Millican but she didn't know where her husband was. He was not around. They spent Saturday night somewhere south of Cedartown. On Sunday, they drove into Alabama, approximately 30 miles from Fort Payne. She did not know the name of the town nor the motel. The motel was "L" shaped. She registered in her own name. Lisa was afraid of Judith so she kept her handcuffed so she couldn't run off. The people from the Harpst Home would be looking for Lisa, and she could get into trouble for picking her up. The handcuffs found in the Adams' home in Murfreesboro were the ones she used. Neelley showed Millican a gun which she kept while traveling, a .38-caliber Smith and Wesson, four-inch barrel, blue steel revolver, six-shot. Lisa helped her pack the car Tuesday morning. Lisa Millican did not try to escape while she was with her.

On Tuesday morning she decided that she could not allow Lisa to go free because Lisa would cause her trouble. Lisa would have been placed in the YDC, and she would rather see her dead than in the YDC.

How could investigators swallow this insane narrative? She couldn't let Lisa go because she would get her into trouble. Yet, she called the authorities and told them she had killed Lisa. She had spent two years in the YDC as an exceptional inmate. Yet, she believed every insane scenario Alvin Neelley concocted in his warped view of reality. It seems the investigators would have realized the folly of her statements.

Smith then went through the Neelley account of what happened at the canyon. Judy did it all, it was all her idea and Alvin was no where around.

She had called the Rome Police Department and the DeKalb County Sheriff's Office. She described other girls she had tried to pick up and admitted that she would probably have killed them if she had been successful in luring them into her car.

Smith questioned Neelley about John Hancock and Janice Chapman. She gave a very similar story to what she had said in Murfreesboro. She told Smith that she had kept Janice Chapman handcuffed. At night, she slept with her husband, and Janice Chapman slept on the bed with her children. She liked to target practice but was not a good shot. She recounted the events happening after shooting John Hancock.

After spending the night, Neelley took Chapman and her children, and drove toward Summerville, Georgia. Alvin Neelley followed part of the way but was not with her when she told Chapman that she was going to tie her loosely. Chapman saw the gun and was scared. She made Chapman turn her back and shot her. Chapman fell on the ground hollering, and Neelley shot her twice more in the chest. Alvin was not there at the time.

Smith produced the photograph taken of Judy Neelley at the time of his interview. Defendant's Exhibit No. 25. Neelley did not implicate her husband in any of her criminal acts.

Smith noticed discrepancies and inconsistencies in the statements given by Neelley. For example, in the statement to Agent Burns, she said Alvin Neelley was with her in the mall in Rome, Georgia. Later, she said he wasn't. The investigation indicated that Alvin Neelley had committed rape in Alabama, as well as a number of other crimes that she denied.

ALVIN'S BIZARRE TALES CONTINUE AND THE STATE RESTS

Alvin had not been charged with any crime. The only motive Judy Neelley could give the witness for murdering Lisa Ann Millican was that she would rather have seen her dead than returned to the YDC. Lisa was not in the YDC; she was a resident of the Harpst Home! There was a great difference between the two.

On October 18, 1982 Alvin told Smith that both he and Judith Ann Neelley had sexual relations with Lisa Ann Millican and Janice Chapman. Neelley said that Judy enjoyed having sexual relations with a woman after he had sexual intercourse with her. Alvin said that Judy came back to the motel and watched him having sexual relations with Janice Chapman. The defendant went into the restroom in the motel, and Chapman followed her in there. According to Alvin Neelley, the two women stayed in the bathroom for some 30 to 45 minutes.

Alvin Neelley said that Lisa Ann Millican approached him and began to kiss and fondle him and solicited sexual relations with him at the Chattahoochee Motel in Franklin, Georgia. This solicitation was made in front of Judy Neelley and the children. Judy and Lisa went into the bathroom, and came out nude. He had sex with Lisa, and then Lisa and Judith had sex on the floor.

Alvin said that he had sexual relations with Janice Chapman at the Oak Hurst Motel in Rome, Georgia, the night John Hancock was shot.

I was sitting at our table unbelieving. How could any officer believe that a fat slob like Alvin Neelley was so irresistible that a 13 year old girl had to have him as well as a woman who thought her husband had just been killed? Nothing put the officers on notice that there was more to the case than what they were learning. Incredible!

More crazy stuff – Judith told Smith that when she left Scottsboro, Alvin had followed her on Highway 35 as far as I-59. When he reached the interstate, he turned south toward Gadsden, Alabama.

The State then introduced Exhibit No. 28, the handcuffs found in the home of Barbara Adams. After State's Exhibit No. 28 was admitted by the Court, the State announced, "The State rests."

With the jury excused, the defense renewed all previous motions filed in the case and denied by the Court. We renewed our motion to suppress, and moved the Court for a verdict by acquittal for the failure of the State of make out a case against the defendant. We renewed our Grand Jury motions, our motion in limine, all other motions, and insisted upon our motion for discovery.

The Court denied all motions, other than the motion to produce the baseball bat. That motion, along with the defense motion to produce the statement of Alvin Neelley, would be considered by the Court later.

MUSINGS BEFORE GOING TO WORK

The evidence of the State had been overwhelming. All we had was Jo Ann Browning and Judith Ann Neelley. We weren't sure what either of them was going to say.

The courtroom was packed with spectators. More than a dozen television crews and innumerable press people were camped out in the elevator foyer outside the courtroom. *The New York Times* and *The London Times* were there. It was like a circus.

The local Democrats kept their rumor mill running wide open. They were traveling the county telling people their "exclusive" Bob French story. People were picketing my office with paper covering Democrat candidate campaign signs saying, "Don't hire this lawyer." "This lawyer likes killers," and so on. I knew it was going to get worse.

A client from Rainsville caught me in the restroom and said, "You know the Democrat machine is smearing you far and wide? Some of them are riding the roads talking about you."

"Yeah, I know it. But there is nothing I can do to stop it."

He continued, "What aggravates me is the Republicans who believe the lies and are spreading them, as well."

"Yeah. It just goes with the territory," I responded.

ALVIN'S FIRST WIFE TESTIFIES

It was time to heat things up with the Defense - If things could get any hotter.

Jo Ann Browning, a 27 year old resident of Dalton, Georgia, was the mother of four children. She lived with Neelley five years and was the mother of three of his children. Two of these children were seized by his mother, who reported them abandoned, and had them adopted by Alvin's half-sister. Sadly, Jo Ann does not see these children at all.

Toward the end of 1973, she met Alvin Neelley at Calfee's Meat Market on Underwood Street in Dalton. Benny Farrington, Alvin Neelley's half-brother, worked there. They began to live together the first part of 1974 while he was employed at Aladdin Carpet Mills on third shift.

The State objected to the Defense going into the details of the ex-wife's relationship with Alvin Neelley.

A long conference was held at the side bar with the Court, outside the presence of the jury, where both sides argued their points concerning the proposed testimony of the witness. The Court decided to allow the Defense to pursue the matter.

Jo Ann was shown an identification tag from Aladdin Mills with the picture of Alvin Neelley as Joseph Henry Parks. She had never known Parks but recognized the picture. Defense Exhibit No. 27, was admitted into evidence. This was another find from Steve's grocery bag from Cleveland.

Browning described her early life with Alvin. The state objected. "Overruled."

When she first met Alvin he was charming, loving and considerate. Then, in the fall of 1974, there was the gas shortage. Jo Ann forgot to buy gas. She drove to Dalton to pick Alvin up from work. She tried to make it back to Cleveland, but ran out of gas. Alvin forced her to walk to his mother's house, and get a neighbor to bring some gas. On the way, some dogs began to bother her, and she picked up a can to throw at them. She still had the can in her hand when Alvin arrived home after a neighbor took gas to him.

Alvin demanded to know where the can came from. She told him, and for the first time, he began to slap her. Jo Ann fled into the bedroom, pursued by Alvin. Neelley's mother attempted to persuade him to stop the beating, but he would not listen. Neelley beat Jo Ann around the breasts and arms. With his index fingers, he stretched the corners of her mouth. Jo Ann was finally able to persuade Alvin to calm down and leave the room.

After that, Alvin beat her every time he became angry. If he was mad about money, or if he was mad at someone at work, he would come home and attack her.

Three or four days after the first beating, Jo Ann was beaten because Alvin accused her of going with other men. When JoAnn denied the accusations, Alvin beat her until she told him the "truth." Neelley would not recognize that she had told him the truth the first time. He would beat her until she admitted seeing other men. He would then force Jo Ann to get into the car and go looking for the other men. Jo Ann testified that she would make up addresses of the supposed men. She and Alvin would look for the men, but they were never able to find them. If she did not make up an address, Alvin would beat her until she told him the address. He accused her of seeing other men while he was at work. It was insane.

Alvin Neelley beat her when she did not do things just the way he wanted. He hit her so many times that if he moved his arms, she would reflex with her arms, trying to protect her head. Finally, after many beatings, all Neelley had to do was threaten Jo Ann, and she would do whatever he said.

Alvin Neelley had a "bad leg." Jo Ann helped him dress each day by putting his shoes on him and helping him with his pants. At times, Neelley would kick her hard in the stomach, particularly when she was pregnant.

He would instruct her to bring something to him. If she did not bring the exact thing he wanted – a shirt or something - he would hit her over and over with his fist.

While Jo Ann was pregnant with Little Al, when he began to beat her, she would scream, and go under the bed. Once, neighbors heard her screams and called the police. Al forced Jo Ann out from under the bed, with a bruised face, to tell the deputies that nothing was happening. The deputies questioned Jo Ann about the bruises, and she told them that she had fallen up against something. As soon as the deputies left, Al began to hit her again.

Alvin would hit her with his fist or his forearm. If she ran into another room, he would break down the door. If she went under the bed, Alvin Neelley would either wait until she came out, or he would promise her that if she would come out he would not hit her. As soon as she came out, he would begin to beat her more. The beatings became a nightly occurrence, whether she was pregnant or not. She was his punching bag.

Alvin and Jo Ann began working at Fritzell Brothers, a carpet mill in Dalton, Georgia. She was packaging yarn kits, and Alvin was working in the shipping department. Jo Ann drove them back and forth to work. If Alvin saw Jo Ann talking to another man, he would beat her while she was driving the car.

Sometimes he hit her in the face with his open palm. He would bloody her nose and black her eyes. She would run the car off the road and tell him they were going to wreck. He didn't care, and would not stop beating her. Al also hit Jo Ann with things in the car, such as ice scrapers, screwdrivers, and his gun. Neelley kept his gun under his seat of the car. The beatings in the car happened almost every day.

Jo Ann knew when Alvin was going to have a mad spell. His voice tone would change, and his eyes had a gleam in them that made them glisten.

LIVING WITH ALVIN NEELLEY

Alvin spent most of his evenings talking on his CB radio. He would flirt with other women while Jo Ann was present. Jo Ann was not allowed to make any decisions for herself or the family, nor would he permit her to make suggestions.

Although I was examining this witness and eliciting this information, I had never heard this before. Jo Ann glossed over the beating details when we found her during our pre-trial investigation. Michelle had given us more information than she did.

In 1976, the Neelleys moved to Albany, Georgia. Alvin sold their furniture to an auction company, even though it had not been paid for. He wanted cash and could not persuade his mother to give him more money.

This move began a series of moves whereby the Neelleys would stay in a town for a month or two months, then move on.

There were three children in the household when the Neelleys moved to Albany. Alvin favored Amy because she looked like the Neelley side of the family. He whipped the children relentlessly for little things. When Jo Ann interfered, he would transfer the beating to her.

When people outside the family noticed the bruises and marks on Jo Ann's body, she would make up an excuse. She did not want trouble.

The Neelleys moved in with Jo Ann's mother for a while, and Alvin did not beat her in the presence of her family. Alvin was always laughing, and cutting up with Jo Ann's mother who would not believe the things Jo Ann told her about him. The three months that the Neelleys lived with Jo Ann mother was the only time since their early marriage that he did not terrorize her.

After residing with her mother, the family moved to Tunnel Hill, Georgia, where they rented a furnished house trailer. Three days after moving into the new home, the beatings began again.

Because he was dissatisfied being paid every two weeks, he began to steal from the store. He forced Jo Ann to take money from the cash register while the clerk on duty was working the gas pumps. Hiding the money under her coat, Jo Ann told the clerk that she had seen a man take the money, and run across the street. Alvin backed her up.

Alvin had made up this story for her, and had rehearsed her for about three or four nights. Jo Ann objected to the crime, but Alvin gave her no choice.

"If I didn't do it and get him some money, I would suffer the consequences."

The crime resulted in about two hundred dollars. Jo Ann sat in the car until Alvin had finished his shift. When they arrived at home, Alvin took the money.

At a Golden Gallon store in Chatsworth, Georgia, Alvin Neelley came up with the idea for Jo Ann to make night deposits by depositing an empty envelope. While counting the money from the final theft, Jo Ann miscounted by twenty dollars. Alvin accused her of trying to keep some of the money for herself. He threw a roll of quarters at her and hit her in the head. Then he started slapping and punching her, telling her that she would do as he wanted her to do. Later, he found the missing twenty-dollar bill. He did not apologize for the beating.

Neelley forced Jo Ann to have oral sex with him, and to perform the sex act with him almost every night. After she had been beaten, Jo Ann still had to perform sexually. She did not enjoy sex, as she was a slave to Neelley. The beatings were extremely brutal and hurt badly.

Jo Ann said that she had never told her story before telling it on the stand under oath.

Alvin said someone had told him about her seeing another man. This was his excuse to begin a beating. After beating her to where she was bleeding from several places, he left to find the other man. He said that he was going to kill her when he returned.

In desperation, Jo Ann called her parents to come and take her away; but they could not find the trailer where the Neelleys were living. She had to hide in a ditch near the residence. Alvin returned and called for her. After she left the ditch, she walked down Highway 31, where she found a woman to take her to her mother's house. Jo Ann stayed with her mother for about a week before Alvin came for her.

He threatened to hurt the children if she did not go with him and do exactly what he wanted.

GOING BACK TO ALVIN

The night she agreed to leave her mother's home and return with Alvin, he insisted that her younger sister return with them.

When they arrived at the trailer, Alvin told her to take some little white pills he had that would make her feel happy. Shortly after swallowing the pills, she began to feel drowsy. Alvin Neelley then brought Jo Ann's 13-year-old sister, Lisa, to bed with them and began trying to have sex with her.

Jo Ann knew what was happening, but she was drugged, and could do nothing to stop Alvin. Her sister was telling him not to touch her, "to leave her alone; and she kept hollering for me, and I couldn't do nothing for her."

Finally, Alvin gave up and Lisa went to sleep in the other room.

Jo Ann was awakened the following morning by her sister's screams. Alvin had placed a sheet over the window and was attempting to rape Lisa. When Jo Ann intervened, Alvin started beating her. Later, he allowed her to call her mother to come take her sister home. When her mother arrived, Jo Ann returned to her mother's home with her sister.

Alvin was arrested for theft by taking from the Golden Gallon store. He telephoned Jo Ann when he was released on bond. Jo Ann returned to him because he threatened to inform the authorities that she was involved in his crimes. They moved into the house trailer with his mother. The beatings continued in the presence of his mother who no longer attempted to help Jo Ann.

Jo Ann and Alvin had been in bed and had not redressed. He accused her of trying to go back to her first husband. He was beating her so severely that she ran out of the room naked. Mrs. Neelley was on the couch but did not offer to help. With naked Alvin behind her, Jo Ann ran on out of the trailer. Alvin followed her out with a mop handle. When Alvin caught Jo Ann, he began to beat her with the handle. Neighbors in the next trailer looked out their window at the naked Neelleys, but they would not come to Jo Ann's rescue. Alvin caused stripes and bruises all over her body. Jo Ann persuaded Alvin to stop beating her because it was time for her to go to work at Southern Binders. He allowed her to return to the trailer where his mother told him that Jo Ann did not need any places on her that would show at work. Apparently, she approved of him beating his wife as long as it didn't show.

WITH ALVIN THINGS ALWAYS GET WORSE

Although Jo Ann and the children rarely had enough food to eat, Alvin ate all day at the stores where he worked. He bought whatever he wanted with money he took from the stores. When Jo Ann cooked at home, Alvin insisted that the food be hot and spicy. He used a lot of Tabasco Sauce. The children could not eat the food because it burned their mouths. When Jo Ann prepared other food for the children, Alvin threw things at her, and cursed her, calling her a "bitch" and a "whore" telling her that she could not get anything right. He seemed to enjoy the suffering of his children.

In 1977, Jo Ann escaped to her mother's home. She was now supporting herself. Alvin called her saying one of the children was sick. He actually wanted her to have sex with him. Once, he called Jo Ann while she was working and said that Mikie needed to be taken to the hospital. When Jo Ann arrived at the trailer, he began to question her about the men she worked with. He took her into the bedroom and began to perform oral sex on her. When she would not tell him she liked it, he bit her until she began to swell. Jo Ann slid out from underneath Neelley and ran into the living room where Mrs. Neelley was asleep on the couch. She dressed and told Alvin she was leaving. She ran out, but he caught her.

On another occasion, Alvin Neelley hit her on her private parts until she was black and blue. He said that he was going to beat her until she was disfigured and no man would want her. He used both fists in beating her. Neelley usually attacked her private parts in the beatings he gave her.

"He would hit me, down there, ah, the main part of a woman, and ah, he would hit me around my breasts, and he bit me on my breasts and" – Neelley bit Jo Ann to the point of bringing blood on the inside of her skin, leaving his teeth marks. He bit her hand so hard that teeth marks could be seen for a week.

After Alvin jumped bail a third time, the family moved to Albany, Georgia. From there they drifted, staying in different motels for two or three weeks at the time. Alvin did not work. He used the money he had stolen from the Golden Gallon. Jo Ann was beaten in the motels. She suffered a serious head injury when Alvin Neelley hit her on the head with a pistol as they were driving down the interstate.

I had her show the scars on her head from the beatings to the jury. They were clearly visible.

In 1978, the family had moved to Lanett, Alabama, where Alvin rented a small duplex apartment. He bought some furniture on credit. Alvin was working as a cashier in a convenience market at the time. Jo Ann was living with him in order to be with her children. Whenever Jo Ann ran away, Alvin would not care for the children, he would take them to his mother in Cleveland, Tennessee.

While working at Matt's Market, Alvin forced Jo Ann to work in the store stocking the cooler, sweeping and mopping the floors, and cleaning up for him. Jo Ann also had to learn the combination to the safe.

One night, Neelley closed the store at 11:00 p.m. and drove down the street. When he came back to the store, making sure the police were not in the parking lot, he opened the door and told Jo Ann to go inside and get the money out of the safe. Jo Ann attempted to talk Alvin out of the crime. She reminded him that he promised her she would not have to do these things. He said she had to do it. Jo Ann continued to resist. Neelley told his wife that she would do these things or suffer the consequences. She took almost one thousand dollars from the safe.

Neelley treated her nicely, when she could supply him with money. When she did not take money for him, he beat her. When she worked, he took her check. Alvin purchased everything that was bought by the family.

When Little Al was born, Jo Ann took some of the rent money and bought some baby clothes and a cradle seat. She mentioned the items to Alvin. He yelled at her and asked her how she got the money. Jo Ann lied, telling Alvin that she had received the money from her people. She then had to ask her father to replace the rent money. Jo Ann's father sent the Neelleys money when she asked for it, and Alvin insisted that she call for money on a regular basis. When the money from her dad arrived, as with all the money from the burglaries or thefts, Alvin took every penny of it.

CRIME SPREES

Matt's Market required all employees to take a lie detector test after the burglary. Alvin passed, and continued to work for the company for four or five months. The company moved him to several different stores.

When Alvin thought the law was closing in on him, he sold the mortgaged furniture, and the car. Jo Ann did not own anything during the marriage.

While living in Lanett, Alvin decided that Jo Ann would burglarize the Fairfax store. He sent her into the store with a walkie-talkie, while he watched for the police. Jo Ann could not fill the bag fast enough with change, and Alvin came into the store and began cursing and acting wild, throwing the money at Jo Ann. She stopped him by telling him the law was going to be there if he didn't stop. The Neelleys ran out of the store and went home where Alvin called the police. He told the police that he had seen two black men looking like they were attempting to gain entrance to the store. The police checked the market and found the door open. Alvin stayed up all night listening to his police scanner finding out what had happened. The next day, he passed another lie detector test.

Alvin was always a CB'er. In those days, he went by the handle, or name, of Plastic Man or Boxcar. He taught Jo Ann how to use the CB and gave her the handle of Lady Plastic man or Lady Boxcar. The CB radio and other girlfriends were Alvin Neelley's only recreation.

He always told Jo Ann who he was seeing and when. He always did exactly what he wanted to do.

When the Neelleys burglarized the Opelika, Alabama, store, they did not find as much money as Neelley had expected. He beat Jo Ann because there wasn't enough money in the safe. He punched her hard while she was driving.

The couple then attempted to burglarize the LaGrange, Georgia, store. They discovered that the combination to the safe had been changed, and they could not take any money that night. Neelley had purchased a van. The family left in the van that night for Tennessee. Neelley beat Jo Ann on the interstate as the family passed through Atlanta because she did not steal any money from the LaGrange store for him.

During the burglaries, Alvin would never go inside the store. Instead, he would holler over the walkie-talkie, "Bitch, why don't you come out? You're not going to get it open anyway. You're doing everything wrong. You're screwing it up."

While driving through Atlanta, Alvin blamed Jo Ann for not trying harder. He said that if she had stayed calm, she would have been able to open the safe in LaGrange. Instead, she became nervous and screwed the whole thing up.

Alvin drove the family on to Nashville, but decided it was too large a town and too crowded for them to stay. The Neelleys moved to Murfreesboro, Tennessee.

Alvin Neelley skimmed the stores where he worked by mixing grocery charges with fuel charges when a customer was buying gas. Al would pocket the difference. Alvin sat at the cash register all day while Jo Ann did his work, down to scrubbing the parking lot when management wanted Alvin to do it. Jo Ann stayed with him on third shift, from 11:00 p.m. until 7:00 a.m. Al would take her into the office and have sex with her. They had sex on the desk, in the stockroom, and standing up in the store. Alvin demanded oral sex.

Neelley rented a trailer for the family about six miles out from Murfreesboro. He was working at the Stop 'n Go in Nashville. His half-brother, Benny Farrington, of Dalton, Georgia, gave him a good recommendation for the job. Alvin was usually fired from the stores where he worked. If Jo Ann was working for the company, he would insist that she quit when he was fired.

Alvin taught Jo Ann to pass a polygraph test by thinking about other things when the questions were being asked. On one job, Alvin made her quit work before finishing the shift. He was dissatisfied, so he took her home and beat her with a rifle butt.

Defendant's Exhibit No. 28, a photograph of Jo Ann and her children, Mikie and Amy, in 1978, was admitted into evidence after the State withdrew its objection to the photograph.

While discussing the beating with the rifle butt, Jo Anne lost her composure on the stand. She began crying and speaking with great difficulty. The state objected and the Court asked defense counsel to take the witness from the courtroom to regain her composure. Direct examination continued after approximately five minutes.

I asked Jo Ann bout her missing front tooth. She said that Alvin Neelley broke her tooth in Cleveland, one night at supper when she didn't do something right.

Asked how Alvin had shot her, she said they were separated at the time. She was working at a carpet mill, and he was working at Calfee's on Thornton Avenue in Dalton. Neelley had Jo Ann's driver's license, and she was unable to cash her check without the license. Alvin met her and retuned the license. He asked her to take him for a hamburger. She refused. Later, Alvin called and tried to persuade Jo Ann to meet him. It was Thanksgiving Day and she refused once more. She went to the store with her brother and sister. She noticed that Alvin was following them. As they were going into Calfee's Market. Alvin yelled to Jo Ann that she was not going to get away with doing him as she was. She heard a loud noise and went on in the store. She did not know she had been shot until she saw the blood. She passed out. Alvin called Jo Ann while she was in the hospital, and said that he was going to kill her when she got out.

In Murphreesboro, Jo Ann had first seen Judith Neelley when Judith was about 15 years old. Alvin brought her to the store where

Jo Ann was working. She had not seen Judith since then until today in court.

Alvin brought Judith around to the store and attempted to make her jealous of Jo Ann by parking his car in front of the store with Judith sitting in it. Alvin then went inside and tried to rub Jo Ann's hair, fondle her breasts, and kiss her. Joe Ann told him all she wanted was to be left alone.

She was never jealous of Judith nor any other girl Alvin brought around. She just wanted to get away from Alvin Howard Neelley.

At home later, Alvin put a gun to her head, and pulled the hammer back. He said he was going to kill her, and be rid of her for good. They were in their bathroom; and Jo Ann told Alvin that she wasn't Christian enough, but she still believed in God. If Alvin killed her, Jesus would be mad at him. She was bleeding from where he had beaten her with the pistol before this incident. He then put her in the car and drove through the night to Georgia.

This was the last time he beat her. She recalled an earlier beating, when she was pregnant, she had tried to hide under the bed to get away from him. He leaped upon the bed and began jumping up and down. The springs were hitting her in the stomach, and it was very painful.

Jo Ann concluded her direct testimony by saying that Alvin came around and took her paycheck after they had separated. She was so afraid of him and gave him all her money.

CROSS-EXAMINATION OF JO ANN BROWNING

On cross-examination, Jo Ann was born on December 3, 1955, and lives in Dalton, Georgia, with her husband, Chauncey William Browning.

Under the pressure of testifying before the crowded courtroom, Jo Ann once more lost her composure and was taken from the courtroom for about five minutes. Upon her return, she said that before Alvin Neelley, she had been married to David Neal Thompson, the father of Michelle, her 11-year-old daughter.

Alvin hit her very hard; yet she had never been knocked unconscious, nor had she suffered any broken bones. He hit her with a jack handle and a tire tool, and she was not knocked unconscious. She said there were many times that she felt faint and almost passed out during the beatings.

During the times Alvin beat her in the car, they did not have any accidents or wrecks. On one occasion, he "carved my leg" with a screwdriver. She did not have medical treatment because he would not allow her to go to the hospital.

District Attorney Richard Igou pointed out that she often went to her mother's. She said Alvin would take her out on the back porch, slap her around and threaten her. He threatened to hurt the children.

When Alvin applied for jobs, he failed the intelligence tests but passed the polygraph tests. He was not truthful, he was cunning, and could outsmart the experts with the polygraph.

Jo Ann's mother believed Alvin instead of her because he would put on an act in front of her family.

She knew taking money from the stores was wrong, but she did it to avoid beatings. She had no choice.

When she could get away from Alvin, he would come for her; and she would go back with him to see her children. Mrs. Neelley brought abandonment charges against her the night she left the trailer when Alvin tried to kill her. At the time, she had to live with her mother, and she could not get her children.

She had not discussed the testimony she had given in this case with anyone before taking the stand.

Jo Ann never fought back. She had an opportunity to do so. She tried to get help from others - the people looking out the window at the naked beating, the people in the next car - but she did not help herself. She was scared to death of Alvin. She never went back voluntarily. He would threaten to do bad things to the children.

Jo Ann had a very difficult time testifying at the trial. Cross-examination was stopped on several occasions in order for her to regain her composure.

She fed the children spicy food because Alvin would not let her take the children's food out first. Alvin knew she loved the children, and he used them against her as a weapon.

Jo Ann admitted that although she had been forced to participate in criminal acts, she had some responsibility for them.

She did not receive any of the money from the crimes, nor did she want any of the money.

She had scars all over her body and head from the beatings. When Alvin hit her with the rifle butt, he hit her hard enough to bring a large knot and cause a bruise. She had a knife mark on her arm where Alvin threw a knife at her. After he shot her she went back to Alvin, but she did not lift the warrant. He was eventually arrested on that warrant.

Before the last beating that he gave her, Jo Ann ran into a store hoping he would leave her alone. Instead, he told her he would shoot her in the store, no matter who was watching, if she didn't go to the apartment. She knew he had shot her once and would do it again so she went to the apartment. She left her children with his mother because of his threats.

DA Richard Igou was just warming to his subject. Since we had never heard Jo Ann Browning's story, we were concerned as to how she would answer. I knew Richard would get into what she would have done if in the same circumstances as Judith Ann Neelley. If she said that she would have reacted differently, that she would have shot Alvin instead of John Hancock, Janice Chapman, or Lisa Millican, our case was dead.

So to borrow an old aviation term, Steve and I had reached the PMP - the point of maximum pucker. We had done all that we could possibly do, and now we were flying blind. We were hopeful the truth would save us.

Jo Ann Browning said that she did not kill anyone because Alvin forced her; but if she had stayed with him, she probably would have killed.

She despised Alvin Neelley. She came to court without a subpoena because she wanted to tell people what Alvin Neelley did, what he could do, and what kind of influence he could have on a person.

She told Richard that we had tried to talk with her when we found her in Dalton. At that time, she was unable to talk about it.

QUESTIONING JO ANN CONTINUES

I took her back on re-direct: she was never allowed to make a decision. She was never allowed to think for herself. He told her everything to do, and she was to do as she was told without question.

Since I knew that Richard was going to pick up speed with his final cross. I tried to prepare her by asking these questions:

Q. You said a minute ago that you were his slave. Were you more than that?

A. It was just like he controlled me. (Crying)

Q. You were like a robot?

A. Right. (Crying)

Q. Mrs. Browning, I ask you one final question. Can you, in your wildest imagination, think of anything Alvin Neelley would have told you to do that you would not have done?

Q. No.

The district attorney took the witness on re-cross and here it comes:

Q. Would you have shot a thirteen-year old girl in the back if he told you to do so?

A. Yes. (Crying)

Q. Would you have injected her with Drano and Liquid-Plumr into her body if he told you to do so?

A. Yes, because I knew what the consequences would be.(Crying)

Q. All right, now, let's talk about that a minute. What would the consequences have been?

A. I would be beat. (Crying)

Q. So, you would have killed a little girl instead of suffering a beating yourself?

A. Please just stop it. (Crying)

Q. Ma'am?

A. Please just stop it.

Q. Yes ma'am. I'll wait for you. I want to get an answer to that question.

A. (Witness is crying)

Q. You tell me when you're ready to continue.

A. I'm ready.

Q. No ma'am, I don't think you are. Let's wait until you are really ready.

THE COURT: All right, go ahead, Mr. Igou.

Q. Mrs. Browning, would you have shot a thirteen-year old girl in the back because you would be afraid if you didn't he would have given you another one of those beatings?

A. Right. (Crying)

Q. Ma'am?

Q. Right.

Q. You would have injected a thirteen-year old girl's body with Drano and Liquid-Plumr because you would be afraid if you didn't he would give you another one of these eight hundred beatings?

A. That's a different story when your mind's being overpowered.

Q. I understand what you all are trying to show, Mrs. Browning, but that's not my question. My question is — Are you ready for me to ask it? Would you have injected that thirteen-year old girl with Drano and Liquid-Plumr because you were afraid that he would give you a beating?

A. Yes. (Crying)

Q. You would have, just like you stole the money because you wanted to?

A. Yes.

READY FOR JUDITH ANN NEELLEY'S TESTIMONY

March 15, 1983, day eight - the trial resumed at 9:00 a.m. The courthouse could not contain the people. At daylight, there were hundreds of people outside the building waiting to get in. The media people were practically in a riot.

The Democratic rumor mill was sayng that I was the father of Judy Neelley's baby, I had impregnated her on the floor of the jail when no one was looking, or through the bars while pretending to interview my client. I thought that the child must be the Second Coming as he was born 2 1/2 months after I met her.

My children were being terrorized at school, and the stress was beginning to take a toll. Democratic beat committeemen made sure that I was the subject of every conversation at every restaurant at noontime. Life was becoming more and more difficult. I was forced to fund the law firm as fees had dried up. People didn't want to cross the picket line in front of the office. Some clients were ashamed to be seen at my place.

This day began with the Court raising the issue of the bat brought from Rome. The State agreed to produce it, and the defendant would identify it.

The Court then instructed the defendant against self-incrimination. The jury was not present. The defendant assured the Court that she understood her rights. The jury was brought in, and I called Judith Ann Neelley to testify on her own behalf.

Like Jo Ann Browning, I had never heard her story before. Steve and I believed she would testify similarly to Jo Ann, and that Jo Ann's testimony had given her enough courage to tell her story. Again, borrowing an aviation term, we were flying IFR - instrument flight rules - flying blind. We had hopes of what she might say, and knew that her fate was in her hands. Jo Ann had told the truth, and although I never saw her again, I appreciated her courage and honesty.

Remember, I said earlier that trials drag on; they are repetitive and sometimes burdensome, even boring. However, in order that you may truly experience this case as it went down, it is necessary that you plod on through Judith's trial testimony.

You have heard the facts as we developed them; the facts as told to the officers; the facts developed by the witnesses; and now you will hear the story of the defendant. I'm not going to repeat a lot of what you already know. I'll summarize Judy's testimony and add what we missed earlier.

The audience was on the edge of its seats in anticipation of what the booger woman was going to say. So was I, and I hope you are because here it comes.

Judith Ann Neelley began by testifying that she was 18 years old, nervous, and scared to be in court. She is married to Alvin Howard Neelley, who is in the Chattooga County Jail in Summerville, Georgia. She had lived in the DeKalb County Jail for five months. She had three children, April and Jeremy - 28-month-old twins and Jason, 2 months old. Her usual occupation was that of a cashier in convenience stores. She was born June 7, 1964, in Murfreesboro, Tennessee. Her father and mother were good parents.

After her father's death, the family subsisted on Social Security until her mother found work.Her mother was fired from her job because she was in an auto accident with the Sheriff's 17-year-old son. They were drunk when she allowed him to drive her car. He was seriously injured.

Her mother was usually interested in CB radios, and although Judy had an older brother and sister, she did the housework after school each day. She did most of the cooking and cared for her baby brother who was four years old. In the summers, she went for walks and kept mostly to herself. She was very shy. Sometimes she went to Franklin Road Baptist Church by riding the church bus. Her older brother and sister were truants with her brother being in trouble with the law when he was 17.

She made mostly A's in school. Defendant's Exhibit No. 29 was a picture of her in the 1st grade. This was admitted over the State's objection, as was Defendant's Exhibit No. 30, which was a picture of the girl in the 8th grade. She was active in FHA, the 4-H Club, and she was a junior high cheerleader.

The press practically went into a riot when it came out that she had been a cheerleader. Their headline the next day was something like, "Cheerleader on Trial for Murder of an Orphan." Plus, the television stations ran pictures of Neelley in her cheerleader outfit. I had no idea where they got the picture. I had never seen it before.

We introduced a picture of Judy that appeared in her yearbook as Exhibit No. 32. She was in the 9th grade.

We were trying to humanize our client, and show that she was once a cute little innocent child. Burns and Danny Smith had portrayed her as a ghoul. We had to rehabilitate her image if we were going to save her from execution.

She told of her early years confirming our earlier conversations with family members, teachers and people who knew her and the family.

Judy Adams had two dates before she met Alvin Neelley. The first boy took her to a movie and back home. The other was her sister's ex-husband's brother, who attempted to treat her like her mother and sister. Judy made him take her home.

Judy's sister, Dottie, married Alan Pitts when she was 14 or 15, after she became pregnant by him. While Pitts was in the hospital, seriously injured from an automobile accident involving her older brother Jimbo, Judy's mother signed for Dottie to marry him. Barbara Adams refused to sign for Judith to marry Alvin Howard Neelley.

Jimbo moved out when he was 16, and Dottie left about the same time. Jimbo and Dottie were both children from previous marriages of Barbara Adams.

Alvin Neelley had left the Adams' home around 7:00 a.m. the morning following his first meeting with Judy. He returned, neat and clean, around 2:00 p.m. with money.

Judy had planned to be the first person in her family to graduate from high school. She had intended to go to college and become a nurse.

EX-CON ALVIN NEELLEY COURTS
A TEENAGER

Around the middle of July that summer, she began to see Alvin Neelley alone. He talked about his children, his ex-wife, and of the dreams that he had for himself and Judy. It was a very romantic time for 15-year-old Judith Ann Adams.

Alvin Neelley began to drive a wedge between Judith and her mother. Each time he took Judith out, which was from two to six times a week, he criticized Barbara Adams. Alvin told Judy that her mother was using her to take care of the house and children while she was whoring around. He reminded her of her mother's reputation.

Judy said that as a child she had been closer to her mother than any other person in the world. She shared her innermost secrets about school and boys with her mother. Yet, Alvin Neelley told her, over and over again, that her mother was a sorry person, and she was using Judy to attract men to the trailer. Although these statements hurt, Judy began to believe Alvin Neelley.

Shortly before school started in August, Alvin and Judith went to his apartment. Judy cleaned the place while listening to Alvin's tape player. She found a bloody bra and some pantyhose. Alvin explained that they belonged to Jo Ann. He said that she had been over asking him to go to bed with her. He refused, and she insisted. He became angry, and hit her in the mouth, causing her to bleed. He promised to treat Judy good, like a woman should be treated. Alvin always portrayed himself as being irresistible.

This story is coming to you straight from Judith Ann Neelley herself. I'm simply asking questions, and, like you, hearing it for the first time.

Alvin drove Judith to Cleveland, Tennessee, to meet his mother and his two children, Amy and Mikie. He explained that he had custody of the children because Jo Ann had abandoned them. Mrs. Neelley gave credence to Alvin's story.

Alvin Neelley was the first and only man Judith Ann Neelley ever had sex with.

I was hoping the press would pick up on that statement as the Democrats were spreading the sex-love rumor about me. This was damaging for my family and me. I was spending my money, maintaining an office of three lawyers, staff and defending a double murderess. All the while, the Democrat beat committeemen were spreading their venom across North Alabama, Northwest Georgia, and Southeast Tennessee. It was unmitigated hell.

The press was not interested in the fact Judith Neelley had sex with only one man in her entire life. It was more newsworthy that the murderess had a romantic interest with her attorney, "that Republican, Bob French." People believed that lie.

Back to the testimony - claiming to take her to a movie, Neelley took her to his apartment, where he talked to her mother on the CB for about 20 minutes. Judy believed Alvin when he told her that he could not get a woman pregnant. He then persuaded Judy to go to bed with him, promising that he would not hurt her. She would later see Alvin Neelley put the same move on Lisa Millican.

After the first sex act, Alvin was able to persuade Judy to go back to his apartment four times. When she ran away from home, Alvin demanded sex on a daily basis. She did not receive any satisfaction from sex as she did not know what an orgasm was.

Alvin told 10th-grader Judith Ann Neelley that school was a waste of time; however, if she would marry him, she could stay in school until she graduated while he took care of her.

READY FOR JUDITH ANN NEELLEY'S TESTIMONY

March 15, 1983, day eight - the trial resumed at 9:00 a.m. The courthouse could not contain the people. At daylight, there were hundreds of people outside the building waiting to get in. The media people were practically in a riot.

The Democratic rumor mill was sayng that I was the father of Judy Neelley's baby. I had impregnated her on the floor of the jail when no one was looking, or through the bars while pretending to interview my client. I thought that the child must be the Second Coming as he was born 2 1/2 months after I met her.

My children were being terrorized at school, and the stress was beginning to take a toll. Democratic beat committeemen made sure that I was the subject of every conversation at every restaurant at noontime. Life was becoming more and more difficult. I was forced to fund the law firm as fees had dried up. People didn't want to cross the picket line in front of the office. Some clients were ashamed to be seen at my place.

This day began with the Court raising the issue of the bat brought from Rome. The State agreed to produce it, and the defendant would identify it.

The Court then instructed the defendant against self-incrimination. The jury was not present. The defendant assured the Court that she understood her rights. The jury was brought in, and I called Judith Ann Neelley to testify on her own behalf.

Like Jo Ann Browning, I had never heard her story before. Steve and I believed she would testify similarly to Jo Ann, and that Jo Ann's testimony had given her enough courage to tell her story. Again, borrowing an aviation term, we were flying IFR - instrument flight rules - flying blind. We had hopes of what she might say, and knew that her fate was in her hands. Jo Ann had told the truth, and although I never saw her again, I appreciated her courage and honesty.

Remember, I said earlier that trials drag on; they are repetitive and sometimes burdensome, even boring. However, in order that you may truly experience this case as it went down, it is necessary that you plod on through Judith's trial testimony.

You have heard the facts as we developed them; the facts as told to the officers; the facts developed by the witnesses; and now you will hear the story of the defendant. I'm not going to repeat a lot of what you already know. I'll summarize Judy's testimony and add what we missed earlier.

The audience was on the edge of its seats in anticipation of what the booger woman was going to say. So was I, and I hope you are because here it comes.

Judith Ann Neelley began by testifying that she was 18 years old, nervous, and scared to be in court. She is married to Alvin

118

Howard Neelley, who is in the Chattooga County Jail in Summerville, Georgia. She had lived in the DeKalb County Jail for five months. She had three children, April and Jeremy - 28-month-old twins and Jason, 2 months old. Her usual occupation was that of a cashier in convenience stores. She was born June 7, 1964, in Murfreesboro, Tennessee. Her father and mother were good parents.

After her father's death, the family subsisted on Social Security until her mother found work.Her mother was fired from her job because she was in an auto accident with the Sheriff's 17-year-old son. They were drunk when she allowed him to drive her car. He was seriously injured.

Her mother was usually interested in CB radios, and although Judy had an older brother and sister, she did the housework after school each day. She did most of the cooking and cared for her baby brother who was four years old. In the summers, she went for walks and kept mostly to herself. She was very shy. Sometimes she went to Franklin Road Baptist Church by riding the church bus. Her older brother and sister were truants with her brother being in trouble with the law when he was 17.

She made mostly A's in school. Defendant's Exhibit No. 29 was a picture of her in the 1st grade. This was admitted over the State's objection, as was Defendant's Exhibit No. 30, which was a picture of the girl in the 8th grade. She was active in FHA, the 4-H Club, and she was a junior high cheerleader.

The press practically went into a riot when it came out that she had been a cheerleader. Their headline the next day was something like, "Cheerleader on Trial for Murder of an Orphan." Plus, the television stations ran pictures of Neelley in her cheerleader outfit. I had no idea where they got the picture. I had never seen it before.

We introduced a picture of Judy that appeared in her yearbook as Exhibit No. 32. She was in the 9th grade.

We were trying to humanize our client, and show that she was once a cute little innocent child. Burns and Danny Smith had portrayed her as a ghoul. We had to rehabilitate her image if we were going to save her from execution.

She told of her early years confirming our earlier conversations with family members, teachers and people who knew her and the family.

Judy Adams had two dates before she met Alvin Neelley. The first boy took her to a movie and back home. The other was her sister's ex-husband's brother, who attempted to treat her like her mother and sister. Judy made him take her home.

Judy's sister, Dottie, married Alan Pitts when she was 14 or 15, after she became pregnant by him. While Pitts was in the hospital, seriously injured from an automobile accident involving her older brother Jimbo, Judy's mother signed for Dottie to marry him. Barbara Adams refused to sign for Judith to marry Alvin Howard Neelley.

Jimbo moved out when he was 16, and Dottie left about the same time. Jimbo and Dottie were both children from previous marriages of Barbara Adams.

Alvin Neelley had left the Adams' home around 7:00 a.m. the morning following his first meeting with Judy. He returned, neat and clean, around 2:00 p.m. with money.

Judy had planned to be the first person in her family to graduate from high school. She had intended to go to college and become a nurse.

EX-CON ALVIN NEELLEY COURTS
A TEENAGER

Around the middle of July that summer, she began to see Alvin Neelley alone. He talked about his children, his ex-wife, and of the dreams that he had for himself and Judy. It was a very romantic time for 15-year-old Judith Ann Adams.

Alvin Neelley began to drive a wedge between Judith and her mother. Each time he took Judith out, which was from two to six times a week, he criticized Barbara Adams. Alvin told Judy that her mother was using her to take care of the house and children while she was whoring around. He reminded her of her mother's reputation.

Judy said that as a child she had been closer to her mother than any other person in the world. She shared her innermost secrets about school and boys with her mother. Yet, Alvin Neelley told her, over and over again, that her mother was a sorry person, and she was using Judy to attract men to the trailer. Although these statements hurt, Judy began to believe Alvin Neelley.

Shortly before school started in August, Alvin and Judith went to his apartment. Judy cleaned the place while listening to Alvin's tape player. She found a bloody bra and some pantyhose. Alvin explained that they belonged to Jo Ann. He said that she had been over asking him to go to bed with her. He refused, and she insisted. He became angry, and hit her in the mouth, causing her to bleed. He promised to treat Judy good, like a woman should be treated. Alvin always portrayed himself as being irresistible.

This story is coming to you straight from Judith Ann Neelley herself. I'm simply asking questions, and, like you, hearing it for the first time.

Alvin drove Judith to Cleveland, Tennessee, to meet his mother and his two children, Amy and Mikie. He explained that he had custody of the children because Jo Ann had abandoned them. Mrs. Neelley gave credence to Alvin's story.

Alvin Neelley was the first and only man Judith Ann Neelley ever had sex with.

I was hoping the press would pick up on that statement as the Democrats were spreading the sex-love rumor about me. This was damaging for my family and me. I was spending my money, maintaining an office of three lawyers, staff and defending a double murderess. All the while, the Democrat beat committeemen were spreading their venom across North Alabama, Northwest Georgia, and Southeast Tennessee. It was unmitigated hell.

The press was not interested in the fact Judith Neelley had sex with only one man in her entire life. It was more newsworthy that the murderess had a romantic interest with her attorney, "that Republican, Bob French." People believed that lie.

Back to the testimony - claiming to take her to a movie, Neelley took her to his apartment, where he talked to her mother on the CB for about 20 minutes. Judy believed Alvin when he told her that he could not get a woman pregnant. He then persuaded Judy to go to bed with him, promising that he would not hurt her. She would later see Alvin Neelley put the same move on Lisa Millican.

After the first sex act, Alvin was able to persuade Judy to go back to his apartment four times. When she ran away from home, Alvin demanded sex on a daily basis. She did not receive any satisfaction from sex as she did not know what an orgasm was.

Alvin told 10th-grader Judith Ann Neelley that school was a waste of time; however, if she would marry him, she could stay in school until she graduated while he took care of her.

ALVIN PERSUADES JUDY TO RUN AWAY FROM HOME

The Court recessed, and Barbara Lankford was taken out of turn when court resumed, she brought the black bat, taken from the trunk of one of the cars. It was admitted into evidence as Defendant's Exhibit No. 33.

Judith Ann Neelley was recalled and said that Alvin told her they would live in Georgia if she would marry him, and that she could raise Michael and Amy. By this time, his child, Little Al, had been adopted by his half-sister, Gwen.

Judy started the 10th grade at Oakland High School. She was dating Alvin. He took her to the movies, drove her to school, and picked her up from school. He took her riding a lot. Although he was nice to her, he insisted her mother was taking advantage of her. He became critical of her entire family, especially her sister. He was very convincing, and he talked about it until she believed him.

During the two or three weeks that she went to school that year, she was proud of her boyfriend, Alvin Neelley. He gave her status, and she discussed him with the other girls. She and Alvin asked Barbara Adams to sign for them to get married, and she refused saying Judy was not ready for marriage. Alvin began insisting that Judy run away from home.

When she was dating Alvin, Judy cooked for him, cleaned his house, helped him dress, tied his shoes, bathed him, and dried him off. She fixed his hair; and if he did not like the way she fixed it, his eyes would turn gray and sparkle and glisten. She learned that look of anger early on in their relationship.

Alvin instructed Judy to pack her clothes and sneak out her window. He also dictated a cruel note for her to leave for her mother stating that she was tired of doing her mother's work, and it was about time she did it herself. Judy did not want to leave this note, but Alvin insisted.

Alvin picked her up near her house, and took her to his mother's, then on to Dalton, Georgia. Alvin returned to Murfreesboro so the police looking for Judy would not know he had anything to do with her leaving. Alvin talked on his CB radio with Barbara Adams as he always did. A week later, Alvin came to Dalton with seven hundred dollars, claiming that it was his last paycheck. Actually, he had stolen the money from the store where he worked.

Alvin told Judy that Jo Ann treated him wrong and ran around on him. Because of that, he had hit her, and knocked her front tooth out. He had shot her when she shot at him. He did time in prison for hitting a police officer in the face with his crutch when he had a broken leg, and the officer had broken into his house. Later, she learned all this was a lie, he was in a juvenile home for stealing an automobile. When Alvin rejoined Judy in Dalton, he continued to talk about her family telling her that her mother was not looking for her. She learned her mother frantically looked for her for six months.

ALVIN PLAYS MINDS GAMES WITH THE GIRL

Alvin used a fictitious Jo Ann as a standard for Judy. He told her how Jo Ann bathed him, tied his shoes for him, and cooked for him. If Judy did not do something Alvin wanted, he would remind her how Jo Ann would do it. The teen-ager, Judy tried to out-do Jo Ann by doing exactly what he wanted.

At the time of the trial, Judy had not seen Jo Ann since chance meetings set up by Alvin in Murfreesboro. When she heard Jo Ann testify, she realized that the things Alvin had done to Jo Ann were identical to the things he had done to her.

Early in their marriage, Alvin began to make Judy fear him by telling her tough-guy stories about how he had hit Jo Ann when she made him mad or ran around with other men. Judy could not talk with her relatives because of Alvin's jealousy.

After Alvin took Judy from his mother's house temporarily, he moved her to Kennesaw, Georgia. There they lived in Smith's Motel while he worked at a Majik Market, across the street. When Alvin was on the job, Judy would go to the store, stock the shelves and cooler, sweep, mop, dust, and clean the parking lot. She did all the work, except run the cash register. Alvin sat and told her what to do. If Judy did something wrong, Alvin would become very angry, curse her, and tell her that Jo Ann would have done it right. Judy would do the work over until she pleased Alvin.

Alvin worked the evening shift, and the couple spent their days in the motel room or house hunting. Judy was 15, and Alvin was 26. Judy was not allowed to make any decisions.

PREGNANT AND EVERYTHING CHANGED

Judy became pregnant in Kennesaw, and Alvln said the baby was not his. He said a woman at the motel had told him she had seen a man go into their room when Judy was asleep. The baby was that man's. Alvin denied every baby he had fathered.

Alvin changed. He became more accusing, jealous, hateful, and frightening. Still, he demanded sex four or five times a day. He would satisfy himself in the store's bathroom, on the concrete floor, or require her to bend over and treat her. "like a piece of meat."

Judy miscarried after five months and required a D and C because of an infection. Alvin continued to satisfy himself and was not interested in her well-being.

Kathy, another clerk in the store where Alvin worked had her deposit ready for the bank. She rode a motorcycle; and while it was warming up, her deposit disappeared. Judy helped look for it while Alvin stayed behind the counter, teasing Kathy about losing it. After Kathy left, Alvin went into the back, came out with the deposit. He told Judy to put it in the car. This was the first theft Judy participated in. Alvin was skimming the receipts by ringing up "no sale" on the register, giving the people their change, and keeping the money from the sale. He was stealing between 30 and 100 dollars a shift. When she tried to persuade Alvin to stop stealing, he became very angry. She did not mention it again.

When Alvin decided he had taken all he could from that store, he told Judy to take the bank deposit, and hide it under the front seat of the car. She did as she was told. They moved to Summerville, Georgia. Alvin watched her very closely when she had the money. He was concerned she might take the money, and leave with it.

Judith had to train herself to avoid going to the bathroom at night. Alvin would accuse her of trying to sneak out. During the day, Alvin followed Judy to the restroom to be sure she was not talking to a man through the window. He forced her to accompany him to the restroom so he could be sure she was not looking at a man while he was gone. She was not allowed to look out of a window, as she might be signaling to a man.

Alvin constantly talked ugly about her family and the employees at the store that she liked. He impressed upon her that these people were a sorry lot, but that he had important friends in high places.

During the time she was living with Alvin, Judy Neelley was not allowed to have any money. Alvin spent it on whatever he pleased.

Alvin began to impress upon Judy that she could never leave him because he would come for her. He would not allow her to live her life alone. Although Judy had not attempted to run away, Alvin began to threaten her. He pointed out that she could not return to her mother's home. There was no place she could go where he would not find her. If he could not find her, he would kill each member of her family until she returned to him. Later, when Alvin and Judy had children, he talked about their children in the same threatening manner. He told her that his mother would take their children, and she would never see them.

He threatened Judith for no reason. It was his way of beginning the indoctrination that would result in her being under his control.

In Summerville, Georgia, Alvin could not find a job. He would look for a job for about an hour a day and then stay in the apartment the remainder of the day waiting for employers to call him. Although she was sick from the miscarriage and attendant problems associated with the D and C, Alvin indulged his sexual desires with her on a continuous basis. Judy complained that he was hurting her, and he told her to get used to it. He told her not to get sick on him. She was treated like something less than a human being. He acquainted her with oral sex. When Judy told him she did not like it, Alvin told her to get used to it.

Alvin instructed Judy how to pass a lie detector test. He also told her that Jo Ann volunteered to steal money for him out of the stores, and that she liked all of the sexual positions that Judy did not like. Alvin told Judy of beating Jo Ann while she was pregnant, and knocking her out the door, and down the stairs. Jo Ann almost went into labor. Alvin said she had been out with another man.

ALVIN BEGINS BEATING JUDY MERCILESSLY

The pair moved from Summerville to Holden's Motel in Rome. After applying for work at the employment office, Judy Neelley was given a job as a waitress in Petro's Pizza Parlor. Alvin agreed that she should take the job. Judy was sent to the workplace directly from the employment office. After working half a day, Alvin picked her up and returned her to the motel room. There he accused her of setting up a date with the cook. Alvin grabbed Judy by her hair and threw her into the floor. He kicked her. He then jerked her up by the hair of the head, and started hitting her in the face with his fists. All the while, Neelley was screaming accusations at his wife, and calling her names. He accused her of being just like her mother.

Judy was dizzy and could not sit up. Alvin ignored her, and began watching TV. Judy apologized for causing Alvin to be angry. She was convinced that it was her fault he became angry and beat her up. Alvin then made her perform oral sex, and said she was just like Jo Ann, screwing everybody in town. Alvin took nude pictures of Judy for the first time.

The beating Alvin gave Judy at Holden's Motel was the first time she had ever been hit by a man. Alvin would not allow her to return to work the next day. He found a job at a Fleet Oil Station as a service station attendant. The couple remained in Rome from shortly before Christmas until after New Year's.

Judy could not accompany Alvin Neelley to the Fleet Oil Station where he worked. He required her to call him from a pay phone at certain times during the day. When Alvin returned to the motel room at night, he would begin accusing Judy of being unfaithful to him. He would then begin to hit her on the head with his fist. After the first beating, Alvin beat Judy on a daily basis. He would come to the room, eat, sit and talk to her for about an hour, then beat her, and have sex with her. If she did not perform oral sex to his satisfaction, he would beat her until she did. Judy began dreading Alvin's return home. She wanted to get away from him but couldn't because she was afraid. If he started to hit her and she flinched, he would become angrier.

On New Year's Eve, he told her to pack the car and come to the service station at a certain time. She did as she was told, and cleaned up the parking lot at the station. He told her that when the shift was over, that they would be leaving town. He was going to take all the money, and make it look like the manager took it since the manager was the only person with a key to the safe. He told her to check the oil and fill the car with gas for a good distance, then gave her the money and told her to put it under the car seat. At 11:00 p.m., he locked the station and left in a normal manner. They traveled to Albany, Georgia, where they lived in the Grand Hotel on Radio Springs Road.

A little later, Alvin Neelley was hired by a convenience store called the Zippy Mart in Dawson, Georgia, forty-two miles from Albany. Pregnant again, Judy was sick on a daily basis. Still, Alvin forced her to go to the store with him, and stay during his shift, stocking shelves, stocking the beer cooler, cleaning the parking lot, and operating the cash register.

The manager of the store did not mind Judy being there. The company was receiving the services of two employees for the price of one. Judy was lifting cases of beer and cartons of groceries. As a result, she could not stand up straight. Alvin accused Judy of trying to upset him, and began to hit her in the stomach saying the blows weren't hurting her. When Judy begged him to leave her alone, Alvin hit her harder.

MISCARRIAGE AND TORTURE

February 14, 1980, when Judith Ann Neelley was 15 years of age, she was taken to the hospital in labor. A miscarriage terminated her five-month pregnancy. The following day, Alvin came to the hospital saying he had sold the car, and had walked across town. He informed Judy that her doctors had told him she miscarried because she had a bad disease which she caught from the man who got her pregnant. He said the doctors checked him for the disease, and he did not have it.

Alvin Neelley took her from the hospital the following day. The couple returned to the motel room, where Alvin became insanely enraged. He beat her with a broom handle until she was bruised to the point she had to wear long sleeves to pay the rent the next day. She still had bruises on her face, and hands so she hid her face when she paid the rent.

After the severe beating, Alvin forced Judy into bed where he had sex with her. She was screaming in pain. The more she screamed, the faster and harder Alvin moved until he was satisfied. He then forced her to get up from the bed and prepare some food for him. The room they had rented had a small kitchen area where she cooked.

The day after she had been released from the hospital, Alvin began to beat Judy again with his fist in the stomach, on the breasts and on the head, while calling her names and cursing her. The doctors had instructed Judy to wait six weeks before having sex. This time would allow her to heal from the D and C. On the second day, Alvin was much more violent. It was as if he was trying to ruin her. When Alvin went to work that day, he forced Judy to go with him. She was bleeding, hurting, and damaged; yet he told her to stock the shelves and forced her to wait on him and act as if nothing was wrong. The third day home from the hospital, Alvin did not beat her, but he did continue to force her to have sex with him. Also, she went to work with him each day. Alvin Neelley now began to instruct Judy how to write like a computer. He still had some money orders in the car that Jo Ann had stolen when they were together.

Judy was hired by the Jiffy Mart. She was now working two shifts a day. She did all of the work on Alvin's shift, and then had to work her shift. Alvin would not help Judy during her shift, other than to sometimes operate the cash register.

One day Alvin came up 50 dollars over on the register. The next day, he came up 30 dollars short. Alvin was stealing money on

Judy's shift as well as his own. Judy objected to the thefts, and he hit her with the back of his hand on the side of her head. Judy was knocked almost unconscious. She couldn't stand.

ROBBERY

Alvin had bragged to Judy that he would always protect her. He told her that he was tough, and everybody was scared of him. He said he ran his section of the penitentiary when he was in jail, and nobody crossed him. He was in the store the night she was robbed.

Alvin was playing the pinball machine in the Jiffy Mart with a loaded .25 automatic in his pocket. A black man, 19 or 20 years old, came into the store asking for rolling papers. When Judy opened the register, the robber took a gun from his pocket and told her to put all the money in a sack and not to push any buttons. Judy called Al's name. He walked over to the counter with his hand in his pocket. The robber took the sack and ran out the door. Another man was outside the door with a shotgun.

Alvin waited until they were gone, checked the front cautiously, and told Judy to call the police. He said he would have shot the boy to protect her, but he was afraid the other guy might hurt her. Alvin would not admit that he was more frightened than Judy. Judy identified the robber at police headquarters, but Alvin would not identify anyone.

The Neelleys were fired for the shortages, the robbery, and sleeping on the job. Taking another job, Alvin made Judy drive the 42 miles back and forth to work, while he slept in the van they owned. Judy was very tired because she still did all the work for two shifts totaling 16 hours.

Alvin went into the back of the store and went to sleep during his shift. She laid down, and they were caught sleeping by customers who thought they had been robbed and called the police. Alvin blamed Judy, stating she should have been sitting up watching the store. They were fired.

––––––

At this point, the Court excused the jury and told the audience that they would have to remain seated from recess to recess. There was too much coming and going in the courtroom. Audience members who arrived early enough to get a seat would sit 10 minutes, and swap the seat to someone waiting out of the courtroom so that person could see some of the trial. The courtroom would seat about 250 people. The judge would not allow standing around the walls nor sitting in windows.

––––––

My allowing Judy to tell her story to the jury continued after the recess. She suffered a beating due to their being discharged.

Alvin told Judy that she should not have given the robber the money. He beat her with his fist, slinging her by her hair and kicking her. After he tired of beating her, he had sex with her while she was still bleeding from the beating. Alvin weighed 300 pounds at the time. Judy weighed 125 pounds, and he could handle her with one hand. When she covered up on the floor, he jerked her up by the hair and threw her across the room as if she were a rag doll. He kicked her in her stomach, in her side and ribs; and when she stood up, he knocked her down again. Alvin was particularly mad about the robbery because the robbers were black. Alvin hated blacks. He bragged that he and a guy named Charles would go into the black section of Murfreesboro and shoot it up with guns. Judy had seen him ride around Dalton's black section, but he did not shoot any weapons there.

During the beating after the robbery, Alvin used a gun on Judith for the first time. As he blamed her for their firing, he held the butt of the pistol and hit her head with the barrel.

Q. You say it did break the skin on your scalp?

A. Yes sir. I never had stitches because he wouldn't take me to the doctor, but I always had sore places on my head where he had hit me with the gun and busted my head.

JUDY TURNED 16 IN ROME

From Albany, Alvin moved them to Rome. There they started using the money orders Judy had filled out. She was now 16.

From March until June, 1980, the couple lived off money borrowed from Alvin's mother. They lived in their car and would sleep near all night restaurants or in a mall. Alvin was not looking for a job. They just went riding around in the car, and he would talk to Judy all day about robbing people, and her unfaithfulness to him. He hit her while he was driving.

When he hit her with the gun and she put her arms up to protect herself, he would beat her on the arm saying he would break her arm if she did not put it down. When she put her arms down, he would hit her in the head again. They spent most of this time in Columbus, Georgia. Judy liked to sleep in the car because Alvin would not bother her for sex in the car.

He constantly talked to her about how Jo Ann took money from the stores. According to Alvin, the thefts were always Jo Ann's idea. Alvin always portrayed himself as the innocent party. He never knew what was happening until it was over. Judy testified that this was his role. He used this act to convince people of his innocence.

After Alvin had exhausted his mother's resources, the Neelleys began using the money orders for money. Judy used her birth certificate to cash the money orders. Alvin did not cash money orders, but he took all the money. When they could afford a motel room, Alvin chose motels having television with porno flicks. He would have sex with Judy like the actors did on TV. She had to act like the girls in the pornographic movies; otherwise, he would hit her and tell her to do it right. Exhibit No. 34 for the defendant was a picture of Alvin Neelley as he appeared at that time.

Judy tried once to escape from Alvin. She kept the change from meals to save enough to take a bus back to Murfreesboro. Alvin went through her purse and found the money. When he asked Judy about it, she told the truth because she feared Alvin. He beat her, and told her she was not leaving.

Alvin took Judy to her mother once – in January, 1980 – for a one- day visit. Her mother wanted to know why she had bruises all over her body. Judy said that she and Alvin wrestled a lot – that she bruised easily – and Alvin bruised her accidentally. Judith would not tell anyone about the beatings for fear of what he would do to her.

I asked her:

> Q. Judy, have you ever told me about these things you're telling the jury here today?
>
> A. No sir.

PREGNANT HOLD UP ARTIST

Judy became pregnant immediately after her miscarriage. She did not have another period. This pregnancy, together with her success with the money orders, caused Alvin to take her to Ringgold, Georgia, and marry her officially.

Defendant's Exhibit No. 35, a copy of the marriage certificate, dated July 14, 1980, was admitted into evidence. Although Alvin treated her nice for four days after the marriage, he would not admit the baby was his. He said she was pregnant by another man.

July 4, 1980, the Neelleys returned to Albany where they were hired in a service station. They took the money from two shifts the first day, netting over $2,000. Alvin took Judy out to Dallas for a vacation trip. When they returned, he drove her to Florida. After the Florida trip, they returned to Murfreesboro. Alvin was charming, sweet, gentle, and kind in the presence of her family. When they left the Adams home, they returned to Rome where he again asked his mother for money.

October 31, 1980, they were in Riverbend Mall in Rome, broke; and Alvin was mad. Judith was eight months pregnant. She was large with the twins. She would deliver them on November 12th - 13 days later. On October 31, Alvin insisted that she rob a woman by taking his gun, and holding the woman up. Judy weighed 196 pounds. Alvin promised her a beating if she did not pull off the robbery. He told her how to rob a woman. He said she should sound calm while her words were harsh. That is how he was when he beat Judy.

Judy walked up to a young woman and said, "Bitch, don't say a word, and you won't get hurt." She took the scared girl's purse. Alvin was parked three parking spaces over from where the robbery took place. Judy got into the car with Alvin, and he drove directly out of town. The robbery netted the Neelleys $10.00 and the victim's checkbook.

Alvin and Judy went to Cleveland, Tennessee, and stayed with Mrs. Neelley for a week. They returned to Rome and Judy was writing checks out of the robbery victim's checkbook. She was going to cash one more check before 9:00 a.m. She was arrested and told the police where to find Alvin. He was arrested at the Seven Hills Motel. Judy was taken to the juvenile detention center in Rome. She went into labor the night after she was arrested. She had not had any prenatal care because Alvin said he didn't have time to take her to a doctor. He told her he would make sure there was nothing wrong with her.

Judy delivered the babies by cesarean section. Mrs. Neelley came for the babies. Linda Adair took Judy, Mrs. Neelley, and the babies to the county jail to see Alvin. She received good postpartum care at the YDC. It was the best care she had received since running away from home. By Christmas, the charges were accumulating against Alvin Neelley. He was charged with the Kennesaw theft, the theft from the Fleet Oil Company, and the shooting of Jo Ann Browning in Dalton.

KEN DOOLEY

Ken Dooley, a teacher at the YDC, was working with Judy teaching her social studies and math. Linda Adair sent Alvin's letters back to him when they were upsetting for Judy. When Judy visited Alvin at the Rome City Jail, he accused her of going to bed with Mr. Dooley because she told him how nice Mr. Dooley had been to her. Alvin told Judy that she was going to get it when he got out - she had it coming.

Alvin had been arrested on November 10, 1980, and remained in jail, with the exception of two days, until March 22, 1982.

Although Judy cleared Alvin of the armed robbery in the mall by taking all the blame for the crime, he was still sentenced to 10 years in the Georgia Penal System.

In January, 1981, Judy was transferred from the YDC in Rome to the YDC in Macon where she stayed for six months. The staff of the YDC was very kind and helpful to her.

July 31, 1981, she was released. She went to her children in Cleveland, Tennessee, and lived with her mother-in-law, Mrs. Neelley.

Alvin wrote to Judith and told her to come and take the blame for the armed robbery. She did so, and he was released for two days. Then he was arrested on another charge. Judy was put in jail for eight days and transferred back to Albany. She was later transferred to YDC Macon.

135

December 1, 1981, she was released once more.

The twins' birth certificates were admitted into evidence as Defendant's Exhibit No. 39. Judy Neelley was 16 years old when they were born at the Floyd County Hospital in Rome, Georgia.

Defendant's Exhibit No. 37, a certificate awarded to Judy for completing a Distributive Education Course in the YDC, was admitted into evidence. A certificate of honor, awarded to Judy on April 17, 1981, was admitted into evidence as Defendant's Exhibit No. 38. Defendant's Exhibit No. 36 was admitted into evidence. This was a valentine given to Judy by Ken Dooley. She put Alvin's picture in it and hung it on her wall in Macon.

While at the YDC in Macon, Albertine Green, a black staff member helped Judy work on her GED to receive a high school diploma. The counselors at the YDC advised Judy to take her children, and get away from Alvin Neelley.

ALVIN THE PROLIFIC LETTER WRITER

Alvin was a prolific writer in confinement. Steve had retrieved a large grocery bag of his and her letters when we were visiting Mrs. Neelley in Cleveland. I began to introduce this correspondence for the jury to back up the testimony proving how cruel, and what a monster Alvin was in his own words.

While Alvin was in jail, he required Judy write to him every day. She was instructed to number her letters, and count her stamps. He also insisted she keep a calendar of her letters, and he began to control her through his letters. Judy told Alvin what she was doing every hour of the day. He was accusing her of all sorts of things. Alvin's letter to her dated June 22, 1981, was introduced into evidence as Defendant's Exhibit No. 41.

Alvin used certain code words or phrases in his letters that had special meanings to her. For example, when he wrote, "You'll prove your love to me," he meant if she did not do what he told her to do, she knew what was coming to her. If he said she was special to him, "no matter what," he was saying he still loved her no matter how many other men she had been with. He also wanted her to tell him whom she had seen. The remainder of the letter contained veiled threats, accusations as a result of an alleged anonymous letter he received from the YDC, and complaints about his physical condition and surroundings.

Defendant's Exhibit No. 41, a letter from Alvin dated June 29, 1981, was admitted into evidence. The State objected to any further reading of letters from Alvin Neelley to Judith Neelley.

After argument of Counsel at the sidebar, the Court allowed the Defense to proceed with its direct by reading the letters.

In this letter, Alvin attempted to make Judy feel guilty of making him have bad dreams in jail. He threatened her if she gave anyone else her picture.

Defendant's Exhibit No. 43, a letter from Alvin dated June 30, 1981, was admitted into evidence. In this correspondence, Alvin was mad because Judith had been with other men. He told her he was planning to get even with the men she had been with when he was released, and they did not know he knew about them. He was referring to men who came to the YDC with a Christian band to help the girls living there. Defendant's Exhibit No. 44, a letter from Alvin dated July 8, 1981, was admitted into evidence. In this letter, Alvin argued about Judy's letters to him, blamed her for their arrest, and threatened her again. He reminded her that he had taken his revenge against Jo Ann.

Defendant's Exhibit No. 45, a letter from Alvin dated August 10, 1981, was introduced. In it, Alvin accused Judy of being unable to wait until he got out of jail. She had to have sex with other men while he was in jail. She had written him that she walked to the store now and then. He accused her of walking the streets. He accused her of having him locked up so she could have time to be free. He accused her of being used and suckered and coming back to him. After a lengthy harangue, he told her to prove her love for him by telling him the truth about her activities.

Defendant's Exhibits Nos. 46 through 56 were letters from Alvin to Judith. All of the letters contained subjects similar to Exhibits 43, 44, and 45. He accused Judy of being unfaithful to him and said that someone, whom he refused to name, was telling him what Judy was doing. He said that he would get even with her when he was released from prison.

Some of the Exhibits set the tone for Alvin's planned activities when he was released from prison. Examples are:

Defendant's Exhibit No. 45 - Alvin blamed the YDC for teaching Judy to think only of herself, "and they're proud of that fact."

In Defendant's Exhibit No. 46, he said:

They're gonna try to hold me until I cool off, but my time will be over before I cool off, I'm gonna kick a-blank-blank-blank when I do get out of here in Albany, Rome, Macon, and some other places, even Cleveland. Let's not forget good old Dalton. Smile."– one d-a-blank thing for sure, I will see that everyone that has made me mad while I've been locked up, I will make sure the rest of their lives will be unhappy and destroyed. I try not to get mad, but every time I see Mixon (his lawyer) or anyone that had had anything to do with us or our case I get mad enough to kill. I'm really gonna laugh when I get the ones who don't even know that I know about them. Smile.

I won't be a fool next time and let them set me up again. I'll break their game playing when I get out. I'm not sure if I'll even bother to come home when I get out until I've settled things I've let things go so long and get so bad the past four years, they have forgotten how mean and nasty and cold I can be. Dalton got a taste of it and they don't want it any more. I even held back on them. I'm gonna go ahead and finish with Jo Ann and a few others in this state, fast.

Enough about my fun. I'm gonna play along with this little joking state for a while, but if I see they're really gonna try and mess over me, I'll just drop out of sight. Then people will start dropping. Smile.

In Defendant's Exhibit No. 49, Alvin continued his threats against the authorities:

They think if our marriage ends I'll forget everything that's happened when I get out and won't do anything when I get out. They're wrong. I'll see them all dead or worse when I get out, and their wives will be fucked, and by niggers, and not just a few. They'll watch too. It's really funny. They're used to doing this and getting away with it, it, but they aren't this time. They've met their match. They can dish it out good and smile, but wonder how they'll take what they dish out. They're gonna, and then some. A little bit more and I'll be out of prison. Then what are they gonna do? They're through dealing.

I'm for real I'm gonna cost this state nothing but money and problems. They've finally made me mad. They've just been bothering me up until now. I may go through some things. I don't want, but I'll do it all my way. I'm a man, not a Georgian. If I have to brand my name on them, they're gonna be sorry for what they done to me. I'm putting my name on you too. You choose how and what way you want it.

In Defendant's Exhibit No. 52, Alvin once more threatened the authorities of the State of Georgia:

They think they're so smart and cool, no one can ever get to them. That's why I'm gonna enjoy getting them so much, is for years they've gotten away with everything they've done.

They've scared people with their talk and the things they've been doing, but I'm gonna prove to them I can get to them and I do know more about them than they think or know about me. I can do my own work well, but they usually talk or get someone to do theirs for them. One of their ways they're planning on getting me is through you, but I promise that that won't work either, but some people won't take a warning. All I can say is everybody give it their best shot. I've done took care of things so well, I don't have to, and I won't be foolish as they are to sell someone short. I'm sure of who I'm dealing with before I ever mess with anyone. They're through dealing, and you're gonna get caught in the middle. I know that's cold, and you must want me to be cold with you 'cause you're cold to me. When I walk out of prison I'm gonna face the fact you never told me anything while I was locked up, and I have—and what love I have left will be gone. I'll come after you like anyone else I'm coming after.

In Defendant's Exhibit No. 56, Alvin wrote to Judy accusing her of failing to tell him everything she had done while he was in prison. This was a constant theme in his letters. He accused her of having sexual relations with other men and "punks" at the YDC. He then went into his usual threats of how he was going to even the score when he was out of jail. In this letter, he told Judy that there is no place she could go where he couldn't find her; that he knew where her family was, and she would find that she was not worth the trouble he would be causing her family.

Over the State's objection, Judy said that Alvin Neelley was convinced that the YDC had sexually abused her while she was there. She tried to convince Alvin that she had not had relations with anyone; but the more she denied it, the angrier he became. The persons he intended to attack out of revenge were the security guards at Macon, some of the teachers at the YDC, and some of the Christians who had visited the defendant with the Bible. The truth that he insisted she tell in every letter was that she had been to bed with security guards, Mr. Dooley, her lawyers, and several other people.

After her release in December of 1981, Judy followed Alvin's instruction to aid him in gaining release in March of 1982.

A FREE MAN

Here is an interesting aspect of the relationship between Alvin, Judy and the authorities. I'll let you read the testimony and see how it plays out. Like Judy, you will be amazed how Alvin pulls it off.

Defendant's Exhibit No. 57 was a letter received by Judy from Mobley Howell of the State Pardon and Parole Board of Georgia. Exhibit No. 58 was a sentence of probation dated March 22, 1982.

Defendant's Exhibits Nos. 59 and 60 were admitted into evidence. Exhibit No. 59 was an order issued by the Superior Court Sentence Review Panel of Georgia ordering Alvin Howard Neelley to serve the original sentence as imposed by the trial judge for theft by taking. This order was dated February 27, 1982. Exhibit No. 60 was an affidavit by the chief jailer of Daugherty County, Georgia, giving Alvin Neelley credit for 104 days of jail time prior to the date his sentence was imposed.

When Judy was writing to the State Board of Pardons and Paroles on behalf of Alvin, she was copying letters he had written, and directed, when and to whom, they should be mailed. Everything about the letters was his idea. Judy did as she was told.

In Exhibit No. 57, Mobley Howell, Chairman of the Board of Pardons and Parole, wrote Judy that Alvin Neelley would not be eligible for "consideration" for parole until February 1983. This exhibit clearly explained the reasons Alvin Howard Neelley could not expect an early parole and might not be paroled then.

Defendant's Exhibits Nos. 57, 58, 59, and 60 were admitted into evidence.

June 2, 1981, Alvin taken to jail.

August 18, 1981, He was released.

September 3, 1981, Alvin returned to jail.

The August release had been due to Judy confessing to the crime. He was returned to jail in September because the authorities did not believe Judy could have committed the crimes alone. Alvin's only accomplishment with this ploy was Judy being returned to YDC for several more months.

February 27, 1982, as shown in Exhibit No. 59, the Superior Court Sentence Review Panel ruled that Alvin would serve the original sentence. With all his charges, he was looking at more than 10 years.

March 22, 1982, twenty-three days later, Alvin Neelley walked out of prison on probation! There were numerous conditions of his parole or probation, including restitution of $3,220.72; reporting to his probation supervisor between the 1st and 15th of each month, unless otherwise instructed; participating in classes, and taking lie detector tests. There were two full pages of conditions of probation.

Now for the rest of the story - Alvin had made friends with an inmate who took him into his confidence, and admitted that he was the one who killed a certain law enforcement officer in cold blood. The State had been working diligently trying to solve the case. Alvin contacted GBI Agent House, and told him that he would give up the killer of the officer if House would get him out on parole. The deal was done. The fellow prisoner was eventually sentenced to die, and Alvin Howard Neelley, Jr. walked out of prison.

You also know why Alvin tried to convince authorities when he was arrested in Murphreesboro that he was working the case for Agent House.

THE HOMECOMING BEATING

Judy met Alvin at the bus station in Cleveland, Tennessee, and took him to his mother's house. Alvin appeared happy to be free, but he was not interested in being home.

After dinner, the family talked until early morning. In bed Alvin wanted sex, and Judy accommodated him. After the sex act, he became angry saying that her body had been ruined since he had been away due to all the men she had been with. He began to slap her, then he used his fist, started kicking her, and "slinging" her around the room. He went to the bathroom and removed the handle from the toilet plunger. Returning to the bedroom he began beating her with the handle. His mother and father were in the house trailer. They did not interfere with the beating. When Judy screamed too loudly, Alvin hit her harder. He told her he would kill her if his mother came in the room during the beating. While he was hitting her with the plunger handle, Judy noticed Alvin had an erection. He had just had sex with her, but the beating had sexually aroused him again. This was the first time she had ever noticed this during his cruelty.

The second day Alvin was home, he beat Judy again. He was nice during the day; but that night he began to question her about being locked up, to whom she had written, and whom she had called. When she denied this activity, he began to hit her with his fist. He forced her to lie on her stomach so he could have anal sex with her. This was very painful; and each time Judy cried out, Alvin hit her with his fist in the back of her neck. He placed a pillow over her face so she could not be heard in the rest of the house. She was bleeding, but Alvin kept on until he satisfied himself.

On the third day home from prison, Alvin found an old phone bill, which showed Judy had made calls to Macon where she had talked to Mrs. Green and Linda Allen from the YDC. That night he forced her to perform anal sex with him again. After he was finished, he finally persuaded Judy to admit that she had had sex with other men while he was in jail. He said that he would not hit her again, and everything would be straight with them.

In truth, the people at the YDC had never hurt Judy; they had treated her kindly. But Alvin refused to believe that. He had convinced himself that the people at the Youth Detention Center had sexually abused his wife. Judy fabricated that she had sex with two white security guards, and one black guard. Alvin stood up and took Judy by the hair and pulled her up out of the bed. He began hitting her in the face with his fist. He pushed her down onto the floor and began kicking her. He picked her up from the floor, and put her back on the bed, and he sat on her legs. He began hitting her in the stomach. He told her he was going to kill her because she had enjoyed "fucking niggers."

He began to try to pull her hair out while hitting her in the face. He grabbed both her ears and tried to pull them off the sides of her head. Then he took his thumbs and tried to gouge her eyes out. He began to beat her on her breasts and tried to pull them off with his bare hands. He pulled her off the bed, and put her in a corner where he began to beat her in the head with his mother's .22-caliber pistol. Judy was bleeding around the face and head, and on various other parts of her body. Alvin took her right hand and bit it, leaving the prints of all his upper and lower teeth. I had her show these scars to the jury. Jurors could see every tooth scar in her right forearm back to his jaw teeth.

Alvin then removed the handle from the plunger, and said that if Judy was going to "screw niggers," he would screw her with the plunger handle. He pushed the handle into her vagina as hard as he could. He kept on while she was bleeding. When he tired of this type mutilation, he took her into the bathroom and made her get on her knees. He said he was going to "piss on her." He did a little; and then he made her open her mouth, and he urinated in her mouth, and made her swallow it. After he beat her some more, he began to laugh at her and made her look at herself in the mirror. She was bloody. Her face was swollen, and she was bruised all over. The reflection in the mirror did not look like Judy Neelley.

Approximately two weeks later, Alvin had sexual relations with Judy again. On this occasion he took some Polaroid pictures of himself and Judy in the sex act.

Exhibit No. 61, a Polaroid picture of Alvin and Judy engaged in sex, was admitted into evidence. The picture showed large black spots on the insides of Judy's arms and legs. There were also black spots on her breasts, and there were long marks coming down to the tops of her breasts where Alvin tried to pull them off her body.

The morning after the beating, Mrs. Neelley asked Judy what had happened to her. The old woman knew before she asked. Judy told her that Al had heard something outside that night before, and he went out to see if someone was trying to break into the cars. He had taken a big stick with him. He had hit her in the face with the stick by accident.

On the fourth night he was home, Alvin made Judy perform oral sex.

Defendant's Exhibit No. 62 was admitted into evidence. This was a color photograph of Judy involved in the sex act with Alvin. The witness stated that she did not consent to the pictures and did not want them. Alvin took the pictures. Defendant's Exhibits Nos. 62, 63, 64, 65, 66, and 67 were offered and admitted into evidence. These exhibits were color photographs depicting Alvin Neelley and the defendant engaged in the sex act. These pictures were taken approximately three weeks from the night he beat her so badly. The pictures depicted bruises all over the Judy's body, and both of her eyes were beaten black and shut. Her mouth was swollen and her nose was swollen.

Judy testified that after the beating of the third night Alvin was home, the tenor of the beatings increased. Alvin used more objects to hit Judy, such as guns, sticks, a leather strap, and a hard piece of plastic. Sexual intercourse always followed the beatings. Whenever she was able to look at Alvin Neelley while he was beating her, she would see that he had an erection. Beating her was a sexual experience for Alvin Neelley.

On one occasion, Alvin was tired of beating Judy with his fists and began using a gun. She was covering her face with her hands, and he was hitting the back of her hands. Alvin told her that if she did not move her hands, he was going to shoot her in the head. When she moved her hands, he hit her in the mouth with a gun and broke her front tooth with the barrel. After he broke her tooth, he continued to beat her while laughing.

Judy was familiar with the black ball bat, produced by the Rome Police Department. Introduced as Defendant's Exhibit No. 33, she had been hit with the bat. On other occasions, he accused her of having had sexual intercourse with blacks. He then attempted to push the bat into her vagina. When the bat would not enter her private parts, she began to bleed very profusely. Alvin started hitting her with the bat.

After the beating on Alvin's third night home, Judy Neelley never again made any move without Alvin. He would not let her out of his sight for even a moment. She was totally and completely terrified of him. Whatever he told her to do, she did it. She never questioned him again. She had scars all over her body from the places where Alvin Neelley had beaten her, including one scar which required stitches when he hit her with a hacksaw.

THE ADAMS FAMILY

After staying at the home of Mrs. Neelley in Cleveland for several months, the family moved to Murfreesboro. They visited with Barbara Adams, the defendant's mother, around the middle of June. They were living off forged checks.

Defendant's Exhibit No. 78 was introduced into evidence. It was a picture of the Adams family during June of 1982. Defendant's Exhibit No. 70 was a similar picture. In this photograph, a big black-and-blue bruise could be seen on Judy's arm. She had been bruised when Alvin Neelley hit her over and over again with the gun. Defense Exhibit No. 71 was a similar picture that showed Judy recovering from two black eyes.

Exhibits Nos. 72, 73, 74, 75, 76, and 77 were admitted into evidence on behalf of the defendant. These exhibits were photographs of the Adams family taken during the Murfreesboro trip. All these data came from the bag of documents Steve took from the Neelley mobile home in Cleveland, Tennessee.

While Alvin was around the family of the defendant, he was always very helpful, respectful, and kind. Judy lied to her family and explained her bruises and beaten body as accidents she sustained while wrestling with Alvin. She told this story out of fear that he would beat her again for telling people that he had beaten her in the first place. In truth, Judy had never wrestled with Alvin, nor did she ever raise her hand to Alvin Neelley.

When they were ready to leave the home of Barbara Adams in Murfreesboro, Alvin volunteered to take the defendant's brothers, Bill and Davie, along with her half-sister, Dottie, to Panama City,

Florida. Judy had written bad checks in order that they might have money to take the trip; however, most of the expense money came from an income tax refund check.

On the way to Florida, Alvin told the defendant that he wanted to have sex with her sister, Dottie. He said that since Judy had been unfaithful to him while he was in jail, he was going to make it worse by doing it with someone close to her, and making her be there and watch. Judy told Dottie that she owed Alvin something, and that Alvin wanted to go to bed with her. Dottie agreed.

In the motel in Panama City, while Alvin was in bed with Dottie, Judy hid in the bathroom. From time to time, her brothers knocked on the door wanting Cokes. Judy gave them Cokes and returned to the bathroom. At one time, Alvin called Judy into the bedroom and forced her to look as he was having sex with her sister. Judy was crying in the bathroom. When Alvin finished with Dottie, he came into the bathroom and had sex with Judy on the floor. The experience was very upsetting for Judy.

Alvin beat Judy during the Panama City trip. He did it at night when there was no one in the motel room other than Judy and himself. He beat her around the breasts and the stomach so that the bruises wouldn't show with her bathing suit.

After the Panama City trip, Alvin left Judy and the twins at her mother's house in Murfreesboro. He told Judy he was leaving her. He stayed gone for a few hours, then came back, and told Judy that she was returning with him. She told him that she was staying at home. Alvin pointed his gun at her and told her he would kill her if she did not get into the van. He reminded her that he had shot Jo Ann.

Alvin drove Judy out into the woods and demanded that she tell him who she had been talking with on the phone. When she told him no one, he placed a .22-caliber pistol to her temple and cocked the hammer back. Judy promised to tell him if he would let her calm down and not kill her. He then placed the gun at the back of her head and told her he was counting to 10 and was going to fire. He counted to 10 and fired the gun near the back of her head. Since she was sitting with the door open, the bullet went out the door. Alvin told her that he would not miss with the next shot. He told her that they were going to her mother's house to pick up the twins, and they were leaving.

ALVIN'S INSANITY INTENSIFIES

The Neelleys went to a motel in Murfreesboro. After they were in the motel, Alvin began to beat Judy severely. She told him she had called Linda Allen, one of the social workers at Macon. Alvin told Judy that they were going to Macon. She was going to lure everyone that had done anything to her to where he was, and he was going to kill them - especially the black security guards.

The Neelleys spent the next night in Chattanooga. Alvin accused Judith of calling Linda Allen while he was asleep to set up a date with a black man in Chattanooga. When she denied this allegation, Neelley took a leather holster and beat her with it.

I showed her State's Exhibit No. 31. She said that was the holster he used to beat her.

From Chattanooga, the pair traveled to Macon. Before leaving for Macon, Alvin told Judith that if she didn't help him kill the people in Macon, he would kill her before they left Macon, Georgia.

In Macon, Alvin stopped at a drug store. He told Judy to buy a pack of diabetic needles and a bottle of Drano. She had no idea what these items were to be used for. The store did not have Drano so she bought a bottle of Liquid-Plumr. Alvin then drove around past the YDC and the homes of the people with whom Judy was supposed to have had sexual relations. He rented two motel rooms, one for Judy and one for himself. The following day, he told her to buy a bottle of Drano.

Alvin now owned, a Ford Granada and a Dodge. He had bought the automobiles with an income tax refund check belonging to Joseph Henry Park, one of his aliases. I showed Judy our Exhibit No. 26. This was an identification card showing a picture of Alvin

Neelley with the name of Joseph Henry Park, an employee of Aladdin Mills. Exhibit No. 26 was introduced into evidence.

Alvin had taught Judy to break into post office boxes by using a large screwdriver. She had broken into several post office boxes in Cleveland, Tennessee. The Joseph Henry Park check was taken from one of those boxes. Alvin always sat in the car while he sent Judy into the post office. He was never in the building. He talked with her by walkie-talkie. Judy would deliver all of the mail taken from the boxes to Alvin. He was looking for checks and credit cards. Through Judy's efforts, Alvin netted a little over $3,000 by breaking into approximately 10 post office boxes in four nights. He did not find any credit cards.

Another source of income was Majik Market money orders. Judy would alter the money orders by raising the amount to $100 or $199. Alvin gave Judith a story to use and opened a bank account in her name. When she cashed the money orders she said that her ex-husband had sent his alimony payments or child support. Judith was cashing from one to four money orders a day across Northwest Georgia. Alvin kept all the money.

Alvin bought CB radios for both cars, and instructed Judy how to install them. When they traveled, he drove in front; and Judy was not to permit a car to pass her and come between them. His reason for requiring her to drive so closely to his car was to be sure he knew where she was looking. He wanted to see if she was looking at other men in other cars or flirting with anyone. When he thought she was looking at other drivers in other cars, he would threaten to blind her, or kill her, or beat her to the point that she could not see anyone else.

Judy had considered driving away from Alvin but was convinced that wherever she went, he would find her; and if he couldn't find her, he would find her family. So she did as she was told.

In support of her testimony that Alvin Neelley controlled all of the money during the marriage, we had Exhibit No. 79 admitted. This was a T-shirt that Alvin had bought with the phrase, "Eat your heart out, I'm married." She did not select any of her clothes nor anything else.

Exhibit No. 80, a sawed-off .22-caliber rifle, was admitted. Neelley had sawed it off to shoot the black man in Macon whom he supposed had been with Judy. He had also purchased high-powered rifles, and a shotgun to get even with the people who had done him wrong.

BACK TO THE YDC

Before going to Macon, they stopped in Rome to even the score Alvin had with Ken Dooley and Linda Adair. He believed that Linda Adair was prostituting the girls at the YDC and Ken Dooley was the pimp. Judy denied these accusations. To get even with Ken Dooley, Alvin drove the Dodge automobile past Dooley's house, with Judy riding in the passenger side. He gave her the .22 rifle and told her to shoot through the window into the room where the Dooleys were watching TV. She was instructed not to hit anyone, just scare them. When she put the gun out the window to shoot, Alvin said that she would miss the house on purpose because she did not want to scare Mr. Dooley. The couple rode by the house several times, Alvin stopped the car, and shot into the house four times.

They checked into the Oak Hurst Motel. Alvin told Judy to go to a pay phone and call the Rome Police Department. Tell them that she had shot up Ken Dooley's house for the sexual abuse she had experienced at the YDC. Alvin told her to call Ken Dooley and tell him that was just the beginning, and he was going to end up dead because of the sexual abuse he had perpetrated on the girls at the YDC. Judy did as she was told.

The next day, Alvin had Judy take him to the home of Linda Adair. She tried to point out the wrong house, but Alvin knew where Mrs. Adair lived. He beat her for trying to protect Mrs. Adair.

That night he told her how to make a firebomb with a soft drink bottle, gasoline, and a wick. Neelley then drove to Mrs. Adair's house, where he instructed her to light the wick and throw the bottle as hard as she could. The bottle landed in the middle of the yard. Because a car started coming down the road, Alvin pulled away, leaving Judy at the scene. She ran down the block, and jumped in the car. At the motel, Alvin was very angry because Judy did not hit Linda Adair's car. He accused Judy of trying to warn Linda Adair, rather than firebomb the yellow car sitting in her yard.

Alvin hit Judy with his gun and his fist, he kicked her as hard as he could, and pulled her hair. He started the beating by accusing her of protecting Linda Adair. He stopped beating her about an hour later when he decided that she should once again call the Rome Police Department, and tell them that she had shot into Ken Dooley's house the night before, and firebombed Linda Adair's house that night. She was instructed to tell the police that she committed those crimes to get back at them for the sexual abuse she went through at the YDC. When the information that Judith had given the police did not come over Alvin's scanner immediately, he hit her and told her to go back and call the county sheriff. When she returned, the information had been broadcast over the scanner. Alvin was very happy about this. He said this was just the beginning. The monster didn't know how right he was.

The next morning the pair left for Macon with Alvin driving the Granada and Judy driving the Dodge close behind him.

Linda Allen, a matron who had befriended Judy, was targeted as the first victim. Alvin said that she had turned Judy against him, against his mother, and against his family. He believed they had hypnotized Judy so that she would do things that she did not know she was doing. Linda Allen was the supervisor over the cottages and the counselors. "She was the top person in the prostitution ring." He then slapped Judy around when he discovered that she had bought Liquid-Plumr. He was satisfied when she went back and bought Liquid Drano.

Alvin sat on the side of the bed and listened to the phone conversation when Judy called Linda Allen. If Judy did not say exactly what he wanted her to say, he whispered in her ear without being heard over the phone. Mrs. Allen said she would come down to see

Judy the next day. That night Alvin told Judy he was going to tie Mrs. Allen in a chair and make her tell him all the details about where she took the girls to meet the men, and who her regular customers were.

The next morning, while they were riding around looking for the home of Mr. Green and other security guards, he told Judy that after he got the information he wanted from Linda Allen, Judy was going to kill her. Linda Allen was supposed to meet Judith at the motel at 5:00 p.m. At about that time, a woman from the YDC called and told Judy that Mrs. Allen had to go out of town, and would be unable to meet her that afternoon. Alvin said that Judy had warned Allen, and he beat her with the baseball bat.

During the beatings, Alvin never hit Judy hard enough to kill her. He would hit her just hard enough to break the skin or bruise her. The following day, the Neelleys drove by the YDC, and Mrs. Allen's automobile was there.

Continuing his insanity, Alvin's next victim was John Brownlee, a security guard. Alvin forced Judy to call Mr. Brownlee, and he agreed to meet her. He was then a maintenance worker at the YDC He finally stated that he could not meet Judy, but he would like for her to meet his wife one day. Alvin beat Judy with his fists and his gun. He took one of the hypodermics, filled it with water, and gave her a shot. A little later, he had anal sex with her.

Alvin told her that he was going to put Drano in the syringes, and give a shot to whomever they were able to get first in Macon. He had been told in prison that to mainline Drano would kill a person, and make it look like they had a heart attack. After spending some time riding around looking for various YDC employees' homes, Alvin tired of staying in Macon.

He accused Judy of warning everybody, so they returned to Rome. It was now September,1982. On the way back to Rome, Alvin told Judy on the CB that the only reason he didn't kill her in Macon was because he was going to wait until he had killed these other people. He was tired of her in bed, and wanted her to find him a woman.

Alvin concocted a plan for Judy to follow attracting women for him. She was to go up to the girl he had selected, ask her if she was someone that she knew, then engage the girl in conversation. After Judy and the girl began to talk for a few minutes, Judy was to tell her she was out riding around and wanted someone to ride with her. If the woman she approached did not want to ride with her, Judith was to ask her if she knew anyone who would. She was then supposed to meet Al, a "stranger," on the CB, and they would meet in person. Alvin would then have the woman as long as he wanted her, and Judy was supposed to get rid of her by giving her a shot of Drano. Judy did not question the plan.

For more than a week, Judy tried to carry out Alvin's plan. They went riding every day looking for someone for him. Each day Judy was unsuccessful, and each night, at the motel, Alvin beat her severely. Judy was unable to remember how many times she tried to entice females to go for a ride with her, or how many times Alvin Neelley beat her for failing to succeed. "It was a lot."

She did remember a 13-year-old girl with black hair near a Majik Market whom Alvin told Judy to pick up. Judy attempted to talk with the girl, but she was not interested in going for a ride. When Judy told Alvin, he hit her in the head with his gun. Judy pointed out that the girl was young and small. Alvin said he was trying to get a virgin. He wanted one that was small. If she wasn't a virgin, she would at least be tight; and that's what he wanted. He wanted a "tight hole."

This was ugly testimony I was presenting to the jury through Judy Neelley, but it was necessary for them to understand what her state of mind, and physical condition was at the time. I knew that the situation was going to get worse.

On the day Lisa Ann Millican was picked up, Judy was visibly pregnant. While Alvin was playing video games, he sent Judy out into the mall to look for women. He spotted Suzanne Clonts and told Judy to try to pick her up. Judy did not find any discrepancies in the testimony of Suzanne Clonts. She added that she was instructed to act as if she did not know Alvin.

KIDNAPING, MURDER AND RAPE AS TOLD BY JUDITH NEELLEY

Now Judy is going to tell the jury her side of the facts of the kidnap, rape and murder of Lisa Ann Millican. She will also recount the events talking place with John Hancock and Janice Chapman. Since you know most of the facts from other witnesses, I will skip most of Judy's testimony, giving you slight changes and additions. Further, it is a little too painful to go through again.

The Neelleys had visited a pawnshop in Macon where Alvin had selected handcuffs. Instead of buying them, he sent Judy to buy the handcuffs. She bought two pairs. The handcuffs used on Lisa were State's Exhibit No. 28. He always instructed Judy to handcuff victims.

Judy said that she had heard the FBI statement from the witness stand. She heard the investigators testify what Alvin had told them. She did not have oral sex with Lisa Millican. She has never had sex with a female.

In Cleveland, Alvin did not go to his mother's house. He stayed at Calfee's Market with Lisa while Judy went for the children, and picked up more clothes.

In the car with Judy, Lisa said that she did not want to have sex with Alvin again. He hurt her. She also asked to call her mother. Judy asked Alvin over the CB if Lisa could call her mother, and he said, "later." After Judy had the twins, Alvin led the way to Scottsboro, Alabama. Judy did not know the purpose of their visit to Scottsboro. Alvin selected the motel and had Judith register under the name of Ben Farrington. He gave her money for the room. While unpacking the car, he told her to take a leather slapjack and hit Lisa in the back of the head with it while she was looking out the window. This would knock her out. And when she came to, Alvin Neelley would be having sex with her.

Judy did as she was told; however, she was unable to knock Lisa out. Alvin took Judy into the bathroom, and told her to have Lisa get undressed while he was in the bathroom. He came out of the bathroom undressed. The twins were playing on the floor. Alvin made Judy stay in the room while he had sex with Lisa. Lisa was crying and begging him not to hurt her. Alvin did not stop until he had satisfied himself. Then he sat in a chair and started watching TV. Alvin told Lisa to take a bath. While she was in the bathroom, he told Judy how good she was. That night, Alvin forced Lisa to sleep on the floor, handcuffed, at the foot of the bed.

The next day, Alvin sent Judith to a dairy bar for something to eat. There was a long line of people at the dairy bar. It took too long. When Judith arrived back at the motel, he started hitting her in the head with his fist and with the gun.

Lisa saw Alvin hitting Judy and beating her as he always did, pulling her hair, kicking her, and hitting her in the head. He said that Judy had been with a black man at the dairy bar. This incident ended Alvin's pretending to be nice in front of Lisa.

After eating, Alvin had sex with Lisa again. This time, he raised her legs and hips up and hurt her more. She was crying again. Lisa was very small, and Alvin weighed over 300 pounds. Alvin told Judy to undress and get in bed with them. She did. And while he was having sex with Lisa, he was sucking the breasts of Judy. He told Judy he was making believe that Lisa was her. When Lisa asked him not to hurt her, he did it that much harder.

Alvin believed that a hit man was going to kill Judy because she could tell the authorities about the prostitution ring in Macon. He was convinced that Lisa was a trap so that the man could keep in contact with her and kill Judy.

Alvin's mental problems had been horrible to this point; now they were escalating into insanity. And, it just keeps getting worse and worse. Yet he knows right from wrong and the nature and quality of his acts. He is a sadistic freak.

Alvin insisted Judy question Lisa about the hit man. She took Lisa into the bathroom and handcuffed her to the pipes under the sink. Lisa denied ever knowing the man; but Judy, sounding like Alvin, continued to accuse her, and demanded that she tell her the truth. Eventually, Lisa said she knew the man from the Harpst Home. She had seen him there once, and his name was Jim.

Judy told Alvin of the conversation. He said that he knew the man. He was a professional hit man whose real name was not Jim.

Later in the afternoon, Alvin had sex with Lisa again. He was very rough with her. Alvin slept from around three o'clock in the afternoon on Monday until seven or eight o'clock that evening. After sending Judy for food and watching TV, Alvin ordered her to put the twins to bed around 11 o'clock and to put Lisa to bed, also.

That night, Alvin took Judy into the bathroom and began to talk to her about the man that he believed was tailing them. He told Judy to take the Drano and put it into one of the syringes and give Lisa a shot.

He showed her where to give the child the shot - in the back of the neck - which he said was the jugular vein, or something like that. Judy did not question him. He told Judy to handcuff Lisa so that she would not fight if the shot hurt her. Judy had never given a shot in her life. He told her to fill the syringes with Drano, put a cap on them and put them in her purse. She poured the rest of the Drano down the sink and threw the bottle away. He told her to pack the car because they were going to leave before daybreak.

Judy took Lisa and the twins, and began to follow Alvin. She had no idea where they were going. At Little River Canyon, Judy remembered that a long time ago, Alvin had told her that he had planned to kill Jo Ann, and leave her in Little River Canyon

He drove to the picnic area near my farm, and what they did there ruined my love for the farm.

Judy took Lisa and laid her face down with her arms around the bottom of a tree. Her hands were cuffed together. Judy told her that she was going to give her a shot to put her to sleep. When she woke up, the Neelleys would be gone, and Lisa would be un-hand-cuffed. Judy squatted down beside her.

When Alvin hollered for her to do it, Judy gave Lisa a shot in the neck. Alvin told Judy to wait for a minute and make sure the shot was going to work. They waited, and nothing happened. Alvin told Judy to give her another shot. Judy went to her car and filled another syringe with the Liquid-Plumr she had purchased in Macon by mistake.

Alvin stayed right near his car telling Judy exactly what to do. Judy bent two needles trying to fill them with Liquid-Plumr. Alvin called her a "dumb bitch," saying that she was as bad as her mother. He called her a "nigger fucker" and told her if she did not straighten up he was going to kill her.

Judy filled the second syringe and walked over to Lisa and gave her a second shot in the neck. Alvin was becoming angry because Lisa was still alive.

Alvin told Judy to get another syringe and give Lisa a shot in the left arm. It would lead straight to the heart. Judy gave her a shot where she had seen doctors draw blood from her arm.

When there was no reaction, Alvin told her to give Lisa another shot. When Judy went over to Lisa to give her the fourth shot, Lisa said she had to use the bathroom. Each time Judy went to Lisa, Alvin went closer to his car. Lisa answered when her name was called. Alvin instructed Judy to give her a shot in the buttocks. He told her to give her two shots to make sure it was done right. He was calling Judy a "nigger-loving slut," a "whore," and a "nigger fucker."

STORY OF HORRIBLE EVENTS CONTINUES

The jury seemed anxious for this horrible story to end. They knew how it came out, and wanted to be spared the gory details. I didn't like it either, but I had to show what a sadist monster Alvin Howard Neelley was, and how much Judith Ann Neelley was under his direction and control. So, I pressed on.

Judy filled the syringes and went over to Lisa and gave her the shots, one in each side of her bottom. She went back to Alvin and told him that she had given Lisa the shots. Alvin was mad because

Judy gave Lisa the shots through her clothing. He slapped her face several times, and hit her head with his fist.

Judy's response to my next question was telling. I asked her why she gave Lisa the shot through her jeans. Innocently, she responded that Alvin did not tell her to pull Lisa's pants down.

Lisa begged Judy to let her go, that she wouldn't tell anybody anything if she would just take her back to the Harpst Home or her mother's. Judy told her that she could not do that and to be quiet. All the while Alvin was yelling.

He yelled, "What's taking so long, bitch?"

Judy told him that she was doing it. She walked Lisa to the edge of the canyon and backed about six feet away from her. She could not pull the trigger.

Watching from his hiding place in the trees, Alvin screamed, "Do it, bitch!" and Judy pulled the trigger.

I asked Judy why, if she had the gun from the time she took it out of the car until after she shot Lisa, she did not shoot Alvin Neelley. Her response was, "He didn't tell me to."

I pressed on, asking her if he had told her to put the gun to her own temple and pull the trigger, would she have done so; and she said, "Yes, sir."

Alvin went to make sure Lisa was dead and began masterbating.

As they were driving away, he said he wanted another girl.

ALVIN'S INSANE DELUSIONS MANIFESTED

Alvin told Judith to call the Rome Police Department from Huntsville, and tell them about the body in order to show them up. In Huntsville, he decided to drive back to Rome to do it. Judy called the Rome P.D. and told them where to find Lisa Ann Millican. "Where I left her."

Alvin told Judy that he was going to show everybody that the Rome Police Department couldn't catch a woman who had done something like that.

Alvin then had Judy call WRGA, and tell them that the Rome Police Department was hiding the fact that a girl named Lisa Ann Millican was dead; that the Fort Payne Police Department was hiding that fact; and that the girl had been killed by a social worker. She told them where to find the body. The call was made with Alvin standing near making sure she said everything right.

When the Neelleys did not hear anything about the death on the radio, Alvin told Judy to call the Fort Payne Police Department. After riding the rest of the day, they went to the Oak Hurst Motel. The next day, they went riding around Rome again.

Alvin used two cars so he could get away in case she was caught. He told her that the cops recorded all calls, and since she had called about the firebombing, they knew who she was. The couple drove to Fort Payne, and Judith called the DeKalb County Sheriff's Office, telling them where to look in the canyon for Lisa Millican's body.

It did not cross Judy's mind that she might be arrested for murder. She just did as she was told. The couple returned to the Oak Hurst Motel.

The following morning, the Neelleys began riding around again. Alvin said he wanted "another woman."

He pointed out various girls, that Judy tried to pick up, but she was unsuccessful.

When the couple arrived back at the motel, Alvin slapped her around. He hit her with his fists, kicked her, pulled her hair, bit her, and hit her with his gun. When he was through beating her, he had very rough sex with her. At times she tried to protect herself by drawing her body up in a ball on he floor. He would kick, and stomp her.

The next day, Alvin insisted that they ride around the children's Open Door Home in Rome. Judy was unsuccessful in picking up any girls for Alvin in that area.

September 25, 1982, Judy Neelley tried to pick up Suzanne Clonts. Later that evening, she was successful in picking up Lisa Ann Millican.

September 28, 1982, Lisa Millican was raped, tortured and killed.

October 3, 1982, Judy tried to lure Diane Bobo, the girl in the Hardee's uniform. That night, she was successful in picking up John Hancock and Janice Chapman.

October 9,1982, a Saturday, Judy picked up a girl named Casey in Murfreesboro. Casey spent the night with Alvin Saturday night.

October 10, 1982, Sunday morning, Judith was arrested at 6:00 a.m. Defendant's Exhibit No. 81, a rough drawing of a calendar showing the events in order of dates, was admitted into evidence.

STOCKHOLM SYNDROME

At long last, Steve and I were beginning to develop the idea that Neelley was the victim of the Stockholm syndrome. The case of Patty Hearst came to mind. That night I finally located Barbara Hart, the woman lawyer in Pennsylvania who represented beaten women. She directed me to Charles Patrick Ewing, a professor at SUNY Buffalo. He had written a book, *Battered Women Who Kill*. Hart acquainted me with a term I had not encountered before, "battered woman." She said that my case sounded like a battered woman case taken to the extremes. "Usually battered women kill their tormentor, rather than some third party. You may have trouble with that."

I found one case where a battered woman had killed a person other than her tormentor. It made sense to me. If a woman was beaten repeatedly, treated like a slave, and reduced to having no independent will of her own, it was reasonable to assume that she would kill as directed - even herself.

JOHN HANCOCK AND JANICE CHAPMAN

Judy's testimony continued describing the facts involving John Hancock and Janice Chapman, the trip to the Coosa Post Office, on to Alabama, then to Summerville, and the trip toward Calhoun.

At the time she had asked for the time check Alvin was right behind them. When the two cars stopped for John Hancock and Alvin Neelley to relieve themselves, Alvin, and told her to walk John Hancock down the road, and shoot him in the back.

He had given her the .38 she had used to kill Lisa Millican and the handcuffs at the Coosa Post Office.

Janice Chapman did not get out of the car, she was handcuffed in the Dodge. Alvin had instructed Judy to handcuff her with her left hand and put the cuffs under her legs so that she could not move her arms any higher than her legs.

When they arrived back in Rome, they registered in the motel as Ben Farrington. Alvin instructed Judy to go for food. When she returned, Alvin was having sex with Janice. Janice did not cry or appear to be hurt. In fact, she appeared to enjoy it.

While Janice was taking a bath, Alvin told Judy to show Janice a clipping from the Rome paper concerning the death of Lisa Millican. He told Janice that Judy had killed John Hancock. Janice did not appear upset. That night the twins slept in one bed, Alvin and Janice slept in another bed, and Judy slept on the floor. The following morning, Alvin told Judy that they were going to get rid of Janice. He said he wanted another woman.

Alvin selected the spot where Janice would be shot. He told Judy he wanted more sex with Janice at the site. He let the front seat in the Granada all the way back. He told Judy to sit in the Dodge with the twins until he was finished. He satisfied himself with Janice in the front seat on the passenger side of the Ford Granada. He then instructed Judy to give Janice something to clean up with and tell her to stand out behind the car. While Janice was cleaning up, Alvin told

Judy to take her out to the left and tell her she was going to tie her up. She was then to walk over and shoot her in the back.

"Just be quick about it, and make sure you do it right."

He drove down the road and parked his car some distance away. Judy heard him yell, "Go ahead."

When Alvin thought Judy was taking too long, he yelled again, "Bitch, what are you doing this time?"

She yelled back, "Just a minute."

He hollered back, "Hurry up."

Judy shot Janice.

Janice was screaming, and Judy shot her twice more. When she got back to the main road, Alvin was laughing. He said that he heard her hollering. He started talking about picking up somebody else.

October 9, 1982, the couple had returned to Murfreesboro. While Judy's mother was washing some clothes, she found a bloody shirt and other bloody clothing. She asked Judy specifically about the shirt. Without explanation nor excuse, Judy asked her mother to call the police, and tell them that Judith Neelley was in town, and would be in a motel on the Nashville Highway. Alvin came in and took Judy riding around again.

HELLO CASEY

The Neelleys found Casey, who was streetwise, and able to handle Alvin.

Alvin told Casey, that Judy was wanted in six different states for murder. Casey asked Judy if this was true, and Judy said it was. Alvin told Judy to take Casey into the bathroom and tell her that she was to have sex with him.

Casey agreed. Alvin told Judy to wait outside the room on a porch or closed-in area. After about half an hour, Alvin knocked on the door and told Judy to come back in. Alvin was acting differently.

He was talking about Casey being experienced and that she knew how to drain a man dry.

Alvin told Judy to handcuff Casey's hands to the top of the bed. He was going to keep her with them for a while. He had enjoyed her.

At 6:00 a.m. the next morning, the police were knocking on the door to the motel room. Judy released Casey and hid the cuffs under a pillow. The gun was hidden under another pillow. The police allowed Alvin to give Casey a ride home. She got out of his car several blocks from where she told Neelley that she lived.

JUDITH ANN NEELLEY ARRESTED

When Judy was arrested, she was told that the county had eight warrants for bad checks. Alvin called Judy's uncle, her grandfather, and several other people, attempting to make bond. As other warrants were found, the bond increased.

Later that day, Alvin visited Judy in jail, saying that he was trying to bond her out. He had hired Bill Burton as her lawyer.

October 11, 1982, Monday, Judy was taken to court for a preliminary hearing involving forged money orders. Alvin was arrested for writing a bad check in 1978. He said Jo Ann wrote the check.

While in jail, Alvin told Judy by letter exactly what to say when she was questioned. He told her to persuade Burton to let him talk to her. He also instructed her to tear the letter up and flush it down the commode.

Bill Burton came to the jail and talked to both Alvin and Judy. He left them alone when he went to check on charges against Alvin. Alvin told Judy to make sure that she did not mention his name about anything - that he was nowhere around when she wrote the money orders, and he didn't know anything that happened with Lisa or Janice Chapman - and to make sure he was not mentioned. He reminded Judy to remember how he had explained this to her before.

After discussing her stay in the Rutherford County Jail, Judy testified concerning her interrogation by Bill Burns, Lester Stuck, and Danny Smith.

Her testimony before the jury was substantially the same as that during the motion to suppress hearing. The statements given to Burns were those she had rehearsed with Alvin, who had prepared the statements to keep him out of trouble. Judy now testified as to the falsity and truthfulness of the statements.

Parts of the statements described what happened. Other parts were lies by Alvin Neelley. Judy gave conflicting stories. Some of the conflicts were given that night, and other conflicting evidence was given to Danny Smith the following day. For example, the she told Special Agent Burns that she told Alvin she intended to get rid of Lisa Ann Millican. Two minutes earlier, she had told him that Alvin was not with her when she was with Lisa. She gave the false statement to keep Alvin out of trouble. This is what she had been trained to do. Burns didn't catch the inconsistencies.

Exhibit No. 82, a letter written by the defendant to her husband that was taken from her attorney's office by the FBI, was introduced into evidence. Judy had written this letter so that the authorities would read it, and clear Alvin.

After almost a day on the stand, I passed the witness to the district attorney for cross-examination.

DA CROSS-EXAMINES DEFENDANT

Keep in mind as you read Richard's questioning, trials are repetitive in nature and sometimes boring. He will re-hash much of what you know in an effort to strengthen the State's case.

Judy said that she had asked her mother to call the police and have her arrested. She did not have a reason for doing that. She could have called the police when she went to the Laundromat, but she was not thinking about the police at that time.

She did not recognize John Hancock as a threat to her. Those were Al's words. She shot him because that was what she was told to do. Several parts of the statement she gave Agent Burns were true.

She did the things she did because Alvin told her to do them. She did not do them because she wanted to do them.

She was more intelligent than Alvin, but he was more streetwise. He could have changed the money orders but did not. Alvin began dominating Judy when he persuaded her to drop out of school and run away with him. She was afraid of him before she left home, but she was more attracted to his gentle side Further, she loved him.

She stayed with him when he treated her badly, and began to beat her. She knew it was wrong when she helped him steal Kathy's deposit. She also knew it was wrong to take the money from the Fleet Oil Station, but she did what she was told.

In September,1980, Alvin brought her to Fort Payne where she applied for a driver's license giving a phony address.

When she robbed the woman at the Riverbend Mall, she did not think of the woman being robbed, nor did she consider whatether she was doing wrong. She was doing as she was told.

When she gave birth to her twins the YDC people were nice to her. She did not tell the YDC how she was being treated by Neelley. When she did tell a "little bit" about the cruelty she suffered, the staff tried to help rehabilitate her. Sadly, she did not take advantage of their help.

Alvin made up the story of the lawyer and guard having sex with her. Judy provided the description of the people involved, and Alvin provided the story of the lawyer having sexual relations with her on the floor, and then inviting the security guard into the room for his turn.

The district attorney questioned the beatings Alvin gave her. Although he hit her in the head, kicked her in her back, and hit her arms with the baseball bat, he did not hit her as hard as he could. He was not trying to kill her; he was trying to hurt her. The only bones he broke were two of her fingers, and he, "busted my head."

The first woman she procured for Alvin was her sister, Dottie. She did not have to force Dottie to have sex with Alvin; she was willing.

Judy did not consider whether robbing the post office boxes was right or wrong.

"I just didn't think about it. I just did it as I was told to do."

On the money orders – she purchased them, she raised them, she cashed them, and the bank account was in her name. She did it all without thinking about it.

"I just did as I was told. I didn't think about if it was right or wrong."

She understood the words in Alvin's letters which were code words because the code had been repeated to her over and over. She was of the opinion that Alvin had serious mental problems, but she could do nothing about it.

She used different names while attempting to lure girls into her car. Whether the girls who refused to ride would have been killed would have depended upon what Alvin told her to do.

When asked whether she wanted to ask John Hancock to help her out of the situation, she said that she didn't think about it. She was just doing as she was told. Alvin kept the guns himself, unless he wanted her to use one.

When she told John Hancock, "Don't worry about Kay. We'll take care of her," she did not have any idea what Alvin had meant.

"Al told me to tell him not to worry about her. I never gave an explanation. I never meant one. I was just repeating what I was told."

She did not hate the girls, she did not enjoy killing them, and she did not receive any pleasure from it.

"I didn't get anything from it. At the time I didn't think about it. Now I do." She said that she was emotional before she met Alvin Neelley. She was not very emotional now.

She thought John Hancock was dead. She meant to kill him. She did not ever think about whether the shooting was right or wrong. She ran to the car after the shooting because Alvin did not tell her to stay where she shot John. Although Alvin did not tell her every single move to make, he did tell her what to do, and she did it.

At Alvin's instructions, Judy handcuffed Janice to the door of the Granada. She had no independent thought on her part. She did not question Alvin, and she did not consider the act she performed; she reacted to Alvin's instructions. The following is an example of the answers given on page 2848 of the transcript:

Q. If she wasn't scared and she was cooperating, why did you handcuff her?

A. Because Al told me to. I didn't ask why.

Q. Did that seem a little strange to you? Did any of this stuff seem strange or odd to you that you would handcuff them, or just because Al told you to?

A. Just because he told me to. I didn't think about it.

Q. Why did you tell her that you had killed Lisa?

A. Al had told her to scare her.

Q. You said you told her too.

A. I said I agreed.

Q. Why did you show her the clipping?

A. Because Al told me to show her.

Q. Why did you handcuff her?

A. Because Al told me to handcuff her.

Q. Why did you kill her?

A. Because Al told me to kill her.

Alvin did not tell Judy to shoot Janice twice more to shut her up. She did that on her own.

"I didn't look. I just shot her."

The Janice Chapman murder occurred on October 4, 1982. After the shooting, the Neelleys went out to eat. That afternoon around 3:00 or 4:00 p.m., Judith tried to pick up "that little red-haired girl," Deborah Smith. The time of the attempted pick-up was placed at five or six hours after she shot Janice Chapman. This is the girl Judy called Michelle. Whether she would have killed Debbie Smith would have depended on what Al wanted.

When Judy called the police concerning the firebombing and shooting in Rome, she did not confess to it. She did not tell the police who she was.

Whether she would have killed Linda Allen would have depended on what Al told her to do - what he wanted. Alvin injected Judy in the bottom with water. "It hurt a lot." He did this before Judy met Lisa Millican.

The routine was the same each time. Her function was to procure the girls. Alvin would use them, and Judy would kill them. Judy never liked sex with Alvin. He was the only man she had ever had sex with. She never had sex with a girl. She did not want sex with a girl.

Judy said that Lisa said she did not want to go back to the Harpst Home. Judy agreed with her saying that she knew what it was like in a place like that. The district attorney reminded the defendant that she had said everything was great at the YDC. The YDC People listened to her, and she had a good life.

She replied that she told Lisa what Al had rehearsed with her until she had it just right. She was accustomed to rehearsing a thing until she had it just right. He did the thinking for them.

The witness was reminded that she went to the Dairy Bar in Scottsboro and did not call the police. Alvin was talking to her on the CB. He had a walkie-talkie, and she had a CB in the car. Alvin had a string on her, even though she had left him physically. When she went to restaurants, he talked to her on the CB.

Richard made the point that Alvin did not talk on the CB to her while he was having sex with Janice Chapman. She did not go to the police at that time.

Richard asked her why she did not attack Alvin with the baseball bat while he was hurting Lisa Millican when having sex with her. Judy said she could not stop him. There was nothing she could do. She never thought of hurting Al. She was too afraid of him to think about that.

When Judy questioned Lisa about the man at the restaurant in Scottsboro, she used the same tone Alvin used with her. The voice was calm, but there was a threat in it. She could not demonstrate the voice in the courtroom because Al was not there to influence her.

Why did Lisa have to be killed? Alvin said that she knew too much, and would get the Neelleys into a lot of trouble. Lisa would tell about him having sex with her. Judy was asked if that was the reason Lisa had to be killed. Judy Neelley replied that she didn't think about reasons. "I had no thoughts."

She did not intend to throw Lisa over into the canyon, as Alvin had said they were going to leave her at the trees. Then, he changed his mind.

Alvin had told Judy the Drano was supposed to make it appear the 13-year-old girl had a heart attack. It was not used to torture her, but that is what it did. She was asked why Alvin let Lisa use the bathroom two different times at the canyon, since Judy was going to kill her anyway. She stated that she didn't ask him why. She just did it.

Judy was asked if she killed Lisa because she was afraid of Alvin. She replied, "I killed Lisa because he told me to." She received threats from Alvin that he was going to kill her, but that was not the reason she killed Lisa. She killed Lisa because Alvin told her to do it.

Richard then went into the old "you questions" to force admissions from the defendant. For example:

Q. How long was that up until you killed Lisa that you had had the handcuffs?

A. We were in Macon right before we picked up LisIt wasn't long.

Q. So, you handcuffed her to keep her from getting away, didn't you?

A. Yes.

Q. And you kept her in a place where she was not likely to be found, didn't you, in a motel?

A. Yes sir.

Q. You didn't want her to run off because you knew that you could get in trouble from her — taking her like that, doing what you had done to her.

A. Yes sir.

Q. But she knew that you had the gun.

A. Yes sir.

Q. You had shown her the gun.

A. Yes sir. The gun was sitting out.

Q. Well, you told the officers that you would keep the gun under the seat of your car and when you went in a motel you put it on the dresser at the motel.

A. Yes sir.

Q. And you did that, didn't you?

A. Yes sir.

Q. And she knew you had it.

A. Yes sir.

Q. And that's why she didn't even try to run away when you had her outside after you parked the car, because you told her not to run away, didn't you?

A. I told her not to; yes sir.

Q. She knew you had a gun.

A. Yes sir.

Q. Let me ask you, Mrs. Neelley, did you always bind your victims with their hands in front of them like this with the handcuffs?

A. Yes sir.

Q. Of course, Janice was a little different. Her hands were between her legs.

A. Yes sir.

Q. Did you always use handcuffs?

A. Yes sir.

Q. You never used any other materials?

A. No sir.

Mr. Igou forced Judith Ann Neelley to admit every facet of the murder of Lisa Ann Millican as her own independent act. She was answering questions from her point of view, and the district attorney was asking questions from his point of view. If I had not been defending, I would have thought that the cross-examination was excellent.

Igou pointed out through questioning the defendant that she had made two mistakes: allowing John Hancock to live and making the telephone call to the Rome Police Department. She knew the telephone calls would result in her being caught.

Q. You didn't give your name on that, did you?

A. No sir.

Q. You never told them your name.

A. No sir.

Q. What you were doing with those was just bragging about it, wasn't it?

A. No sir.

Q. Because you had enjoyed doing it and you wanted to tell everybody else about it.

A. No; I did not.

Q. Then, what was the reason for it?

A. Al was calling — had me call the police department and tell them that they could not catch a woman that was doing that, and the YDC knew what I sounded like anyway, whenever there were — the calls were made to the Rome Police Department about Ken Dooley and Linda Adair, and they had the recordings to compare.

Q. You knew that at the time, didn't you?

A. Al told me; yes sir.

District Attorney Igou asked the defendant two questions in one and narrowed his next question to obtain the answer he wanted for the jury.

Q. And you did target practice, and you did use wad-cutter ammunition.

A. Not in target practice.

Q. Just in killing?

A. Yes sir.

Judy was asked to identify several photographs: State's Exhibits 53 through 71, which were admitted into evidence. Some of the pictures were taken in the Barbara Adams home in Murfreesboro in July the year Alvln took Judy, Dottie, and the boys to Panama City, Florida. This was July before September, 1982, when Lisa was picked up. These pictures showed various members of the family playing with handguns and a rifle. In one picture, Judy is holding a pistol to Davie's head. She was posed by Alvin in each picture. He told her what to do and he supplied the guns.

The district attorney then once more questioned Judy as to her enjoying killing Lisa, having sex with women, and enjoying sex with Alvin. He mentioned the handcuffs, injections, torturing Lisa, Lisa's pain, Lisa's crying, more injections, shots, Liquid-Plumr, Drano, and things Judy did not tell Lisa that she could have told her.

Each series of questions ended with Judy testifying that she was only doing what she was told. "I'm just telling you, I didn't have any feelings."

Judy was then questioned about the effect of the shots of "concentrated lye stuff" on Lisa. She described a bruised knot under the skin. Although she remembered seeing it, Judy didn't think about it at the time. After the shots, Judy wiped off the needles and syringes with a towel and threw them off in the canyon.

She did it to wipe off fingerprints? No, she did it because Alvin told her to do it.

Judy Neelley then testified once more as to almost all the details of the facts at Little River Canyon. Alvin directed all the events at the canyon. She did not think about the handcuffs nor any of the other facts of the murder. She was doing as she was told. Lisa asked for a shirt. Judy asked Al if Lisa could have a shirt.

He said, "Tell her no." So Judy told her no.

Richard questioned her about the terrain at the canyon, the distance of the drop, Lisa's height, and Judy's gun. Lisa was instructed to stand on a spot that Judy marked with her foot near the edge of the canyon. Judy did not think about being near the edge of the canyon herself. She took Lisa to the very edge of the canyon because Alvin told her to do it.

> Q. You got close enough so that she would fall off into the canyon, you thought, when you shot her?
>
> A. She was supposed to; yes sir.
>
> Q. That was the plan, wasn't it?
>
> A. That's what Al said; yes sir.
>
> Q. That was the plan, wasn't it?
>
> A. That's what Al said; yes sir.
>
> Q. You and Al had discussed it hadn't you?
>
> A. There was no discussion; no sir.

Q. Well, what do you call it?

A. Al told me what to do, what would happen, and I did it.

Richard tried to force Judy to say that she intended to shoot Lisa and let her fall into the canyon. She knew the meaning of intent. She did not have any intent. She was doing what she was told to do. She could not allow Lisa Millican to return to the Harpst Home because Alvin did not tell her to do that. She did not make any decisions at the canyon nor any other time; she did not have any feelings for anything; and she knew that she could not allow Lisa to return to the Harpst Home.

She said that Lisa's feet were two inches from the edge of the canyon. She backed off and shot her with a .38 pistol. The district attorney questioned her intent once again. Judy said that she intended to do as she was told. She admitted pointing the gun and pulling the trigger, and Lisa was supposed to fall into the canyon.

Q. Were you upset about that, Mrs. Neelley, about the whole thing, about the killing of Lisa?

A. I didn't have any feelings about it.

Q. I didn't ask you if you had — I asked if you were upset about it.

A. I had no feeling.

The district attorney pointed out that she sounded very calm over the telephone when she reported the incident to the Rome Police Department a few hours later. She agreed.

When asked if she knew kidnaping Lisa Millican was a criminal act, she said that she didn't think about it. It did not occur to her that murder was a criminal act. She did not think about killing Lisa when she pulled the trigger.

Alvin Neelley told her when to change the babies, and when to feed them.

Cross-examination ended with Judy testifying that the only thing she ever did on her own was go to the bathroom; Al usually watched her do that; and if they had something in the motel, she would eat.

THE DEFENSE RETURNS

On re-direct, the State's Exhibit No. 60 was identified as part of a roll of film taken in the search of the red Ford Granada. Judy had never seen the pictures before. In one picture, Judy's eyes were swollen, there was a bruise in the corner of her eyebrow, and there was a bruise on her arm. State's Exhibit No. 63 showed the bruise on Judy's forehead a little clearer. The bruise on her forearm was visible in the photograph. Judy testified that she was just getting over two black eyes. Judy was shown State's Exhibit No. 55.

Q. What do you see there, Judy?

A. On my wrist you can see where I had been bit, and on my eye you can see where I have been busted in the eye. It's swollen and dark, and there's a bruise on my left forearm.

In Exhibit No. 71, Judy is holding the .22 rifle Alvin purchased and sawed off the barrel.

The picture showed that she had teeth marks, where each of Alvin's upper and lower teeth dug into her arm. The picture was taken when, "I was just getting well where he had bit me."

She had two black eyes and a bruise on her left forearm. Exhibit No. 69 depicted Alvin as his eyes were beginning to glisten. State's Exhibit No. 70 was another photograph of Alvin starting to get mad.

Judy was asked about her talent, as well as her intelligence. She was able to draw. Exhibit No. 83 was hands clutching through some bars. She felt that was how her life was. Defense Exhibit No. 84 was a cartoon drawn by Judy depicting two porcupines. One is talking to the other, "Just once I'd like to be petted."

Casey was not killed because Alvin did not tell Judy to kill her.

She had never told her story before the trial. She did not feel free to tell her story.

The Court overruled the State's objection, and allowed the defendant to testify that she had told her lawyers the same story she had told Danny Smith and Bill Burns. Her lawyers did not believe the story and tried to gain her trust so that she would tell the truth, and allow them to prepare a defense. They bought a new TV for her, and provided clothes for her trying to gain her confidence.

She first realized that Alvin Neelley controlled every aspect of her life when she heard Jo Ann Browning testify. She realized that Alvin had done the same things to Jo Ann that he had done to her. He even said the same words.

Alvin Neelley never called her Judy after she ran away with him. Usually, he didn't call her. He just told her what to do. If he did call her, it was "bitch" or "slut" or "whore" or something similar. He never called her name.

When Judy was released from the YDC, she returned to Mrs. Neelley's to care for her twins. She did the cooking and attended church. During the time Judy was living in Cleveland, she was baptized. She wrote to Alvin announcing her baptism, and he told her to stop going to church. Judy attended church one more time. Alvin told her that she had better not go again, and she did not go.

When she was under Alvin's control she did not think of right or wrong. She just did what she was told.

On the morning the police came to the motel room door and arrested Judy, Alvin directed all the activities in the room in preparation for opening the door.

After a short re-cross-examination, the Defense rested and renewed all motions, including all motions previously ruled on by the Court. Additionally, the Defense moved the Court to quash the indictment and grant a mistrial. All motions were denied.

The courtroom crowd was restless. The Court called a longer recess. Steve and I met with Judy, and thought that we had developed a defense. It had been difficult work.

Now, thanks to nightly research and calls around the country, the defense was morphing into the battered woman syndrome taken to extremes. We had to fight on.

CHAPTER NINE

REBUTTAL – CROSS-EXAMINING THE EXPERT

————◆————

Before the State begins its rebuttal, let me set the stage for you. Richard is going to produce evidence that Judith Ann Neelley intended to kidnap and murder Lisa and Janice. To do this, he is going to use the State of Alabama Psychiatrist who had originally examined her and found her capable of standing trial. Realizing that our chances are little and none, I am going to try to use this same witness as an expert for Judy to develop the battered woman's syndrome as a defense. We need to convert this psychiatrist into our expert rather than an expert for the state.

Most of the testimony is going to be directly from the record as taken down by the court reporter at the trial. You are going to be reading a court transcript.

Alexander A. Salillas, M.D., a psychiatrist with the Department of Mental Health, Tuscaloosa, Alabama, testified that he was asked to see Judy Neelley at Bryce Hospital.

The doctor testified as to his qualifications and experience. He examined Judith Ann Neelley and did not find any mental disease or defect whereby she lacked the substantial capacity to appreciate the criminality of her conduct. He did not find any mental disease or defect whereby Judith Ann Neelley lacked the substantial capacity to conform her conduct to the requirements of law. In the opinion of the doctor, Judith Ann Neelley committed a deliberate act, "done, ah, with premeditation." As a staff physician for the Alabama Department of Mental Health, the witness was of the opinion that Judith Ann Neelley was not committable to the mental hospital under psychiatric criteria.

HERE'S THE CROSS EXAMINATION

The cross-examination of the State's expert had to be lengthy as he had to make our case for us. His cross-examination had to be slow, deliberate and devastating. Try not to be bored with this cross as it is lawyering in desperation.

I began casually enough by exploring the qualifications of the doctor after his graduation from Santo Thomas University in the Philippines.

The doctor was then examined as to his familiarity with the term "*coercive persuasion.*" I didn't know enough about the Battered Woman's Syndrome to question him about that at that point.

He said that coercive persuasion happens every day around the world. An example of coercive persuasion is the school principal or teacher who directs the action of the students. The doctor agreed that coercive persuasion occurs when a husband tells his wife to do something and threatens or intimidates her or beats her into doing it.

Another form of coercive persuasion is called "brainwashing." Soldiers in the Korean War experienced this. I then questioned the doctor as to the elements of coercive persuasion.

> Q. I want to ask you some items or some elements that
> I'm wondering if you would consider as to whether

a person might be a victim of coercive persuasion. The first element being the isolation of the victim and the total control over her environment. If you were determining whether a person acquired a mental defect whereby the persuader imposed his will on the person being persuaded, would you consider the isolation of the victim and the total control of her environment by the person doing the persuading? Would that be one of the factors to consider?

A. Yes.

Q. All right. The second factor: control of all channels of information and communication. Would that be a factor you would consider?

A. Uh-huh. That's correct.

Q. Third: psychological debilitation by means of diet control, insufficient sleep, poor sanitation, or other physical conditions. Would you consider that?

A. Yes, I would.

Q. Fourth: assignment of tasks of a repetitive nature.

A. Uh-huh.

Q. Five: manipulation of guilt and anxiety.

A. Sure.

Q. Six: threats of annihilation by the all-powerful persuader who insists that the victim's sole chance for survival lies in identifying with the persuader. Would you consider that?

Q. Yes.

Q. Seven: degradation of and assaults on the preexisting self. Would you consider that?

A. Yes sir.

Q. Eight: peer pressure, often applied through ritual or struggle sessions.

A. Yes sir.

Q. Nine: required performance of symbolic acts of self betrayal, betrayal of group norms and confession.

A. Uh-huh.

Q. Ten: alternating harshness and leniency. Would you consider those?

A. Yes sir.

Q. Now, acting alone none of these forces would prove irresistible to a person of ordinary resolve, particularly if he was aware of the attempt to influence him, would they?

A. That is right.

Q. All of us could overcome each one of these individually, couldn't we?

A. Uh-huh.

Q. But rather it's the concentration of the multiple forces, both physical and psychological intensively applied over a period of time, which gives coercive persuasion its particular power, or peculiar power, doesn't it?

A. A. You said it all.

Q. All right. Now, if that's the case, then a determined persuader possessing total control over the life and environment of the captive, or a person to be persuaded, can produce behavioral and attitudinal changes in even the most strongly resistant individual, can't they, Doctor?

A. They can.

Q. And the thing that really gets them is the breakdown of the victim's identity and will in the latter stages of coercive persuasion destroys the very mechanisms that the victim might use to fight back with, doesn't it?

A. It may.

Q. Then past experience, though, in the field of psychiatry, has demonstrated that most coercively persuaded victims, once removed from the coercive environment, soon lose their inculcated responses and return to their former modes of thinking, once they are far enough removed from the persuasive techniques, aren't they?

A. They may.

Q. In the case of the coercively persuaded defendant it is appropriate to ask also whether the intent the actor possessed can properly be said to be his own.

A. Yes.

Q. Let me ask you this: Would you agree with this: That where a person has been coercively persuaded, the ten factors that I have discussed with you, the guilty mind with which the person acts is not her own, but rather, her mental state is more appropriately ascribed to the captor, or persuader, who instilled it in her for his own purpose.

A. I grant that.

Q. Okay. But part of coercive persuasion would include stretches of relentless and incessant interrogation, wouldn't it?

A. Uh-huh.

The doctor agreed that coercively persuaded victims usually resist the process initially, but they finally give up. One of the things the doctor would look for to determine if a person has been coercively persuaded would be whether the criminal acts benefitted the captor. This is particularly true when the actions induced were dangerous and were actions the individual showed no interest in performing before falling under the control of the captor.

The doctor then attempted to distinguish his prior testimony by stating that in the final analysis the actor made a decision that he is responsible for. He did agree that human beings can be subjected to a conditioned response.

Pavlov's dogs were discussed. The doctor admitted that because of the conditioning, the dogs salivated when Pavlov rang the bell, whether the dogs were given food or not. It was this experiment which brought about the idea of the conditioned response to a known stimuli into psychiatry.

The rules of the trial debate do not allow one to immediately ask an expert witness his opinion of the facts of the case. The cross-examination must turn to a hypothetical question covering all the relevant facts of the life of the defendant and her relationship with Alvin Neelley. Then the expert can render an opinion based upon the assumptions presented.

I established assumptions touching Judy's life from Murfreesboro to Kennesaw, Georgia, where Alvin denied he was the father of Judy's pregnancy.

The witness stated that, "from a totally charming — ah — prince, he had turned now to something like a monster or an ogre."

I then gave the doctor assumptions leading to the first beating in Rome, Georgia. He was asked what the psychological effect of that beating must have been on a 15-and- a-half-year-old pregnant girl in a strange town.

The witness responded, "It must have hurt like Hell, I'm sure. She must have been depressed and — I can sympathize with her is all I can say."

After discussing the possible avenues of escape for the young girl, including calling the police and considering all the assumptions available to the girl, the witness stated that he could not figure out what kept her from doing what she ought to have done.

Q. QAnd what should she ought to have done, Doctor?

A. I don't know.

The witness testified that in the end the decision to stay in the painful situation was the girl's. The witness stated that it was her choice to stay on and be the patsy.

The doctor then agreed that there may be as many as 40 million American women who are beaten, and the beatings go unreported. The witness was asked the reasons these women remain in the situation where there is domestic violence. He responded that the women did not want to report it.

It is the victim's choice. Various reasons other than the choice of the victim were discussed with the witness. Some of the reasons were: Their desire for marital privacy, emotional dependency, low self-esteem, fear of their husbands, shame, a lack of confidence to reach out to the authorities or others for help, economic dependency, the false hope the man will reform, and the woman has no place to go.

Dr. Sallilas agreed with each and every one of these reasons. He admitted that the factors in the defendant's hypothetical case were much more severe than the ones battered women usually experienced.

He testified that in his opinion battered women still have a choice. Although the hypothetical "little girl" (Judith Ann Neelley) was a wife and a captive, she still had a choice to continue to stay with her husband. Additional assumptions were given to the witness:

A. Granted that all these are present, Mr. French, still it is the victim's choice to stay, you know. Assessing her chances for escape, the risk involved, the consequences, still it is a matter of choice in the end.

PHARISEES AT THE GATE

The Court recessed and, before bringing the jury back, informed the interested parties that two jurors were having difficulty visiting with their families over the weekend because of work schedules. It was agreeable with the State and Defense that the jurors visit those family members when court recessed at the conclusion of the day's testimony.

If I didn't have enough pressure going on, two members of my church visited me during the afternoon recess and suggested that it might be a good time for me to take a sabbatical from teaching my Bible Class. I had been teaching the Baraca Class at the First Baptist Church for 17 years. It was the largest Sunday School class in North Alabama with more than 100 members. I knew the church was feeling some of the heat from my representing Judith Ann Neelley, but I didn't ask to be put in that position. I questioned the gentlemen whether the Board of Deacons, of which I was a member, had sent them. No. Then did the minister suggest they encourage me to quit teaching? No. It was their idea "for the good of the church." I respectfully declined and suggested that now was the time for my church to stick with me. Nothing like a little more pressure.

BACK TO THE SHRINK

Resuming the trial before the jury, I decided to see what I might mine from his Philippine background during World War II. He was familiar with the use of Kamikaze aircraft against American vessels. He was also familiar with the plywood aircraft without wheels. He said they were called Baka. The result of Kamikaze and Baka missions were the same - suicide, a one-way trip. When the pilot sat in the cockpit of the airplane loaded with the bomb, he knew he was not coming back. According to the witness, the freedom of choice for the young pilots flying the suicidal missions was volunteering in the first place.

The doctor volunteered that, "We cannot judge Japanese by our own standards. They have a different way of looking at life and death."

Q. Okay. Can we judge Jonestown by our own standards?

A. Maybe you can. Maybe—

Q. Can we judge the Moonies by our own standards, Dr. Salillas?

A. If you are living in a society where you want to exist, certainly I would say you can.

I pointed out to the doctor, and he agreed, that in Jonestown there were medical doctors (three of them), retired, and practicing lawyers, school teachers, engineers, other professionals, along with working people. There were people of different races and ethnic and cultural backgrounds.

Q. And yet when Jim Jones told them to drink the cyanide, they not only drank it themselves, they gave it to their children, didn't they?

A. (Nods head, affirmatively.)

Q. Now, Doctor, at what point in time did the residents of Jonestown have a free choice?

A. I would say all the way down to the last thoughts died.

The witness stated that the only thing a person can do in life is make choices. Everything is a free choice. The witness was asked if choices are ever taken away by others.

A. Never is. I would — I could choose not to come here, but I'm not about to be put in prison, Mr. French. To me this is livable. I mean it is something I can live with, coming up here, driving a hundred and fifty miles.

Q. But as I started out with you earlier, there are times during coercive persuasion that the choices we make are directed for us, aren't they?

Q. Directed, but still a choice, Mr. French.

Q. Yes sir. We always have a choice whether we live or die, don't we?

A. Yes.

Q. Do the people that you work with at Bryce —

A. Taylor-Hardin.

Q. Taylor-Hardin - the people who see reality totally distorted due to mental incapacity, do you tell us that they still have the right to make a choice?

A. They are choosing behaving the way they want to based on their own perceptions. It may not be in tune with reality, but it's a choice they make.

Q. Right. It is a choice they make, but the perception of the reality affecting that choice is changed, isn't it, or different from ours?

A. It may be different.

Q. All right. So, now we're speaking the same language. What we're talking about is the reality in which we operate our choice-making mechanism, right?

A. Uh-huh.

Dr. Salillas then agreed that the reality of Jonestown was different from that of the courtroom, and the reality faced by Patricia Hearst was different from that ordinarily faced by people every day. The reality that a battered wife sees reflects in her choices and attitudes.

I then returned to additional assumptions added to the original hypothetical question. The revenge of Alvin Neelley was discussed. The witness stated that revenge is a very strong emotion, overpowering at times. Since the past is gone and the future is not yet here, the present reality is all a person has. The person who brings the past into the present through memory wastes the present. Revenge, hatred, and recrimination may distort one's view of reality. All religious traditions teach love for others.

The witness agreed that a person with a capacity to love sees more of what is reality than a person bent on revenge.

Additional assumptions were once again added to the hypothetical question. The witness agreed that a person may agree with another because of threats while knowing that the facts are different. Continued threats make it easier for the person to accept the conception of reality held by the person making the threats. It finally becomes easier to find out what the threatening person wants and do it immediately. Eventually, the acts become habitual with the actor and becomes learned behavior.

Q. Yes, sir, and it becomes like Pavlov's dog, a conditioned response to a known stimuli, doesn't it, Doctor?

A. Yes sir.

Q. And the stimuli is the fact that I know what's going to happen to me if I don't tell you what you want to know.

A. Uh-huh.

Q. But my free choice, if I have lost it in my reality, my free choice now becomes simply a response, doesn't it?

A. Maybe.

The witness described the assumptions regarding Alvin Neelley as "sexual sadism," named after the Marquis de Sade. Anyone who receives sexual gratification from inflicting pain on someone else is a sadist. Alvin Neelley fit the profile of a sadist.

Additional assumptions of the hypothetical were added for the witness, down to the Neelleys sleeping in the car, and Alvin's obsession for revenge.

Q. He constantly told her how he was going to get his revenge, and he constantly told her to the point that she accepted that as reality. Now, Doctor, under those circumstances, would it seem consistent to you as a psychiatrist that that girl's reality could be deformed to the point where she would assume what he was telling her was reality itself?

A. I can say that she was fearful of him and would agree to everything that he would probably say.

Q. All right, assume that she agreed with everything that he said and she did everything that he told her to do. That would be consistent, would it not, Doctor?

A. It would be.

Q. At this point in time would you say, and I don't want to rush you, but would you say that this girl was in the company of a maniac?

A. It certainly sounded like that to me.

The doctor then traced the development of sadism from toilet training to the characteristics of cruelty, compulsiveness, and rigidity. The person chooses this as his method of sexual gratification.

I added additional assumptions of facts placed in the original hypothetical question.

Q. There is no genuine reality here, is there. Doctor?

A. I'm asking you — I fail to see the connection between what's real and what she needed to do. She obviously would have to follow directions that he gave her. That is the reality of the thing now. Reality — you're asking as to whether the girl's reality ended?

Q. No. You have answered my question. Her reality is what he told her to do. Her reality is his view of reality now, isn't it?

A. She was just following his orders.

Q. So, at this point in time, as he attempts to attract these women through the use of his wife, or this young girl who is seventeen years old, as a decoy or bait, would it be consistent with your experience that she would do precisely what she was told, when she was told to do it, exactly as she was told to do it?

A. Yes, it appears that way.

Q. And would she do that without question?

A. At that point in time, yes.

Q. All right, and would she do that without feeling?

A. Probably.

The witness assumed from the hypothetical question that Lisa Millican would refuse to have sex with Alvin.

> Q. And I want you to assume that he — he told the other woman, his wife, to threaten her, to do whatever was necessary to make her have sex with him, and would it be consistent with the profile that we now have of the wife of the sadist that she would do exactly what she is told and tell the little girl she must have sex with him?
>
> A. The wife knows better than to go against her husband.

Alvin's imagined hit man at the restaurant in Scottsboro and his requiring Judy to question Lisa in the bathroom until she admitted the man was a hit man was consistent with Alvin's personality.

> Q. All right. I want you to assume further that the wife went into the bathroom and used the same words that he had used on her to interrogate Lisa. Would that be consistent with her personality, Doctor?
>
> A. Could be.
>
> Q. All right. Well it is, isn't it?
>
> A. Well, with the assumptions that you are giving me, Mr. French, anything's possible.
>
> Q. That's exactly right. Doctor, and the assumptions are what you are limited to.
>
> A. That's correct.
>
> Q. They're assumptions. And with those assumptions in mind, it would be consistent with the personality of the wife to take Lisa into the restroom and use the same words that he used on her over and over gain to make her admit things, isn't that correct?
>
> A. That's right.

Q. And she would do it without any feeling, wouldn't she?

A. Uh-huh.

Q. And she would do it because she had been trained to do it, wouldn't she?

A. Because she had been told to do it.

Additional assumptions were added to the hypothetical question. The facts of removing Lisa to Little River Canyon and Alvin's direction of the activities at the canyon were added. The witness was asked if it would be consistent with Judy's personality to do what she was told by Alvin at the canyon. The witness responded that it could be true.

Additional assumptions were added leading up to the injection of the Drano into Lisa's buttocks without removing her pants. The question ended with:

Q. Would it be consistent, with the hypothetical and with the facts that you have in mind, that the wife would not pull the pants down if the husband did not tell her to?

A. It's probable.

The doctor was reluctant to say that Judy would pull the trigger at Alvin's command. He wanted additional assumptions to the hypothetical. He wanted to find some reluctance on the part of the 18-year-old to kill the 13-year-old girl. Those facts were not in the hypothetical as they were not in Judy's testimony. The questioning proceeded:

A. Again based on the assumptions she didn't try to talk her husband into letting the girl go at all?

Q. No; she did not.

A. She did not at all?

Q. She did not suggest anything to the husband, because she never suggested anything to the husband.

A. Just followed him automatically?

Q. Yes sir. She followed him automatically.

A. Now what were you trying to —

Q. I asked you if, based upon the hypothetical that I gave you, if it is consistent with her personality that she would go ahead and pull the trigger.

A. Probably not.

Q. Well, tell us why not. Doctor. You started to tell us a minute ago. We're waiting.

A. My own way of saying — My only way of answering your question, and I hope this will be satisfactory to the jury as well. She had been through all these beatings before. No big deal. She had been through it and survived. Fine. The little girl could probably withstand it too, you know, and carry on afterwards. At that point, when the act of killing — because it is of such — regardless of any way you look at it, wherever you come from, it is of gravity and such finality that once that step is taken there's no turning back. Ah — What I'm trying to say is that there wasn't enough sense in her to judge that this is something she had not done before, and the gravity of the act itself, to my own way of saying, has not failed to put an impact on her at all.

Additional assumptions were added to the hypothetical question. This series of additions terminated with Alvin reaching an orgasm while looking at Lisa's body in the canyon. The Doctor said that such an action was consistent with a sadist.

Q. Would it further be consistent with that personality if you assume that within ten minutes of that moment, as they were driving back down the canyon road with her less than a car length behind him, he's driving away, that he says to her on the CB words like this or to this effect, "Let's go to Rome and find another woman."

A. Quite possible.

Q. That's consistent with it, isn't it. Dr. Salillas?

A. Yes sir.

After the noon recess, my cross-examination continued with the John Hancock and Janice Chapman facts added to the hypothetical question. The doctor stated it would be consistent with Alvin Neelley's personality to have sexual intercourse with Janice Chapman as soon as possible after Alvin thought John had been murdered. This would continue to be a sadistic act, just as the act at the canyon.

The assumptions of the rape of Janice Chapman in the Granada and her subsequent murder were discussed with the witness. I asked him if these acts were consistent with the sadistic personality of Alvin Neelley. He said it was consistent. He then added that it was also consistent with individuals with an absolute disregard for the rights of others, constantly violating the rules, just bent on self-gratification.

Doctor Salillas described Alvin Neelley as " having been a Frankenstein before and is one now," and he did not see any deterioration, per se, into being more normal. Neelley had been violent all of his life, and that was his nature. It was the path Neelley chose to take.

Additional assumptions were added to the hypothetical leading down to Barbara Adams' reporting her daughter to the police. The doctor was asked:

Q. Remember in the hypothetical she did not approach her mother. Her mother approached her with a bloody shirt, and it was that occasion that she took to get out.

A. Granted. The assumption again is that many people want help, will not cry for help until it is presented to them. You have heard about a cry for help in suicide. They want to die, but they want help at the same time. This is not uncommon at all.

Q. Well, here we see in our hypothetical a mother who just fortunately finds this shirt, and the daughter being alone with her mother one time while her husband was in the front bedroom. He allowed her to take the laundry to her mother, and the mother says, "What is this," and she cannot even tell her. She says, "Call the police and tell them I'm here." Now, would you assume, then, that — I mean, would your conclusion be, based on these assumptions, that once she had been placed in the security of confinement would you assume that she would still continue to parrot what the husband had told her?

A. If the husband is significant enough to her, yes.

Q. All right. Would you presume from what I have told you that she would write him a letter on the 15th, saying it was all her fault, that he wasn't even there, and he had nothing to do with it? Would that be logical?

A. That is consistent with the way I've pictured her so far.

The witness testified that in his opinion the relationship between Alvin and Judith Ann Neeley was not all that bad. "There was love in it, although it was a love maybe handled in the wrong

kind of way. She did find some - for her husband was the significant person, and it's instinct to be protective of somebody whom
you cherish."

    Q. Tell us where in the hypothetical she had any reality
        of her own.

    A. The reality that you speak of is that if she doesn't do
        what her husband tells her to do she loses his love,
        his attention, his affection. Affection, I grant, is
        rather sadistic, cruel, but still there. For her, at that
        point in time of her life, that is important, regard-
        less of what she has to do. If she has to kill, based
        on the assumptions, to keep her husband, she will.

Other assumptions were added to the original hypothetical
question. The doctor was now of the opinion that the defendant
stayed in the situation because she needed the love Alvin Neelley
had for her. He said that she would be mentally deficient after going
through all the abuse she said she experienced. However, the witness
did agree that a sadist would want to inflict pain rather than kill.

    Due to the doctor volunteering testimony, and due to my offer-
ing a number of new assumptions into the hypothetical, the examination turned from a discussion into bordering on argument.

    I thought that I had gained all the good testimony I was going to
get from the doctor. My cross-examination turned toward impeaching the witness.

    The doctor admitted he had spent the lunch hour in the office
of the district attorney with the assistant district attorney, and the
other doctor from the Department of Mental Health. He stated that
his testimony of the morning had been reviewed and suggestions
and comments had been made as to how he might answer the questions when the cross-examination continued. The witness admitted
he was employed by the State of Alabama and was being paid by the
State to be present in court and testify.

Some inconsistencies in the witnesses' prior testimony were discussed:

    Q. Let's look at this distinction. You will recall this morning I told you, or you understood that he had told her that if the Drano were injected into a person it would kill them right?

    A. (Nods head.)

    Q. That's right, isn't it?

    A. Yes.

    Q. And then I asked you if she gave her a shot of Drano through her blue jeans would that be consistent with the personality, and you said "She would just be doing as she was told." You recall that?

    A. Yes. Again —

    Q. Let me finish my question.

MR. IGOU. We object.

    Q. I'm gonna let you say anything you want to.

THE COURT: Finish your question, Mr. French.

    Q. So, she knew that the Drano would kill her in your assumption. She gave her the shot through her pants because she was doing as she was told, but the result would be the same; the child would be dead. And you said that she was just doing as she was told; yet when I asked you when she was standing on the canyon and she said he said "Pull the trigger," and she pulled the trigger, you said she made an independent choice. Now, that is not consistent, is it, Doctor?

    A. Again the decision to go with the order, that is the choice, Mr. French. To inject — It was a willful

— Injecting the Drano or pulling the trigger was a violation or willful act.

Q. But the person would be dead either way, wouldn't they. Dr. Salillas?

A. That was the purpose of the whole thing.

Q. Yes, and one, you didn't see what the person would be thinking, but they would be just doing as they were told, but when I marched her up to the edge of the canyon you could see individual thought, couldn't you. Doctor?

A. Mr. French, you were trying — it was very hard in the first place to follow you. I have to make notes. But you were trying to impress upon me whether the defendant saw the reality as her husband saw the reality — I disagree with you on that. The reality for her at that point in time was that she would be beat and slapped if she didn't do what she was told to do. Now, injecting — Granted, the plan was to do away with the victim. That has been decided upon. I will grant you injecting a substance and shooting are two different actions, Mr. French.

Q. Sir?

A. Shooting a gun is a lot more distasteful to some than merely an injection. It's much more cleaner.

Q. Perhaps it might be to you. Doctor. I cannot conceive injecting someone with Drano being clean under any circumstances. Maybe you're used to giving shots and I'm not. I want to go back to your report. Doctor. You're familiar with your report of this woman, aren't you?

A. It is mine, so I should be.

The witness discussed his work and the way the Lunacy Commission functions. He had interviewed Judith Ann Neelley for "an hour, give or take a few minutes." Dr. Salillas found Judy to be an average, normal woman of high intelligence. He did find, under Axis II, a dependent personality disorder. He described this as a serious condition where one "subrogates his or her interests to that of the person that is important to her. It could be a child, 'a husband,' a father, a friend, et cetera." It is a neurotic kind of disorder.

> Q. Well, can you tell how it manifests itself in a person generally? How did you find out this woman had a dependent personality disorder?
>
> A. The description itself, I guess, is explanatory enough. Persons with this kind of disorder have a tendency to — ah — They attach themselves to somebody. It's a kind of emotional attachment. As I have stated, they would do anything for this significant person in their life. We all have some certain kinds of dependency, all of us. It may be to somebody — a friend, a family member, but there are certain degrees of this.

The doctor testified that he did not have any difficulty in assessing and evaluating that Judy had a dependent personality disorder. Additional assumptions were added to the hypothetical question, and Dr. Salillas agreed that the girl in the hypothetical had a dependent personality disorder.

> Q. And you would say once — Would you say, then, based upon the hypothetical, that she is perfectly normal, that she has a high intelligence?
>
> A. Mr. French, you keep bringing up all this. It's very hard for me to answer you. If you would stick down to the facts I would be able to arrive at the formulation much better. If you keep bringing in loose ends all the time, I have to change my opinion every

time. That would leave us no end to the discussion. We could stay here for a week, and I can give you what you want.

Q. Dr. Salillas, when a person has a dependent personality disorder to a high degree, to an intensity, will you describe for the ladies and gentlemen of the jury how that person's normal behavior might be in ordinary day to day affairs?

A. I give the assumption that Mr. French has given me would suffice as an example.

STATE ATTEMPTS TO REHABILITATE

On re-direct, District Attorney Igou asked Dr. Salillas if the defendant had been programmed to commit murder. The witness said, no, that murder was a drastic desire regardless of the culture you come from.

The district attorney then added assumptions to the hypothetical question. These assumptions added vacation trips to Florida, Texas, and incidents with the children. He then added the shooting of John Hancock and the threat to take care of his girlfriend. He added the murder of Hancock's girlfriend as she was shot in the back and "flopped over" and the " defendant went over and put two more bullets in her chest because she said that she had to shut her up." Casey was added, and the witness was reminded specifically of the killing of Lisa Ann Millican. The district attorney then asked Dr. Salillas if the defendant was exercising her own choice in doing so?

The witness testified that the act was a volitional one. Considering all the facts, the text of the conversation between her and the attending psychiatrist, and the social history, Dr. Salillas said it would be hard for him to find her insane at the time of the crime.

In his examination of the defendant and the hypothetical's presented at the trial, Dr. Salillas could not find that she lacked the substantial capacity through mental disease or defect to conform her conduct to the requirements of the law.

GOING FOR THE JUGLAR

Mike O'Dell and his fellow doctor from the State had coached the good doctor at lunch. Since he had acquiesced to the coaching and was back helping the State, I thought I might as well do him in. My re-cross-examination concluded with the following:

Q. I asked you if you had a preconceived notion before you came here that she had the mental capability to do the act. Did you, or did you not?

A. We all have our preconceived ideas. I'm just human.

Q. I understand that. Doctor.

A. It seems to me that you are trying to picture me as something else.

Q. No sir. I'm simply trying to picture you as a human being who was biased and prejudiced against the defendant before you took the stand, and I believe you ought to admit that you are.

A. I am, but I try very hard to try and remain impartial.

That was enough. The State was not going to rehabilitate that. However, Mr. Igou tried by asking the doctor if he had examined the defendant before coming to court to testify. The doctor stated that he had, and his opinion had not changed.

I hated to gild the lily, but I might as well throw one more lick in to round it out. I asked about the number of defendants entering a plea of not guilty by reason of insanity that the doctor had examined.

He had examined 15; of that number, he found 2 who were insufficient to stand trial.

Neither the State nor the Defense had anything further.

The Court announced that all the evidence was now in. The jury was excused until Monday. With the jury out of the courtroom, the Defense renewed all motions denied by the Court.

CHAPTER TEN

THE VERDICT

———————◆◆———————

It was now time to start attacking Juror Hargis who was obviously prejudiced against the defendant. We moved that juror, Eileen Hargis, be excused before the jury began deliberations and that an alternate be put in her place.

The grounds for our motion were that she was inattentive; she was obviously prejudiced against the defendant; she mouthed objections to the state; and she would seek to manipulate and control the jury. You may read the grounds for our motion as we knew them at the time in **Appendix 2**.

The State argued that if the juror knew when to object, she must be paying attention to the trial. The State did not see what the defense described. He did not object at the prompting of a juror. The argument seemed ridiculous to him.

We had several alternate jurors who could take her place and she would never know that she wasn't an alternate. The State's strong opposition to our motion put me on notice that there was more going on here than meets the eye. There was.

The judge said that he did not see the conduct raised by the defense soliciting an objection from the district attorney. Due to the length of the trial, some of the jurors appeared more attentive than others. Juror Hargis looked away from the witness who was testifying on several occasions. He concluded that he had not observed anything out of the juror that would be justification for her removal at this time.

We objected to the jurors visiting with their families over the weekend because of the conduct of Juror Hargis. The defense also asked to take the jurors on voir dire individually, at the end of the trial, to determine the facts surrounding their deliberations.

The Court stated it would take that matter up later.

We argued for the removal of Hargis more strongly, stating that we had been the object of her aggression since early in the trial. We moved our questioning position of witnesses away from the area of the juror. Juror Hargis led the jury in each day, and took the same seat each day - the one nearest the audience and the examiner's podium.

The district attorney responded that he stood at the same podium and never heard a word from the juror or any other juror.

I told the court that I did not believe Juror Hargis was committed to the State. It was our position that this juror would interfere with the jury process. By the middle of the trial we had considered asking that the juror be excused. This was not mentioned to the state until her activities became so blatant that we had to get on the record with it.

The Court pointed out that she was the only member of the jury panel who did not have a family visit the weekend before. Steve and I suggested that Hargis be replaced by an alternate, and then the Court could go forward with the family visits over the weekend. Her replacement could come by agreement between the State and Defense or by order of the Court.

The State informed the Court that it would not agree to any substitution of jurors. The district attorney was of the opinion that only the Court could order the replacement of a juror. We responded that the juror had disqualified herself.

I had tried to be sort of magnanimous about the removal of Juror Hargis, but with Richard acting out of character, I was beginning to smell a rat. Something had passed me by. Steve and I had to get into Juror Hargis a little more thoroughly.

Usually, when there are alternate jurors if the conduct of a juror is questioned in the slightest, the Court simply moves an alternate onto the panel. Here, for the first time in my legal career, the Court denied the substitution of an alternate juror, but did cancel the family visitation. If the State had stated our grounds, I believe that the Court would have removed the juror immediately. I have been in two different cases in federal court where one side or the other complained about a juror doing less than Hargis, and the alternate immediately went on the panel. I did not like how this was going down.

The parties and the Court then discussed the Court's jury charge. The requested charges of the Defense were denied. The Court stated that it would give the defense of duress to the lesser-included offenses of kidnaping in the first degree and kidnaping in the second degree. The Court was also going to charge on aiding and abetting and the plea of insanity. The verdict forms were approved by the parties.

FINAL ARGUMENT

March 21, 1983, Monday, the thirteenth day of the trial. The Court informed the jury that arguments of the lawyers would begin. O'Dell argued for the State. French argued for the Defense. Igou closed for the State.

I objected to the State's argument when Mr. Igou said the following:

MR. IGOU: Because of Mrs. Neelley's desire to please Alvin, two people are dead and one more, she thought, and she said, "I had a good reason." That's what she's telling you. We're here today in this courtroom, as we have been for lots of days, and it's impersonal. It's formal sometimes here, and it's nothing like that morning that she had Lisa out there at the canyon. You have been in here so long that you have been sitting in these chairs, and you can't really think about that. You can't really put yourself there.

MR. FRENCH: May it please the Court, I beg your pardon, Mr. Igou. This is improper argument asking the jury to put itself in the place of the victim.

MR. IGOU: I'm telling them they cannot do so.

MR. FRENCH: That's just a back door asking the jurors to put themselves in the place of the victim.

THE COURT: I'll overrule the objection.

At the conclusion of the State's argument, the jury was given a recess. The Court announced to the parties that with regard to the motion of the Defense to remove Juror Hargis, the Court had carefully observed her during the arguments and found her, for the most part, to be very attentive to both arguments. The Court was convinced that her demeanor today was appropriately attentive. The Court was willing to give the Defense the opportunity of an evidentiary hearing on the motion made earlier concerning Juror Hargis. The Court was allowing the Defense the opportunity to substantiate evidentially the allegations made as grounds to the motion.

The Defense stated that it would like to do that but would not want to burden the record with a useless act if the Court had made up its mind. The Court could not say what it would do as a result of the evidence which might be offered. We didn't know what we might learn later.

The Defense then made a showing or proffer of the evidence that it would show at such a hearing. The Court said it was asking the Defense if it wanted to take that kind of evidence. The Defense said it would prefer to wait until after the verdict.

The disposition of the alternate jurors was discussed, and the parties and Court agreed they would be retained by the Court until the jury reached a verdict.

There was no objection to the Court's oral charge.

The jury commenced its deliberations at 4:25 p.m. The alternates were kept separate and apart from the other jurors. At 6:10 p.m., the Court called the jury to recess for the night. Eileen Hargis had made herself foreman of the jury!

THE JURY DELIBERATES

While the jury was out, that night my dog was barking, and we kept hearing this "thump, thump, thump."

Celeste went to a window and said, "There are four people out there throwing rocks at our house. They're going to break out windows!" Some hooligans had decided to throw rocks at my house.

I ran to the closet and got a rifle and started toward the front door.

"Don't kill them, Bob!" Celeste was genuinely concerned.

I went out on the front porch and shot a couple of rounds up into the night sky, and the rock throwers jumped in their car and sped off. That was the last of the rock throwers; however, the animosity against me and my family was growing every day. My twins were having a very difficult time in school.

March 22, 1983, the jury resumed its deliberations at 8:30 a.m. At 9:50 a.m., the jury requested the judge give the intent portion of the oral charge again. The note was signed by the Foreman Eileen

Hargis. By agreement, the Court gave its intent portion of the oral charge again.

At 10:40 a.m., the jury reported it had reached a verdict:

"We, the jury, find the defendant guilty of the capital offense charged in the indictment. Eileen H. Hargis, Foreman."

SETTING THE SENTENCE HEARING

The Court adjudged the defendant guilty and announced that the sentence portion of the trial would begin at 1:00 p.m. This portion of the trial would deal with whether Judith Ann Neelley would be given death or life without parole. The jury was returned to the jury room.

The Court placed in the record the agreement of the State and Defense that the sentence portion of the hearing would not involve any evidence. It was agreed the State would open the argument, the Defense would argue, and the State would close; and the Court would charge the jury.

The Defense asked the Court about the evidentiary hearing concerning Mrs. Hargis. The Court said that at this point in the proceedings, the motion for new trial would be the appropriate time to have it.

CHAPTER ELEVEN

THE SENTENCING

———►◆◄———

The Court opened the sentencing hearing with the statement that the parties would not refer to the fact that the jury's opinion was advisory in nature.

The State asked the jury for the death penalty. The Defense argued. The Court charged the jury in the penalty phase of the trial, and the jury retired to deliberate at 2:55 p.m.

At 3:55 p.m., Foreman Hargis announced the jury had reached a decision. It recommended life without parole. The vote was 10 for life without parole, 2 for death. We learned later that the two death penalty votes were Hargis and her roommate. The Court announced it would conduct an additional hearing after a pre-sentence investigation. The jury was excused and the trial was concluded.

April 18, 1983, at 9:00 a.m. the Court commenced the sentencing hearing by reminding the Defense they had been given a copy of the pre-sentence report.

It was a very detailed report rehashing the State's entire case during the trial. It did not have any new information and Walter B. Smith, the probation officer preparing the report, made no recommendations.

The sentencing hearing began with the Defense making an opening statement. The State responded in opening.

Judith Ann Neelley was called to the stand to save her life. She told Judge Cole that she really didn't know how she wound up in the situation she was in. She was at a loss as to how she got here.

A. I just — fell in love with the wrong man and after ah — after I ran away with him, then I had no - no control — ah — Up until I testified on the stand I said that I still loved Al, but now I don't really know if it was love after — ah — he started beating me and after everything happened. I don't know if it was more fright or being so scared of him more than it was love or dependency.

She did not think of murder; she did not think of anything other than doing things right, exactly as she was told to do them. Alvin Neelley trained his wife by repeating instructions over and over again. If she did not do it exactly as he said, she would be beaten, screamed at, or cursed.

She believed that she still had a contribution to make to society by helping stop something like the Millican murder from happening again. She said she could help battered wives and abused children. She testified about her life and said that she did not want to die in the electric chair. Judy Neelley did not receive one single thing from the murders and shootings. She did not have any idea how they occurred.

The State did not cross-examine. The State did not put on any evidence. I guess they knew something I didn't know.

The Court allowed unlimited argument from each of the parties. Court recessed at 12:00 noon.

Upon reconvening at 1:30 p.m., the Court read its sentence in open court. Due to aggravating circumstances outweighing the mitigating circumstances, the Court found that Judith Ann Neelley must die!

This really bothered me. Judge Cole forced me take the worst case in Alabama History, other than perhaps the Scottsboro Boys Case, at my own expense. Then, after all the work, all the expense, all the pressure, he entered an order overriding the jury and gave me my only death loss in 17 murder cases.

You, the reader, have now been through the investigation, the trial, and the jury verdict. What would you do? Would you take the jury's verdict? Would you raise it to death in the electric chair, or would you find her not guilty? Or, perhaps guilty of a lesser-included offense such as kidnaping? For the record, I have included the complete order of Judge Cole's as **Appendix 3** for your review.

It's a tough life, folks. This was a bad case from the beginning. Now it just became Worse – much worse.

CHAPTER TWELVE

AFTERMATH

———◆———

By the time of the sentencing hearing, the public roar had died down a little, and some of the old clients were coming back; however, the trial had taken a financial toll on the firm. The hours, the travel, and the other expenses had cost the firm in excess of $320,000.

I had always kept four months' office expenses in the bank. Now we had no reserve, and we were living week to week, barely surviving.

Steve said that he was tired of the case, and he would not help with the appeal. He would stay through the motion for new trial.

SURVIVAL

I'm going to take you with me as I tried to survive Neelley. There were many adventures before the case would go to the U.S. Supreme Court.

Edgar Hammonds, owner of National Truck Service, Inc. and other ventures, employed me to negotiate an oil contract in Nigeria. Contrary to popular belief - mineral and mining law is my specialty.

I had worked in Johannesburg, Nairobi, Pretoria, Rhodesia, Nigeria, and the Cameroons dealing in coal, oil, gold and diamonds. I had formed corporations in Liberia. I had been listed in *"Who's Who in International Law."* So I was familiar with the players.

I'll put the dates before my diary entries. Understand that while I was trying to survive financially, Neelley continued to be my expensive responsibility.

FLYING HIGH

April 19, 1983, the day following the sentencing, I was at 31,000 feet over the East Coast en route 3,805 miles to Dakar, West Africa, on the Pan Am Great Circle Route.

The pain of losing was real, even in a 747 with more than 300 people on board. I consoled myself with the wretchedness of the snuffing out of the lives of two females who died simply because of their sex. Then there was John Hancock, who didn't deserve to lose the love of his life, and suffer being shot in the back. Yet I was forced into their existence by being duty-bound to do the best I could as a protagonist.

There were two ways of looking at the case - look at the victims, or look at the hapless, hopeless life of Judith Ann Neelley. The Courts, and most folks, chose to look at the victims. They did not consider Judy Neelley was a victim as well.

April 20, 1983, 9:25 a.m. in Monrovia, Liberia. The termite towers are scattered around the airport like small dirt castles for termite sentinels to view the comings and goings of the human beings in those funny looking machines. The mounds were 10 to 12 feet high. I counted 23 mounds near the airport.

Ragtag natives stood beside the runway to watch our aluminum whale take off. Thatch-roofed native huts forming villages in the jungle slid under the wing of our 747.

April 21, 1983, 1:50 a.m. at the Eko Holiday Inn, Lagos, Nigeria. We were to meet the Chairman of Nigerian O.P.E.C. later that morning. I was trying to sleep on the couch, miserable to the bone, when in walked the Assistant to the President of Nigeria.

He came in, all smiles, dressed in beautiful light blue flowing robes with lizard skin backless shoes. Almost all African shoes were like flip flops, or had no back in them, to be slipped in and out of easily. The Assistant to the President quickly slipped his feet out of his expensive lizard skins.

While he and Edgar were discussing the oil deal, I stumbled into the shower. Typical of Nigeria, most days there was only cold water. That day, there was only scalding hot water. In desperation, I jumped around in the shower enough to get half wet and half soaped. The steam was blinding. I dried the soap off and dressed.

I slept in the presidential limousine on the way to the Executive Office Building. I was abruptly jolted awake when a car broadsided our limo. The driver jumped out of his car cursing our driver for all he was worth. When he spotted the Presidential flags flying on the front fenders of the black Lincoln, he jumped down into a kowtow begging Allah's compassion. Then he thought better of it and ran into the gathering crowd abandoning his vehicle. Our host said the police would come and take the automobile, return it to the owner, and the driver would be jailed for leaving the scene of an accident.

We worked on very complicated contracts at the president's office, and later went to Elijah Muhammad's office. We were negotiating with the finance minister and the president of the central bank.

All day we worked amid the stench, filth, and noise of Lagos – the beggars, the lepers, open sewage ditches, the squalor, the noise, the sullen black faces, and the constant commerce -- in the African heat, and we reached an impasse.

Someone suggested we engage the services of a facilitator, a man who could make things happen. The delegation visited Abdullah, a Lebanese black-marketeer, and deal maker. I had known Abdullah for a number of years. I always enjoyed being with him, as his home was cool and comfortable.

The last time I was in Nigeria, I had been invited to his daughter's wedding. He had always given my clients' his best effort. I had never had a client who put a deal together. Nigeria was, and still is, a country of cutthroats, thieves, pirates, smugglers, and other dangerous men.

April 26, 1983, we dallied in Lagos six days as guests of one of the most powerful men in the Country. Elijah operated five or six large companies, including the country's Mercedes Dealerships. One of his brothers was a Supreme Court Justice; another was a Senator; and another was Chief of the Housa Tribe. The Chief was the most powerful of the brothers.

This trip had been very expensive for Edgar. If we did not transact business tomorrow through Abdullah, we were leaving.

April 27, 1983, Elijah came to the room early. He had checked with the bank and we could do business right away. Abdullah would let us know by 3:00 p.m. if the financial package I had prepared was in order. We'd be there one more day.

At shortly before 5:00 p.m., Edgar declared the trip a failure. Since I had worked in Third World countries on numerous occasions, I expected little from the trip. Although I had prepared a package of foolproof documents, I had advised Edgar against it.

GOING HOME

April 28, 1983, we went to the airport for our flight to London. Surprise! Abdullah was going to London on the same flight. He was full of apologies for the failure of the oil deal.

The price of oil had gone up $1 a barrel, and the Nigerians weren't going to do business under their original enticement offer to Edgar. The finance minister and banker disappeared after the financing and shipping documents were approved. They had a better deal than when they told Elijah to entice Edgar to come to Nigeria.

April 29, 1983, 40 hours later, I arrived back at my office to face our Law Day Banquet that night. I would be with Judge Cole and the other lawyers and judges.

Tom Gordon, of the *Birmingham News*, wanted me to go to Tutwiler and visit Judith Neelley with him. He would clear it with Tutwiler. Good luck!

A number of people had called that day and told me that I had done a good job. Representative Euclid Rains said he had been there for the entire trial, and seats were sold for as much as $10 each. He was very complimentary of our defense. A trial lawyer from Minnesota sent me a copy of the *Huntsville Times* and asked me to autograph it for him. I did.

When Representative Euclid Rains called, I flipped on the telephone speaker so Steve could hear what he had to say.

He said, "I sat through almost every minute of the Neelley trial. I watched every move you made. You presented the most brilliant defense I have witnessed in my lifetime. The excitement of that trial was the most interesting event of my life. I would take nothing for the experience. It almost defies description. I thought your performance was sheer brilliance; it was genius."

"Why did you dress her so finely? Why did you keep her on the stand so long?"

"Mr. Rains, there is a rule in trial law – always talk to the jury as long as you can. They will not tolerate crime. Therefore, you must talk with them. The reason I kept her on the stand so long - you must make the jury adopt your client. Otherwise, they will burn your client. Although she did horrible things, I did not want her to look like a murderess."

"I'm getting the idea now. I can see how you kept it so exciting. You didn't know that seats were selling for $10 each in the courtroom?"

"No, I didn't know that."

"Until the Judge ruled that if you left your seat you could not return to the courtroom, we were paying people $2 each to sit in our seats while we went to the restroom or to lunch. After the second day, he ruled that if you left your seat for any reason, someone else could get it. Most of us did not leave our seats. I sat there every day from 7:00 a.m. until after 5:00 p.m. without going to the bathroom, getting a drink of water, or eating lunch. You can see that you held my interest, Sir?"

"I didn't know that was happening."

"Using only the two women as witnesses had to be one of the most brilliant maneuvers I have ever heard of in a courtroom."

"Thanks, those were my two queens. But the State had five aces."

"It was beautiful to see the system work. I thank you for the sacrifice you made in presenting the defense and will continue to make during the remainder of the process. I believe in handing out flowers while people can smell them. I want you to know I appreciate what you did.

"Now, I wanted the girl convicted, but not the death penalty. I must admit, Mr. French, I did learn something about our society. We are truly a bloodthirsty bunch, aren't we? Weren't you shocked that the middle aged women and elderly men were the ones most adamant for killing your girl?"

"I found it interesting. I also learned a lot about my Christianity."

"And I learned a lot about mine, Sir."

BACK TO WORK

When I had returned from Africa, I had sat up with Celeste listening to all the horrible things that had gone on while I had been away. It seemed like the world collapsed. The next morning Anita came in and we talked - more grist for the mill – then the day started at 7:50 a.m.

It was a hard day – a generally insane day. I did my usual, sat in the eye of the storm, and let her run.

At the Law Day banquet, one lawyer's wife told Celeste, "We're glad Bob came. We know he has jet lag and should be in bed, but we needed to have him here."

Most everyone said nice things like that.

After the event, we packed, and drove to North Carolina for four hours through the Smokey Mountains. Paul and Virginia Hyde, long-time clients, had attended the trial. They were buying another restaurant, and they wanted me to handle the paperwork.

April 30, 1983 we arrived in Maggie Valley after 2:00 a.m. I got up at 10:15 a.m. and went to the real estate office.

After negotiating a $300,000 lease-purchase deal, we went back to the Hydes' and I was determined to relax. I reclined in a beach lounge on their deck high above the valley floor.

Driving west through Nantahala Gorge, Celeste moved the car into the curves along the banks of the Ocoee River. I watched white-water rafters splash down the river.

It was 4:00 p.m.; we were 96 miles from home. As we passed through Cleveland, Tennessee, we were within less than one mile of Judy Neelley's twins, April and Jeremy, at the home of Mrs. Alvin Howard Neelley. Another painful memory.

WELCOME TO TUTWILER PRISON
FOR WOMEN

May 1, 1983, at 10:20 a.m., Steve Bussman and I were on our way to Wetumpka to visit with Judy Neelley. Celeste had stayed up until 3:30 a.m. preparing the box that a prisoner was allowed to have when she processed into Tutwiler Prison for Women.

At 1:07 p.m., downtown Wetumpka, Alabama, I remembered walking those streets twice in political races. I had walked them with Jimmy Holliman in 1964 when I ran for Congress. Later, Edgar Weldon's father walked these streets with me campaigning for Lt. Governor in 1970.

The staff at Tutwiler treated Steve and me rudely. The warden came out and ordered the guard to inspect my boots. They went through the box, like it might contain a secret weapon. They then took the box into a separate room for a closer look at each item.

I noticed the inmate roster posted on the wall. There were 14 more people than the prison had capacity to hold. Both inmates on death row were not considered to be living in the prison. They were dead.

Warden Holt appeared to have stepped out of a B-grade movie. She was wearing neat but dowdy clothes, and boxy medium-heeled black pumps with a plastic bow. She had a round scar on her nose. Looked like she just had something removed. She was tough, and she meant for me to know it.

Tutwiler was built at the turn of the twentieth century and built to stay that way. What a hellhole. Everyone fit the movie script. Steve was amazed. Finally, we were allowed to see Judy.

Steve and I took home almost as much as we had brought down there in the box of approved items. Tutwiler made its rules as it went.

May 2, 1983 the office staff was angry that the prison staff did not allow Judy to have the things that were on the list they provided for the inmate. I told them, "That's prison."

I had a message to come to the county jail. Everyone in the jail was interested in Judy Neelley. The guys in the six-man cell wanted to know all about our visit to Tutwiler and how Judy was getting along. Troy Rogers, wanted to know if she had mentioned the two dollars he owed her. I told him to forget it.

Cheely, Judy's favorite boyfriend, was most concerned about her. He and Lamar came to the bars of the bullpen and tried to talk to me about Judy. Someone wrapped up in blankets on a bunk in the darkness asked me if her pussy was good. He didn't come out of the darkness so I didn't know who he was. The remark hurt Cheely as he was in love with Judy. I told Cheely the most contact I had ever had with the lady was to put my arm around her when she was sentenced to die.

May 3, 1983, Judy's aunt called me. Her son had been killed when he rode his motorcycle off the rim of a rock quarry owned by Hoover, Inc. I would look at it.

May 7, 1983, at 7:59 a.m., Raul Oyarzun, a Cuban ex-patriot from Mobile, was driving Celeste's Volvo toward Hardee's to buy breakfast. Raul's uncle owned the largest engineering firm in the Caribbean. He was another client in need of African representation. From breakfast we were going to Nashville where we were meeting with a Cameroon Envoy. He was flying into Nashville to meet us.

At Hardee's, everybody looked at me as I came in. Since the assistant manager was on the Neelley jury array, he knew me. I learned that 15 minutes of fame sucks.

The morning was beautiful, crisp, spring in the mountains. All of the green was fresh and popping out of the branches; the sky was clear blue; the interstate was ringed with mountains; and Raul began to talk of Cuba.

"This looks like Cuba, man," he remembered. "We have little mountains down there. Castro hid in mountains just like these. The farmers protected him. Look at this. It's beautiful, just like Cuba. Damned Castro! That is one man I would like to kill.

We met the envoy and negotiated for more than three hours. Typical of African, corruption we could not make a deal. He wanted us to come to the embassy in Washington and deal directly with the Ambassador.

I didn't think Raul could muscle up the fee to visit the embassy, but a few weeks later we flew my Baron into DC for the meeting.

May 8, 1983, I taught my Bible Class and sent Raul back to Mobile, Mother's Day gift in hand. After lunch I worked at the office until 10:30 p.m.

EXPLAINING TIME

May 9, 1983, I received a letter from Judith Neelley asking me to describe time for her. I wrote to her: Assume you have a cardboard tube that carpet or rugs are wound around. Take the tube and a ball only slightly smaller than the diameter of the tube. Lay one end of the tube on a chair and the other end on the floor. On the elevated end place a sign, "In the Beginning." At the lower end of the tube place a sign, "The End." Write on the ball, "Now." Place the ball in the elevated end of the tube and allow it to roll down from the beginning to the end. Notice that behind the ball, in the past, there is nothing. In front of the ball, in the future, there is nothing; the tube is empty. There is nothing in the past but wasted space, void. The future is also empty, as now has not arrived. Thus, the present is all there is. There is nothing to be done about the past; it is empty and gone. There is nothing to be done about the future; it is empty awaiting the present. All you have in life is the "now." Without the present, time and space are empty. What you have done is gone forever. Those actions exist only in a fading memory. Yearning for the future is a waste of the "now" because there is nothing you can do to hurry the ball down the tube. The "now" moves in its own time. We want to fool ourselves into thinking we can manipulate time. We can't. We can only measure a false idea of time. We don't really know what time is.

THE WORK NEVER STOPS

May 11, 1983, I received a letter from Ben Hunt of Birmingham asking me about the sociological questions raised by the Neelley trial. I replied that less than 5 out of 100 persons ever considered the destruction of Judith Ann Neelley. Most were preoccupied with the destruction of Lisa Millican and Janice Chapman. They believed that they would have fought back or killed Alvin Neelley. They wouldn't have. The role of defense counsel in our judicial system is not understood.

Judith Ann Neelley was back in the papers. She and Alvin had been indicted in Scottsboro, Alabama, for the rape of Lisa Ann Millican. There was also an article in the Birmingham papers about Rep. Rains and his resolution to stop electrocutions until a new electric chair was purchased.

The night before, some potential clients had flown in to see me from Indiana. They felt they had been libeled by a newspaper in Muncie. The husband was a public figure, no case.

My greatest problem with Judith Ann Neelley was to forgive her. I am not sure I was ever successful with that, but I continued to struggle. I liked Judy as a person, but – what she did was horrible. I couldn't reconcile how I felt about the case – still can't.

May 12, 1983, Ron Adams, Judy's uncle, called. He said Judy's grandmother was upset about the news of the Scottsboro indictments. Ron was at the jail that night of the confession and, "it was a joke." He also told me about the accident of Judy's cousin, Joe, who rode the motorcycle into Hoover's rock quarry. He was sending pictures and other material down regarding the possible case.

I told him about the case I had against Hoover for taking coal belonging to my clients that was washed by Hoover. Hoover people opened up the washer and caused a tremendous waste of my client's coal that was freshly mined. Later, they mined the gob pile and sold my client's coal. The jury gave us a large verdict. Judge Cole took the judgment away from me on a Motion for Judgment Notwithstanding the Verdict. That was his first JNOV. Neelley was his first death sentence. I wished he would quit using me for breaking new ground in his judicial career.

The Neelley case was in the *National Examiner* that day. I wished the press would abandon this case for a while. Are there any true journalists left? Or were they all muckrakers and sensationalists?

Jerry Barksdale, called. He had visited with me during the trial. Jerry had been in my life to some degree since 1962. He practiced law with me for a while. He wanted me to move to Huntsville and go into law practice with him.

May 13, 1983, Friday, a bad-luck day, but I felt like something good was about to happen. I didn't know what it might be. I needed to make some money.

My mind returned to Barksdale. He said that I was Rembrandt, painting barns. He had me thinking about that Huntsville office. I would be returning to my roots. My immediate family left Huntsville in 1939. I had two ancestors who fought with George Washington and settled in what would become Madison County – Owens Crossroads and New Hope. The idea definitely weighed heavily on my mind.

May 14, 1983, I was planning on tilling my garden and planting it. TNT (Tammy and Tommy) needed to know how to garden. So I was going to teach them.

I went for a haircut that morning. I had a choice, get a haircut or buy a fiddle. Afterward, I dragged out the tiller, and TNT. The garden was on our northernmost property line. It was about 75 feet wide and about 100 feet long. We prepared the land, and then we went to the seed store and bought the seeds and plants everyone wanted. We bought only hybrid stuff. Then we went back to the garden, hooked up all the hoses to the faucet at the house, and began planting. Celeste came out and helped us plant. We had a great time. TNT learned how to garden. I hoped that they would remember it. It was a duty of the fathers to teach the children survival. So they would hoe, cultivate, fertilize, spray, pick, and put away whatever we grew here. We'd done it all before. Children learn by repetition.

May 15, 1983, I taught the Baraca Bible Class that morning.

May 16, 1983, Monday, I started working on Judy Neelley's Motion for New Trial. It looked pretty good. I put in every ground I could think of. I include it in this work as **Appendix 4.** If you want to skip over and look at it, feel free. Maybe you can think of something I left out.

May 17, 1983, I mailed Judith Neelley a copy of her Motion for New Trial. Then, I tried to catch up the office work as I was scheduled into the Atlanta Federal Prison the following day.

I went on to spend the night near the prison. I was called to the desk and told my American Express Card was not valid. I was surprised. I had the card since the 60's. Fortunately, I had enough cash to pay for the room. They kept my card. It would have been embarrassing, but I was beyond that point at that stage in my life. A similar experience would soon happen with my Shell card. After that one, I took control of the books and knew when we were – broke.

BRONCO BILLY

When I returned, Raul had found a premium buyer for Nigerian oil in mobile. Since I had introduced him to Edgar, I hoped the deal would come together. Both of them had spent a fortune trying to make it work.

At 9:58 p.m., Raul called and said, "I love it, man. Here we are in this international oil deal, so damned close to having it put together that I can almost smell the $300,000,000. I can't believe it - a trucker from Ider, Alabama, who barely finished high school; a Mobile Cuban who works in an insane asylum; using a hick town lawyer from Fort Payne, Alabama; about to rock the international oil market. It's fantastic. I love it."

I told him that I would love it also when the deal came together.

He started calling me "Bronco Billy," after the character played by Clint Eastwood in the movie by the same name. Bronco Billy lived by the code of the Old West in a world of make-believe that he always made come true.

Edgar had contracted a tanker loaded with 5,600,000 barrels of oil ready to sail for Mobile, Alabama. They were burning up the telex machines. They were using my old contract package. Since it wasn't my money, it was fun. With Bronco Billy everything was fun.

May 18, 1983, Wednesday, at 10:21 a.m., Edgar called. During the night here, day over there, he had cut a deal for 10,800,000 barrels of Nigerian oil. The buyers in Mobile were going wild. Raul was beginning to call every three or four minutes. I would have to go to Montgomery immediately and meet the parties. They were wanting to blend Nigerian oil with oil from the Alabama Citronelle Oil Field.

Edgar was originally buying Nigerian oil to blend with oil from his wells in Kansas. Being the wheeler-dealer that he was, he had renegotiated the deal, and could make more money off selling the oil in Mobile. Me? I was just a hired negotiator who drafted documents. Or, as I like to say, "Just a journeyman trial lawyer trying to hawk a fee."

RETURN TO MAGGIE VALLEY

Paul Hyde called in the middle of the oil storm. He had his deal concluded and was interested in closing as quickly as possible. I told him that I would have to drive over there in something other than the little "Roll Tide!" Porsche. It was in the shop. It was running a little rough. I guessed the Volvo and I would go through the gorges to Maggie Valley.

Late that evening Eddie and I left for Paul's place in North Carolina. Brown decided to make a confession to me.

He said, "French, you know all those tight-assed times you were flying that damned airplane at midnight in all that ice and thunderstorms, and you thought I was asleep?"

"Yeah, I remember the times. I was sitting up there watching that radar, working those deicers, hoping and praying the plane would keep flying. The auto pilot went out, and I had to manually fly that sucker at 18,000 feet, and you laid over there in the right seat with your hat down over your eyes sleeping. Yeah, I remember those times."

"Well, French, I wasn't asleep. I was making like I was asleep to keep the other passengers off your ass while you managed to get us out of a mess."

We arrived at Paul's around 1:00 a.m. He fed us sandwiches and wine. We talked until about 4:00 a.m. I jumped into his almost famous hot tub, and from there to bed.

May 19, 1983, I was sitting in the car with Virginia in the rain in Maggie Valley, North Carolina. Paul was in the real estate office. He went in to set up the closing later in the day.

Earlier Edgar had called, and I had to dictate an international non-circumvention agreement for the oil deal to my secretary Cindy by phone. Sometimes I wondered how I did those things. When she read it back to me, it sounded like a real lawyer had written it.

We couldn't get the real estate agreement everyone wanted - too many lawyers present. You know the old saying, "Too many lawyers spoil the business deal?" We left friends and vowed to continue negotiations until the deal was consummated.

May 20, 1983, Friday, was the end of a long hard week. Mail came, and Judith Neelley said that the guards had told her that she could not have any contact with the other prisoners. They had received death threats from some of the people in the population. What difference did it make? She lived in solitary confinement.

Paul and Virginia called. I had to go back over there, and try to close their deal.

May 23, 1983, I returned from North Carolina. The restaurant deal was finally off. The developers were convinced they had a gold mine and they were going to make sure they reaped the rewards of their deal. When it came down to signing and writing the check, Paul refused to give them the profit override they were demanding. So that one went down the drain. Paul was still working on a motel. I suggested that he and Virginia look elsewhere for investments.

TROUBLE IN PARADISE

I couldn't make enough money off the few clients I still had. Celeste was going to take up nursing again. She had been out of the field for more than 16 years. Now we were talking about her going back to work. She had been doing a little private duty work over the years to keep up with advancements in medicine.

We had made money in the legal business, real estate investments, and mineral development. We had a Rolls-Royce, a Merlin Prop-jet, two other twin engine airplanes, property in the mountains of North Carolina at a ski resort, property on an island in the Gulf, and a lodge with a stone guest house at DeSoto Park. We had stocks, bonds, and money in the bank. I had learned that happiness was not found in material possessions. Now we were slipping financially; it wasn't a catastrophe.

May 24, 1983, Raul called. He wanted to know if Bronco Billy still believed in the oil deal. He was having trouble with his buyers. They were impatient with the Nigerians.

Due to firm hardships, I posted a card: THEM THAT DON'T BELIEVE CAN LEAVE! Someone wrote below it, "THEM THAT STAY WILL PAY." I thought it was Steve.

The oil deal depended upon Nigerians, and I did not have a high regard for Nigerians. I could not recommend the oil deal, but I could earn a fee as we went along.

After lunch I went to the bank, and on to interview a potential client whose wife had just been killed in a car wreck. It sounded like the wreck was her fault; plus, it sounded like she was drunk.

May 26, 1983, before I went to Tutwiler to talk to Judy Neelley, I went to see Gary Lance at Kilby Prison down the road in Montgomery. What a difference 15 miles makes. Going from Kilby to Tutwiler was like going from the electronic age to the Stone Age. The guards at Kilby apologized to me for taking so long to bring my client out to me. At Kilby, the people were doing a job professionally. At Tutwiler, there was an undercurrent of sadism and cruelty. Warden Holt believed in punishment.

May 29, 1983 I awoke to good news. The people from the Cameroons weren't interested in oil, they wanted me to come to their embassy in Washington, and make a presentation on the housing project Trans-World Associates developed for emerging African nations. I was going Wednesday, and taking Tommy with me.

Barksdale and I represented Congressman Phil Crane's wife, whose case I needed to settle. We had a tentative offer of $500,000. That fee would cure my ills for a while. I believed I could smash two birds with one rock on the trip.

After the Cameroon call, the day went into the tank:

Anita was concerned with the bills that had been piling up since we had geared up for the Neelley case. She had to deal with the bill collectors. Nita suggested I set aside one hour a day to work on the Neelley case, and the rest of the time forget it. Make money - probably not a bad idea.

Celeste said, "You have to look out for your family first. You have to stand by those who love you, your friends, and your other clients. You can't let this case become a way of life. You always go down into the valleys of deep depression when you lose a case. What about Whisenant? You didn't go overboard on his case."

"Judy Neelley was an instrument used by a maniac. And she got the chair. She is a victim of the system, and I will beat the system."

"You've been fighting the system ever since we've been in Alabama. You have never been part of the 'in' crowd."

"I told you. Judith Neelley will not be executed."

April 30, 1983, I had two cases in Scottsboro. After court, I went to Edgar's office to work with him on his oil deal. It was not promising. As usual, the Nigerians were pulling their old tricks. Once they find you are interested in their oil, they keep changing the price and the terms.

May 29, 1983 the Rome, Georgia, newspaper called me. They were doing a background story on Judy's time spent in the Youth Detention Center in Rome. Apparently, the people who knew Judy while she was in the YDC told the press that she was a fine person as long as she was kept out of contact with Alvin Neelley.

June 1, 1983, I looked at the sign on my office wall, "ILLEGITIMI NON CARBORUNDUM." Loosely translated from the Latin, it says, "Don't let the Bastards wear you down." I tried to live by that motto, but it was getting more difficult.

Bobby Lee Cook, Jr. called from Summerville, Georgia. He had been appointed to represent Judy Neelley in Georgia. The prosecutor was planning to bring her to trial in August. Cook was concerned about the testimony of John Hancock. I told him to wait until Georgia extradited Neelley.

June 2, 1983, 4:00 p.m., I had just returned from Huntsville where I had appeared on a radio talk show with Barbara Lucero. We I had been Nixon delegates to the GOP Convention in 1968. We had a nice time between calls remembering. Most of the questions were about Judy Neelley. The public was divided over her fate.

My youngest sister, Rebecca, an executive with Intergraph Corporation, heard the show and left her work to take Tommy and me to lunch.

It seemed that there was no way I could come up with the money to finish the week. My banker was screaming, and the office expenses just kept piling up.

I told Anita to pull my old American Light and Power file. There might be a few shares of stock in that file. I was slowly cashing out everything I had. Sure enough! I had over $18,000 in utility stock that I could cash out. I couldn't believe I had that much utility stock lying around. The Lord just kept helping me survive. It was nice, but my 15 minutes of fame were becoming an hour of torment.

Joe Trotter was a union executive when the garbage workers union asked Martin Luther King, Jr., to come back to Memphis to help with the strike. Trotter had left the motel to go for hamburgers when James Earl Ray shot Martin Luther King.

Trotter brought clients who were the descendants of a black woman and a French nobleman who got together more than 100 years ago. The whiter heirs abandoned the blacker members of the family. As a result, an oil company took over the land left to these people by the French nobleman. He had recognized all of his children before he died, but the land was lost due to a bunch of smart white lawyers. I was hired to get the land back for the folks and collect all of the back oil royalties they were entitled to receive. Tough case.

June 3, 1983, Friday, I talked with Arlene Crane, trying to convince her to settle. If not, she was going to have to replace Jerry and me with local DC attorneys.

I drafted a second amendment to the Motion for New Trial. I then went to court and tried a divorce case. I needed some real money involved.

June 6, 1983. The Democrat rumor mill was cranking out the same old stuff – nothing new - but very effective. People drove by on the street in front of my house and yelled, blew their horns, and threw trash into my yard.

Time to leave for Mobile. I had a case to try down there involving a ship with 7 tons of marijuana that ran aground at Pirates Cove. Got to keep on keeping on.

June 7, 1983, back from Mobile. My client came from San Francisco, but the State was not ready. The Baldwin County DA and Sheriff who had stolen part of the load were either in jail or otherwise disposed. Court granted a continuance. My client was bent out of shape. I wasn't too happy myself. $500 in expenses went down the drain.

June 8, 1983, feeling bad, losing weight, extremely nervous all the time, and my eyesight was giving me trouble. Something was going on. I needed to see a doctor.

HOMECOMING

Judge Cole had entered an order requiring the State to produce Judith Ann Neelley in Fort Payne by the 13th for her Motion for New Trial hearing. Glory be! Judy was going to get a vacation. A reporter came in and interviewed me about the fact that Judith Neelley was being brought back to DeKalb County.

I went to the jail and talked with Muscles. He was providing a special cell for Judy. The DeKalb County Jail was planning a "Welcome Home Judy" party.

Judge Cole called and said that Sheriff Richards wanted to talk to me about Judy's visit to his jail. When the High Sheriff arrived, he reminded me how we had always gotten along, and we visited pleasantly for several minutes.

Then he got down to his subject. He did not want any visits with Judy after 8:00 p.m. due to security. I told him fine. We talked some more, and the Sheriff satisfied himself that I was not going to break Judith Neelley out of jail, nor was I going to have sexual relations with her on the floor of the jail. So he said we could visit with Judy until 9:00 p.m. in the visitor's room.

He thought I did a good job working for Neelley. A lot of people had criticized me for the way I went about it, but he told each one of them, "Well, what would you want him to do if he were representing you? Would you want him to lay down on the job? If he were representing me, I would want him to do his best. And that's what he did for her." I felt pretty good hearing that."

Being a Democrat, I had tried to put him out of office when he had stood for election. But we had never had any harsh words. He ran things in a laid-back fashion, and was honest. We were fortunate to have a good Sheriff, DA, and good judges.

I went after Eileen Hargis in the papers that day. I had always intended to go after her. I laid the groundwork for her downfall early on.

June 10, 1983, 10:30 a.m., Celeste and Anita were going through Judy's things to have her box ready to carry to her cell. Anita had called Mr. Snow, and he said that the car they sent for Judy broke down, and they had to send another squad car to Wetumpka to pick her up. The sheriff went for Judy personally. He took a woman with him to attend to Judy's needs on the way back. Hummm, the sheriff might not have been as clean as I thought.

The local paper was carrying a headline that Judy Neelley was coming back to DeKalb County. All of the TV folks were going to be on hand when she arrived. The TV people wanted me to be there when she was brought in. The sheriff said they would radio ahead when the car was 30 minutes out, and Steve and I could come to the jail and give them their pictures. Cindy and Nita had made a "Welcome Home Judy" sign, which they had put in her cell. We had taken all of her favorite things over to her cell for her - the TV, curlers, etc.

The way everyone was acting, you would think a celebrity was coming to Fort Payne rather than a convicted murderess. Eddie heard it on television, and he was coming down for the occasion.

I was trying to obtain the services of some psychologists out of Atlanta who could testify as to the Battered Woman Syndrome.

Several University of Alabama Law Students had volunteered to do the research for us for the new trial. They were doing a great job – Roll Tide! The researchers were convinced that the FBI preventing Bill Burton from seeing his client in the Rutherford County, Tennessee, jail was error.

If the case could be reversed on failure to allow the accused to have her counsel, all cases would probably have gone by the boards, other than the shooting of John Hancock. I was anxious to see how the courts would dance around that one.

I was sending the little "Roll Tide" Porsche to Chattanooga for repairs by Eddie that day. I hoped it would come back in one piece.

June 11, 1983 at about 1:22 a.m. I was just finishing a meditation before going to bed. The phone rang, and I answered it in the kitchen on the first ring. A deputy said, "Is this Bob French?" I stated that I was.

He said, "Do you own a red and white Porsche?" Again, I answered in the affirmative.

"Do you know where your car is right now?"

I told him that as far as I knew, it was in Chattanooga at a repair shop being worked on. It had been taken to Chattanooga earlier in the day.

He said, "Well, I have Jim Mays on the radio, and he and five other groups of law enforcement have been chasing your car for the better part of an hour."

I asked him where they were chasing my car. He said they were chasing it on the north end of Sand Mountain. It had avoided several roadblocks. I told him to tell Mays not to shoot up my car or tear it up.

There was nothing more I could do so I went to bed.

At morning I went to the sheriff's office. They had finally stopped my car about 2:30 a.m. after someone had driven it into a Mr. Wooten's backyard, bogged down in his garden, and ran. My car was towed in.

Naturally, it was front page news under the title, "Lawyer's Lament." I think the only thing I said was, "What else can happen now?" I should have admitted that I knew that much more could happen.

The engine was blown in the Porsche; and Richard tried to connect me to the escapade. Igou and O'Dell brought the garage man down from Chattanooga who said he had left the car on the street by mistake. They had intended to have it inside, but someone else was supposed to take care of it and didn't. Apparently, they left the keys in the door. Insane!

The battery was either missing from the car or disconnected. So someone went to a lot of trouble to run the law in my little "Roll Tide" Porsche. The lowest estimate was about $4,800 to repair the little car.

I decided to find out who did it. It took Eddie Brown about an hour. It was just a bad scene - and even more bad publicity. Everyone was impressed with the driving skills of the driver. I wasn't.

The media opined I might have been driving the car. Mr. Willie Hammons saw me a few days later and said, "Bob, I don't care what anyone says, I know you weren't driving that car. And I have told everyone I could prove you weren't driving it." He winked at me.

"How would you be able to prove that, Mr. Willie?" I asked.

He laughed an elderly gentlemen's sly chuckle, "It's simple. If you had been driving that car, they would have never caught it."

I agreed with him. I wouldn't have blown the engine either.

After the Sheriff's office, I had to work the June Jam. The Alabama Band held a jam with country singers for a festive occasion. I had worked in the event each year to help the Fort Payne Band Boosters. TNT were in the band. So Celeste and I did our part.

Usually about 50,000 people showed up. Most of the proceeds went to charity. I was spotted by photographers, and became most of the story, "Judy Neelley's Lawyer Works the Jam." They pictured me in a paper hat dispensing hot dogs.

TRIP TO WASHINGTON

June 16, 1983, Washington, DC, Tommy, Paul Hyde, and I were in the Sheraton in Silver Springs, Maryland. We had a meeting that morning at the Cameroon Embassy. We were to make our African housing presentation to the Ambassador at 11:00 a.m. They wanted to resurrect the building project developed by my Liberian client, Trans-World Associates, Inc.

The presentation at the embassy was well received. They said the project should go forward quickly. The deputy ambassador said he would accompany me to the Cameroons in about 6 to 8 weeks. We were allowed 20 minutes of the Ambassador's time. Instead, he gave us 34 minutes, and I packed a three-hour presentation into that time. They wanted my passport so they could provide a visa for the trip. I was holding off until I saw green pass from black hands to white hands.

I enjoyed Washington. I saw Eric Starks of the Booker T. Washington Foundation; a friend of his, Bruce, who was recently in the Cameroons; J.B. Trotter, my buddy from Memphis; and Dr. Alfred Hoyt, who held numerous patents and was the head of the Engineering Department at Howard University in Washington.

June 17, 1983, although we had a straight shot out of Washington from Embassy Row, I told Paul we had to show Tommy the capitol. We drove back down Massachusetts Avenue, Constitution Avenue, and Pennsylvania Avenue to let Tommy see the sights of Washington. When he saw the Capitol Building, he said, "I've been there before, Daddy."

I told him, "No, you've just seen so many pictures of that building and the Washington Monument that you think you have been here before."

WORKING ON MOTION FOR NEW TRIAL

I pushed hard preparing for the new trial hearing. I wanted to have a battered woman expert testify. This search plugged me into the family violence movement that would later be called domestic abuse. Right now, very few people knew anything about wife beating other than those women who were being beaten. I learned that there were 30 million women beaten everyday in the USA.

I talked with Lenore Walker in Denver, Barbara Hart in Pennsylvania, and others before I selected a psychologist expert from Atlanta - Margaret Nichols, Ph.D. I was going to use her as newly discovered evidence as it was clear we knew nothing about battered women, and neither did the Court.

I finally discovered that trial "smell" I had noticed earlier. It was the collusion between Lawyer Charles McGee and Assistant DA Mike O'Dell. McGee was Hargis' lawyer in her pending criminal cases, and O'Dell was prosecuting her!

I had been puzzled why McGee came into the courtroom in the middle of the trial and visited with O'Dell at the State's table. Now I knew that it was McGee's charade with O'Dell that swayed Hargis for conviction.

When she saw her attorney pal around with the DA, including reclining in a DA staff chair for most of an hour, she got the message. She was still in trouble and she saw her way out. It was really a cheap trick, but nothing was too low for Charles McGee. I was not sure O'Dell did much more than take advantage of an opportunity. Still, he knew what he was doing, and he knew better. Innocently, I had thought McGee was interested in the trial; and that he sat with the State rather than sit near the jury. I should have remembered what a trickster he was.

The days were very hectic. Witnesses were having conflicts, and doing the things witnesses usually do -- didn't want to become involved. A lawyer really never knows what is going to happen until the day of the hearing. So, we were busy.

Judy was enjoying her status in the "Dekalb County Hilton." I did get by to see her once. She became involved in several "jailhouse romances." Although she was in a cell by herself, she was the sweetheart of the jail. More than one inmate fell in love with her while she was there.

Jeff West, the rapist, who allowed me to first interview Judith Ann Neeley in his laundry room/jailhouse suite, fell for Judy. He watched her, was very friendly, did favors for her, and lusted in his rapist heart for her body.

One night, around 3:00 a.m., using his trustee key, Jeff let himself into Judy's cell wearing a robe. Judy came awake when Jeff attempted to kiss her.

Judy said, "Jeff West, don't touch me. You know that I already have a murder conviction, and one more won't hurt."

Jeff pleaded for just a little affection, but it did him no good. Finally, in desperation, he left the cell.

Judy wanted to report it to the sheriff. She felt violated. I told her to just let it cool and take it as a compliment. No need to burst into the papers with that kind of story. She agreed. Jeff got off the hook and never went back.

I kept working on the Motion.

CHAPTER THIRTEEN

MOTION FOR NEW TRIAL

You are going back to court with me for this hearing. It will drag a little, but you need to know what we were trying to do to save Judith Ann Neelley.

June 21, 1983, the defendant's motion for new trial hearing was called to order at 10:30 a.m. The Court swore the witnesses, and excluded all but one from the courtroom. I called her father's brother, a convenience store owner in Murfreesboro.

Ronald Adams, was 37 years of age. October 14, 1982, between 5:00 and 5:30 p.m., he was called to the Sheriff's Office where he was met by 15 to 20 officers, and questioned about Judith and Alvin Neelley.

Adams saw his Attorney Bill Burton, and knew that Burton was representing Judith Neelley. He heard Burton asking to see his client. Burton was told that she didn't want to see an attorney. Burton insisted, but was refused. Adams heard the agent call his superior.

Burton was considered the family attorney.

Burton asked, "Does Judy know that I am here and available?"
He was told by officers, "Yes."

Neither Adams nor Burton was allowed to see Judy Neelley that night.

On cross-examination, Adams said Burton had been retained on an earlier matter. He did not retain him for Neelley. Burton was at the jail to protect Judy. Alvin had called Bill Burton and asked him to come to the jail and represent Judith Neelley.

I submitted pages 1 through 93 of our Motion to Suppress hearing, which contained the testimony of Burns, Smith, Burton, and Neelley.

Lou Stevens said Mrs. Hargis appeared to have the trial tuned out of her mind, looking around, or looking at her fingernails. During the cross-examination of Dr. Salillas, Hargis looked at the state and mouthed the words, "Object, Object."

The jurors heard the comments of the audience - - "I'll pay the electric bill to barbecue her;" and "They should do the same thing to that lawyer and Judy as she did to Lisa." A woman thought she was funny by answering before Judy could answer from the stand, by saying, "Al made me do it." She did this over and over again, and each time she did, the audience laughed.

Stevens was so disturbed by the audience and Mrs. Hargis that she came to me immediately at the close of the case and volunteered to testify.

On cross-examination, Stevens admitted she did not read lips, and that all the jurors didn't pay attention all of the time. She was less than 10 feet from Mrs. Hargis, and it was obvious that she was not participating in the trial. After the verdict Stevens was crying, and told Judith Neelley that she would do anything she could to help her. That didn't mean she would lie to help her.

Bob Dunivant, a writer for the *Birmingham Post Herald*, from Athens, Alabama, heard comments from the audience from the second and third row -- extra-loud stage whispers. One spectator said, "Barbecue her ass." The jury heard it.

Hargis did not examine the evidence.

Paul Hyde, a motel and restaurant owner, who showed horses, was from North Carolina. He came to Fort Payne on business, and stayed three days observing the trial. Eileen Hargis was looking around, smiling at some of the audience, nodding her head, humming to herself, and having eye contact with certain people in the audience. He saw her mouth, "Object, Object," to the prosecution. It was inaudible, but anyone who saw it knew what she was saying.

One person held up a newspaper for Mrs. Hargis to see that had a headline derogatory to the defendant. He also heard the woman answering before the defendant could answer. Three jurors looked directly toward the woman. He knew that the jury heard the audience's statements. Several times someone said, "They ought to use Drano on her."

On cross-examination, the witness admitted he was a client of Bob French, and that was his interest in staying for the trial. He was hard of hearing; and if he could hear the comments, he knew the jury could hear them.

Anthony Spurgin, a self-employed plumber from North Sand Mountain, heard the audience comment, "Al made me do it." The woman made this comment over and over all day. Hargis was more interested in the courtroom than she was the trial.

On cross-examination, Spurgin admitted that he was a friend of Eddie Brown, an investigator for the defense firm. However, he had not discussed his testimony with Brown. He had told Bob French what he knew.

Barbara Adams, the mother of Judith Ann Neelley, had known Bill Burton for 15 or 20 years, and considered him the family attorney. When Judy was arrested, she rode to town with Alvin to retain Burton to represent Judy. She saw the receipt where Alvinl Neelley had paid Burton to represent her daughter.

On October 14, 1982, a Sheriff's Deputy, David Grisham, came to her house with six or seven officers. She was frightened, and signed a consent to search her home.

On cross-examination, she admitted that Burton was retained to represent Judy on charges of bad checks and forged money orders. At the time he was retained, on October 12, 1982, neither she nor Burton was aware that Judith might be a suspect in a murder case.

There was no doubt in the witness' mind that Burton was Judy's lawyer for whatever her charges. That was the reason he was called to go to the jail on the night of October 14, 1982.

JUROR HARGIS EXPOSED

Jimmy Lindsey, Circuit Clerk of DeKalb County, Alabama, brought with him the files involving criminal charges pending against Eileen Hargis where O'Dell was the prosecutor and Charles McGee was Hargis' lawyer. There were five bad check cases against Eileen Hargis who was juror No. 46.

Exhibit A was a case against Eileen Hargis that was settled before the Neelley trial.

Exhibit B was settled April 9, 1983, after Hargis served on the Neelley jury.

Exhibit C was concluded on April 7, 1983.

Exhibit D was concluded the same day - April 7, 1983.

Exhibit E, was also concluded April 7. No year was shown. The State and McGee settled a total of four Hargis bad check cases on April 7th.

Remember, the Neelley trial began Monday, March 7, 1983. McGee settled her cases with O'Dell on April 7, 1983. Someone carefully omitted the year of settlement. Quite cozy, huh?

Circuit Clerk Lindsey prepared a table concerning the handling and disposition of the Hargis cases. This table was introduced into evidence as Defendant's Exhibit F.

The clerk did not hear the Defense question Mrs. Hargis as to her involvement in "criminal acts, something nobody was prosecuted for." He did not recall hearing me ask Mrs. Hargis if she knew Richard Igou or Michael O'Dell.

On cross-examination, Lindsey said the jury cards were drawn in the presence of Defense Counsel Steve Bussman. The district attorney was not represented.

On re-direct, Jimmy said that in January 1983, he knew Eileen Hargis. On trial date, he had seen her in the hallway. His memory was reinforced when he saw her sitting in the jury box. He remembered then that the Assistant District Attorney Mike O'Dell had told him in January that Charles McGee was her lawyer.

The district attorney or a staff member checked the records in the clerk's office to ascertain whether potential jurors had criminal records.

Now, I knew that O'Dell and McGee had conspired - by agreement - or it was understood, that McGee would visit with the state and indicate to Hargis, who was not paying much attention to the trial, that she needed to be in favor of the state. Had O'Dell agreed to an alternate in the place of Hargis, all the effort with McGee would have been wasted.

After a discussion with the Court concerning the flow of the evidence of due diligence in jury selection by the Defense, I testified as attorney for the defendant. My testimony is a bit lengthy discussing how we researched the individual jurors, what we concluded about Mrs. Hargis, and other aspects of jury selection. **Appendix 5**.

On cross-examination, I stated that I could not identify all the jurors by the defense profile. However, there were certain ones who were easy. The Defense had expected Mrs. Hargis to appear in court wearing an Alabama jacket. Wearing that with high-heeled shoes and blue jeans indicated to the Defense that she was her own person; she thought for herself and didn't care very much about other people's opinions. She was a strong-willed person. Had she admitted to the pending charges, she would have been excused.

Virginia Hyde heard the audience comments, "Alvin made me do it," and "She should be shot with Drano," loud enough for the jury to hear them.

The woman in the T-shirt, jeans, and black jacket, Hargis, always sat in the first chair on the front row nearest the audience. Witness sat a few feet from her. When the audience made comments, Juror Hargis acknowledged that she heard them by smiling back to the person making the comment. Hargis mouthed the word "object."

On cross-examination, the witness came to the hearing at the request of the Defense. At the trial, she was sitting on the front row. The person saying, "Al made me to it" was behind her on the third row. The witness believed she was a lip reader, "I guess we all think we are."

After this witness, I told the Court the various matters of proof we were relying upon in support of the motion for new trial. Among these were the denial of counsel, illegal confession, lack of intent and juror misconduct. I then moved the Court to recess the hearing until July 1, 1983, in order that the testimony of Dr. Margaret Nichols, a psychologist and consultant with the Atlanta Counsel for Battered Women, might be presented to the Court. The Court said it would grant the request of the Defense. The State should go forward with the evidence it wished to present.

THE STATE'S OPPOSITION TO THE MOTION FOR NEW TRIAL

Bill Burton said that after he represented Judith Ann Neelley in her preliminary hearing regarding bad check cases or money order cases, he was called by her husband. Alvin hired him at night to go to the jail to protect Judy Neelley. The witness recalled Ron Adams being present at the jail the night Judith confessed. The witness did not recall saying to officers, "Does she know I'm here and available?"

Charles McGee, said Eileen Hargis hired him after being arrested on bad check charges. He called Michael O'Dell, and they agreed that Mrs. Hargis would have 90 days to pay the checks and the court costs in each case. The court costs were more than the checks. McGee told Hargis that he felt they could win some of the cases.

> A. ...but she didn't want to do that. She didn't want to take the time and trouble to go to court, and didn't want the publicity or the embarrassment of having

to go to court. So, she said she was willing to do whatever, pay the court costs and the checks, and that's what she agreed to do...

McGee testified that all the checks passed by Mrs. Hargis were written around the same time.

> A. ...In checking it out, all these checks, the cases that I talked to Mike about and the one prior case, were all written basically right around the same time, within a short period of time difference. I believe some of them were written possibly in September and some of them were written in October, the latter part or the first part of the next month. And so, I relayed this to Mike when I called him. I told him that she did have a prior but that the checks were all written basically at the same time, and apparently the people who had gotten the warrants just waited later or possibly they hadn't been served until later. I don't know -- I don't guess I checked to see when the warrants were taken out, but for some reason there was some several months difference in the arrest date, and I relayed that to him, and he said if that was the case, assuming she wasn't a repeat offender, someone they had trouble with in the past, that he would agree to let her pay the checks and court costs. Because the court costs were going to be a pretty big amount, I did ask for 90 days to pay it.

In late January or early February O'Dell agreed not to set the Hargis cases on the next docket. If she had not paid it in 90 days, it would be reset, and she would be tried. Hargis wasn't in the room when McGee talked with O'Dell.

The next time McGee mentioned Mrs. Hargis to O'Dell was during the Neelley trial. McGee came to the courtroom a day or two after the trial began and saw Eileen Hargis on the jury.

> A. Well, anyway, I mentioned to him that one of the persons on the jury -- He could have mentioned it to me. I don't remember who started the conversation. But that Mrs. Hargis had had a case that I had talked to him about, about a month or two prior to that.

I discussed the juror with the assistant district attorney because I thought she might be a good defense juror. There might be some animosity toward the state because of the juror having been involved in the bad check cases.

The juror was going to be against the state because she had charges pending? The juror was going to be for the state in order to get a break.

McGee knew O'Dell knew the name of Hargis and the charges against her in late January or early February. She had paid off a pending criminal case on November 17th. She kept passing bad checks, and another complaint was issued against her on January 21st and another on January 27th. Ms. Hargis was an active bad check writer. O'Dell was very familiar with the criminal activities of Mrs. Hargis when McGee talked with him.

McGee said that if an attorney knew that there was something adverse about a juror pertaining to his client, then he thought he did have an ethical, moral and a legal obligation to disclose it. He didn't.

Michael O'Dell, Deputy District Attorney, said that he had not met Mrs. Hargis before her appearance with other jurors in this case. He did not remember her name at the time of *voir dire*. He knew her when Charles McGee, and he talked about her. Earlier, he had talked with McGee on January 31st about settling the cases of Mrs. Hargis. He did not pay any more attention to Eileen Hargis until McGee asked him about her at the trial. At that time, he told McGee that he was concerned about one juror and pointed to Mrs. Hargis.

He told McGee that the State had found out after striking the jury that Hargis had some criminal worthless check cases. McGee refreshed O'Dell's recollection of the transactions concerning Mrs. Hargis.

> A. I expressed some dismay at first before he told me we had settled those cases. And then I felt at that point that we didn't have to worry about Mrs. Hargis anymore - that those cases were disposed of, and she did not enter a guilty plea, and she was not sentenced, she was not fined. It was disposed under the circumstances back in January, and I felt at that time that that matter was disposed of.

On cross-examination, O'Dell knew that Hargis was the person with whom he had settled the cases. He knew that information at the time the defense made its argument to substitute an alternate in her place. He knew the history of Hargis when the Defense accused her of mouthing "object, object," and when the Defense complained that she glared at Defense Counsel for 20 to 30 seconds. He knew the Court was wrestling with the problems raised by the Defense concerning the juror; however, he did not make it known to the Court that charges were pending against Juror Hargis.

If Mrs. Hargis had failed to pay the costs and checks as agreed within the 90-day period, he would have placed her name back on the docket for prosecution. Eileen Hargis had not paid the checks and costs at the time the Neelley case proceeded to trial.

> Q. And at that point in time you did not tell the judge then, when we were again re-insisting that this juror be excused, and you did not tell him that she had had these criminal charges pending against her, did you?
>
> A. No sir; I did not.
>
> Q. In fact, you and Mr. Igou both insisted on keeping that juror on the panel, didn't you?

A. I saw no reason to have her removed; no sir.

Q. My question was–

A. Yes sir; we did not insist. The judge asked for our feelings on the matter and we gave them to him, just as we had a right to do. Our colloquy was very short, Mr. French. We told him what our feelings were and that was it. Evidently he agreed with them.

Q. But you never told him all of your feelings, did you?

A. I don't know what you mean by that.

Q. You never told him that this lady at this point in time had four cases still outstanding that she had not paid off.

A. No sir. As far as I was concerned they were not still outstanding.

Q. And you stood and listened to Mr. Igou tell the Court that this juror was a good juror and you agreed with him, right?

A. I certainly did. I may have been the one who told him that.

O'Dell said that it was his responsibility to "make sure we didn't have anybody on the jury that was prejudicial toward us, and obviously we had one on there who had been charged at one time. So, if it was my duty to disclose it would have been to Richard for my making a mistake."

When the juror was challenged during the trial, he was of the opinion that she was as attentive as any other juror. Because the Defense objected to her being on the jury was the main reason the deputy district attorney asked Richard Igou to leave her on. O'Dell said that if the Defense had wanted her removed during the first week of trial, the State would have been probably more than happy to do so. [That would have been before he made a tacit deal with McGee.]

The witness was asked if he would have disclosed the information about Hargis had he been aware of it during *voir dire*. He testified he was not sure, but he might have felt compelled to tell the Defense.

O'Dell, McGee and Hargis knew exactly what they did. They probably didn't overtly conspire to show their relationship before Hargis; but McGee, a man without scruples, saw an opportunity to help himself. O'Dell saw an opportunity to persuade a juror and went along with the charade for one reason only – to influence the future Foreman of the Jury. This was the cheapest of the cheap shots! The Court had to really do legal gymnastics to get around my questioning of Hargis during jury selection. She lied, and knowingly lied in order to get on the jury.

While Neelley was in progress, the Alabama Appellate Court reversed a case of mine from down on the coast. A juror did not reveal that he had served on a jury before.

Eileen Hargis, said that there were two instances of bad checks against her. All of the checks were dated about the same time, one in November and three others after the first of the year. This was not true as borne out by the testimony of the Circuit Clerk, Jimmy Lindsey.

Hargis said that she had only lived in Fort Payne a few months when her checks were turned over to the Sheriff. She visited Judge Hunt concerning the first check. He told her to pay the check and the costs. This was another untruth. A judge would not talk to a defendant without counsel, and the district attorney present. Further, Hunt was out with surgery.

When the second set of three or four checks came up, Eileen Hargis went to see Charles McGee. A day or two later he told her she would have 90 days to pay the checks and the costs.

I was interested to see just how far she would go from the truth. She said that she did not have any communication with any members of the audience during the trial. She did not stay in any particular seat in the jury box each day. She did look at every piece of evidence. She was not a singer and did not sing while in the jury box. She did not smile at the Prosecution. She did smile at "pretty well" everybody.

She did not hear any other comments from the audience other than two reporters asking about lunch. She did not hear any derogatory comments made about the Defense or the defendant during the trial.

Trial lawyers try to select the foreman of the jury when the jury is chosen. We had chosen George Westmoreland.

When the jury retired, Mr. Westmoreland was nominated as foreman of the jury because he had served on juries in the past. He was the oldest person on the jury, and he was a very nice man, but he did not want to serve. He suggested that Ed Moses be foreman. Mr. Moses did not want to be foreman, and two or three women said they did not want it. Ed Moses suggested Eileen Hargis be foreman.

A. The eleven of them weren't going to be and that left me, and I said, 'Well, if taking it would get it started so we could get to what we were supposed to be doing, I would take it, but I didn't particularly want it either. I don't see being foreman of the jury as any prize either,' but I said if that's what they wanted and it was an eleven vote quick that I take it, and so, I became the foreman of the jury.

Hargis admitted that she did not speak up when asked as she did not think she had any relationship with the district attorney's office when she was questioned on *voir dire*. She had not talked with anyone from the district attorney's office before the beginning of the trial. She did not see a newspaper while the trial was in progress, neither did she see an Alabama Band record jacket held up by a spectator. No one tried to talk to Mrs. Hargis during the trial.

Finally, Eileen Hargis said she was not influenced in her decision in this case by anything other than the evidence.

Nothing in the courtroom had anything to do with her decision, and she was not biased or prejudiced against the Defense during the case by anything.

She was not for any reason biased or prejudiced in favor of the Prosecution in this case.

On cross-examination, Mrs. Hargis said that she had about five years' experience selling concessions for an entertainer. The work is hard and quick. The noise level is high, and customers are in a hurry.

The lighting is dim, and it is crowded. It is organized pandemonium, according to the witness. She sold T_shirts by "small," "medium," and "large."

> Q. And actually, as you sold these items, even if you couldn't hear the person, if you could see their lips move and say "small," you could know what they wanted, couldn't you?
>
> A. No sir. I'm not a lip reader. I'd had to hear it. I don't think I'd try to anticipate what they were trying to tell me if I couldn't hear it.
>
> Q. At no time when you were selling those concessions did you ever learn to hear people just by the formation of their lips as to small, medium or large, or record or shirt or whatever?
>
> A. No sir. I've got to be able to hear what they say that they want.

Those answers contradict reasonable thought. But, she was not through, Mrs. Hargis said that she did not have any communications with anyone in the courtroom. She did not remember glaring at the examiner over the lectern. She said that she did not glare at anybody.

Eileen Hargis was shown Defendant's Exhibit B, a case against her for a bad check in the amount of $125.00. The check was written on September 10, 1982. It was returned September 13, 1982, "insufficient funds." Witness testified that she took care of the bad check as quickly as she could. The witness could not explain why a complaint was taken in the case November 9, 1982, and she paid it off on April 7, 1983. Other warrants had been taken against her for several months. At the time of jury selection, she knew she had outstanding warrants against her for the checks.

> Q. Surely, and they were still pending at the time that the Neelley case came on for trial, weren't they, some of them, all of them except one?

A. One had been paid off and the others I had made arrangements on and paid part of them.

Q. All of these four cases were still pending at the time the Neelley case came on for trial, wasn't it?

A. Yes, sir.

Q. And you knew that, didn't you?

A. Yes sir.

Q. And I want to ask you if you remember me asking you this question: "Mr. French: I talked with you earlier about non-violent crimes and about violent crimes that had perhaps affected you. I want to now ask you, just in case I missed it - I'm not even going to talk about crime. I'm just going to talk about criminal acts, something nobody was prosecuted for. Have any of you or any of your close relatives or close friends ever been involved in a criminal act, and I'll exclude Terry on this. I'm talking about a criminal act that had affected your life." You remember me asking that question, don't you?

A. Yes sir.

Q. And you did not respond to that, did you?

A. No sir.

Q. But you knew at that time that you had these check cases outstanding, didn't you?

A. Yes sir.

Q. And let me ask you if you would recall that the judge told you, when you took your seat on the panel - Do you remember the judge saying this to you? "All right, ladies and gentlemen, I am now going to give the lawyers an opportunity to ask you some additional questions. Their questions would be lengthy. You may be asked some things you've never been asked before or you've never had an occasion to think about before, but please understand that this is a necessary process, necessary part of what we're here to do. I cannot over-emphasize to you the importance of your understanding the questions that are asked and your answering the questions fully and frankly and honestly. Your failure to do so could result in this case having to be tried again at some later time. So, if you have any doubt as to whether a question applies to you and whether you should answer it, please do not hesitate to have the matter clarified so that when we leave here you would be satisfied that you have given a full, frank, and honest response to every question asked. All right, Mr. Igou." do you recall the court saying that?

A. Yes sir.

Q. And you understood that, didn't you?

A. Yes sir.

Hargis admitted that there were really not any nominations or votes for foreman of the jury. Someone suggested Mr. Westmoreland, who felt he shouldn't take it; and he suggested Mr. Moses. "I just remember it went from Mr. Westmoreland to Mr. Moses to me." Eileen Hargis did not remember any other suggestions other than several of the women saying they did not want to do it.

When she was in the jury room she sat in the chair to the left of the head of the table.

Ed Moses brought her name up for foreman of the jury. No votes were taken. No one was nominated. She was not elected by any balloting.

G. L. Westmoreland did not hear any comments from any spectators. The evidence influenced him.

On cross-examination, he said that he was a little hard of hearing and sat at the end of the box away from the audience. Eileen Hargis sat nearest to the audience. In the jury room, she sat near or at the head of the table. He thought that at least two people should be nominated for foreman. He withdrew his name and suggested Ed Moses. Ed did not withdraw his name from nomination; he said something about handwriting. Moses then said, "I appoint Eileen." Hargis took the position. There was never an election, and there were no votes taken. Everybody was satisfied. No complaints.

Charles E. Moses, when Westmoreland was nominated for foreman of the jury, he said, "Let Ed take it." Moses did not have the handwriting required for the job so let Eileen take it. "Just so happened she was sitting at the head of the table in the jury room. Nobody really wanted the job."

Mary Shankles, Eileen Hargis' roommate during the trial, did not hear any comments out of the audience during the Neelley trial. There was no election of a foreman. "No; we didn't vote."

The motion for new trial hearing was recessed.

CHAPTER FOURTEEN

THE BATTERED WOMAN

---◆---

July 1, 1983, 9:00 a.m., the new trial motion hearing continued with the Defense proceeding.

Steve and I had been educated as to the term *Battered Woman*. Judith Ann Neelley was a battered woman that Alvin took to a new level.

We searched the country to find an expert in the field to testify at our Motion for New Trial. That person found us right next door in Atlanta.

I'm going to quote from Dr. Nichol's testimony in order that you can hear from her how an average woman becomes a battered woman, what the abuse does to her physically and mentally, and how she reacts in certain circumstances. It is a phenomenon that occurs in poor homes, rich homes, educated homes, red neck homes, weak homes and powerful homes. You may be one of them. It is usually a family secret. So track the testimony of Dr. Nichols and learn about this horrible occurrence. I'm putting it here in detail for educational purposes.

Margaret Nichols, Ph.D. was a clinical psychologist in private practice in Atlanta. Educated at Emory University and the University of Connecticut, she received her B.A. degree in 1967, a Masters in 1971, and her Ph.D. in 1975. All three degrees were in psychology. For six years she was on the faculty of Emory University Medical School in the Department of Obstetrics and Gynecology. From that experience, she developed a specialization in the development crises of women.

For six and a half years she has worked with the Council on Battered Women in Atlanta. They have a hotline and receive two to four thousand calls per year. The Council has between 100 and 150 residents per year in their emergency shelter. In her supervisory role at the shelter, Dr. Nichols administered therapy or evaluation to between 75 and 100 beaten women. The mental health profession has recently formulated a syndrome, or a set of behavioral characteristics, that typified the abused woman called the battered woman syndrome.

I asked her to describe the battered woman syndrome:

A. There are several things that characterize the battered woman. One -- Probably the hallmark of the battered woman is even though she is in a situation where she is repeatedly being abused time after time after time, she says very clearly that she loves her husband, that she wants to stay with him, that she feels committed to him. Another characteristic of battered women is that in general the abuse starts relatively mildly and builds up, becoming more and more severe. What happens in this case is that the woman gets more and more used to rougher and rougher and harsher treatment, so that she finds herself, some period of time down the road, being willing to put up with more severe abuse than she probably would have been early in the relationship. Battered women also classically feel that they have no real options but to stay in that situation, that they had no place to go, they had no support from family or the community, they had no skills of their own where they could take care of themselves without the man who is supporting them. Over the period of time, also, as the battering increases, their self-esteem gets lower and lower. They begin believing, even if they didn't believe it at the beginning, that they deserve the beatings, that their husbands are telling them that the reason they are being beat is because they did something wrong, and they believe that. They continue to try to please him, to find ways to take care of him so that the beatings would stop. Another thing that happens is that -- very, very, frequently -- is that the battered woman becomes convinced that the man who is their batterer can do anything, is capable, either emotionally or personality-wise or physically, of all kinds of super human feats. He is given, in the woman's mind, absolute knowledge, the ability to know things and be correct about aspects of the world that the man would really have no way of knowing but the woman begins to believe this more and more. And I think that more than anything else the real hallmark of the battered woman, who is fitting this sort of classic syndrome that we're talking about, is that she is very, very afraid, usually terrified for her life and/or for the life of others and feels that she had no choice but to submit to the treatment and the regime that her husband had set up.

Q. Dr. Nichols, at my request -- I believe we became acquainted with each other by phone some time after the Neelley trial, and at my request did you come over and interview Judith Neelley?

A. Yes; I did.

Q. And have you -- From the time that you spent with her and talked with her, had you been able to formulate any opinions concerning her?

A. Yes; I have.

Q. Okay. Let me ask you just a few questions. First, let me go at it this way. Does she fit into the battered woman syndrome?

A. Yes; I believe she does.

Dr. Nichols was not surprised that Judy Neelley did not tell the doctors performing the psychiatric evaluation the truth about her situation. She was not surprised Judy was not honest with her attorneys, as she was protecting her husband.

A.Usually some event changes the woman's opinion to the extent she can let go of complete reliance of the man. Prior to that event, it reaches a point where it is not okay to go to the bathroom unless the man believes that the woman's bladder is full enough to be able to allow her to go to the bathroom. There can be that completely overriding control over the woman's life. A long time is required for the woman to get over the effects of that and let go. Although Judy Neelley is not over her reliance on Alvin Neelley, the major event necessary to change her attitude toward him had happened.

Battered women are ashamed of being battered. "They feel they have done something very wrong, that if they were not such horrible people, their husbands would not treat them like this. They frequently take full responsibility for their abuse."

Dr. Nichols became acquainted with Judy Neelley through Susan May, a founder of the Council on Battered Women. May was the executive director of the Council until approximately a year before the Neelley trial. Susan said she was going to contact Judy's lawyers as she felt Judy Neelley was a battered woman from news accounts of the trial. She told Dr. Nichols she was going to suggest that Nichols evaluate Judy's case. This conversation was after the trial and one day before the sentencing of Judith Ann Neelley.

The witness stated that it was happenstance whether or not any particular attorney happened to know that there is a battered women's syndrome or if there is help available for battered women. "It's even more happenstance to know that this is now beginning to be seen as a legal defense."

The psychologist was asked if the finding that Judith Ann Neelley had a dependent personality disorder was consistent with the battered women's syndrome.

> A. First of all, I was not at all surprised. When I saw the diagnosis on the report and knew at that point that she had not talked with the doctors at that hospital about the abuse, about the situation in reality and truth with her doctors there, I thought the dependant personality was probably the best diagnosis that they could have come up with. It is very consistent with a woman who had been in a battering situation for a period of time. It primarily speaks to, again, that profound emotional day-to-day reality dependence and seeing the man as the ultimate authority in her life.

The doctor said that Judith Ann Neelley probably fit the battered women syndrome to the most severe extent she had seen. In reaching that conclusion, the witness found that not only did Alvin Neelley isolate and control Judy; but he also did that progressively more and more and more. "Again, this is very typical of the more extreme cases of battered women, that their whole lives become centered around this one person."

One of the primary things being attempted by isolation is the sense of wanting no communication between the woman and the outside world. "Usually, in most cases, the man puts that in terms of if she communicates with somebody, then that means that she's flirting and/or being sexual with another man. Sexual infidelity is a profound obsession with battering men."

"The battered woman is made to feel that the beatings are her fault, that she is to blame, and if she were better the beatings would stop, he would love her, and everything would be wonderful. There is an on-going consistent manipulation of guilt and anxiety and responsibility."

Q. Some of the things that we've discussed so far, would they be classified under a term that I've heard used since I've been in this case called learned helplessness?

A. Yes.

Q. Could you discuss learned helplessness at all?

A. Learned helplessness occurs -- well, first of all, was found in laboratory experiments, primarily with dogs, and what they did in these experiments is that the dog was put into a cage and random electric shocks, that were very painful, not enough to kill, but were certainly very painful, were administered to the dog. There was no way that the dog could escape. There was no way that the dog could control the severity of the shock or when the shock occurred, and even more important, there was no way that the animal could predict when the painful stimulant was going to occur. Once this was done enough, what they found that happened with the animals was that the animal stopped -- initially was pacing, trying to find a way out, looking for alternatives. After a while, the animal stopped looking completely and just laid down in the cage, and at the most, whimpered when the painful shock occurred, sometimes did not make any sound at all. It was as if part of the animal had gone. When given -- With these animals, when given then, the opportunity to escape, when a door to a safe cage was opened, the animal would not move, even when the animal was forcefully moved to the other cage and allowed to stay there and then put back in the shock cage with the door open, knowing that that was a safe place, the animal would not leave. He would simply lie down on the grid floor and accept the shock.

Q. And that is how learned helplessness came into our psychological vocabulary?

A. Yes.

Q. Now, had that been applied to domestic violence?

A. Yes; it had. It had been applied in situations of usually the more extreme nature where because of the inability to control the beatings, the inability to escape from them, and again -- and I think this is probably the most psychologically debilitating thing -- the inability to predict. Battered women who are in this extreme and get to the learned helplessness place, when asked, "Did you know what would make him mad enough to beat you?" universally say, "No; I had no idea. I never could tell when I was going to get a beating and when I wasn't going to get a beating." And so, what happens is after a while they give up. They don't think about leaving any more. They don't think about any alternatives. They simply give up, and usually I think they try to numb themselves in an attempt to not feel.

Q. In your examination of Judith Neelley, is it your opinion that she had reached that point in learned helplessness?

A. Yes.

The witness was asked if she could pinpoint any one particular aspect of Judy's life that was the turning point in making her into a helpless individual as far as Alvin was concerned.

"When Alvin gave Judy that very severe beating on March 26, 1982. From that beating, Judy did not know whether she was going to live or die. This was the most extreme beating I have ever heard of. However, an important part of the beating was the humiliation and degradation Alvin practiced on Judy."

Dr. Nichols said that the degradation of the pre-existing self of Judy Neelley started a couple of months after they left Murfreesboro and grew progressively worse and worse. This activity was consistent with the battered women syndrome. Requiring performance of degrading acts of self-betrayal or betrayal of group norms and confession was part of the syndrome at the more extreme end. Judy Neelley was at the extreme end of the syndrome because of the things Alvin Neelley did to her.

When asked for an explanation as to the motivating force causing Alvin Neelley to perform horrible acts on women, Dr. Nichols said that humiliating and degrading another to look and feel subhuman made Alvin feel stronger and bigger. He also received a great deal of sexual arousal and excitement from beating or degrading Judy. That was sadism.

Judy had tried to leave Alvin but was forcibly detained. Once this happened she felt she had no choice but to stay. Even if Judy could leave, she had the feeling that she had no place to go. She had burned the bridges with her family, she had no skills, so there was nothing she could do.

> Q. In your discussions with Judith Neelley, immediately leading up to the death of Lisa Ann Millican, could you determine, from your discussions with her, that immediately prior to those acts that she had any identity, or would have any process, whereby she might control her acts?

A. No; I believe she did not. At that point she was completely and totally under his control. She didn't do anything that he did not tell her to do, and whatever he said, she did.

Q. And she offered no resistance?

A. No. Alvin Neelley substituted his mental state for Judy's.

Q. Under those circumstances, would she be able to exercise any freedom of choice?

A. No; I do not believe she could.

Q. If she could not, under those circumstances, exercise freedom of choice, could she, in your judgment, formulate any intent to kill?

A. She had no intents of her own.

Q. Was it consistent with the syndrome that the acts engaged in would only benefit the batterer?

A. Yes.

Dr. Nichols could not find anywhere that Judy Neelley benefited from the acts performed on Lisa Ann Millican.

On cross-examination, the witness stated that she developed the term, "development crises of women." She did not know whether the term was recognized generally in the field of psychology and psychiatry. She had seen in excess of 1,000 women who had a psychological problem that would fit into the developmental crises of women.

Dr. Nichols had direct case consultation supervision of in excess of 12,000 women. She worked for four years at the student mental health service at the University of Connecticut. She served an internship at Duke University Medical Center and received two years' supervision with an eminent psychologist in Atlanta. Most of her training was in diagnosis and treatment. She was not an expert in persuasive coercion; however, she was an expert in learned helplessness.

She had testified in six cases. There was an assault case, and the other five involved the wife killing her husband. She had testified for the Defense each time. This case was the first case involving the killing of a person other than the spouse. It was not uncommon for the battered wife to kill her husband. This was consistent with the battered wife syndrome. She had never been involved in a case where someone used the battered wife syndrome as an excuse for killing a thirteen-year-old child.

Dr. Nichols based her opinion on background information furnished by the defendant's attorney and an interview with Judy Neelley which lasted more that three hours. The doctor was of the opinion that she had a better opportunity to evaluate Judy Neelley than the multiple psychiatrists from Bryce Hospital because Judy was more cooperative with her than with the psychiatrists.

Dr. Nichols had never encountered beatings with more physical violence than the one Alvin gave Judy in March of 1982.

Q. What injuries did she sustain?

A. She sustained multiple bruises and contusions. A lot -- and I don't know the extent of whatever internal injuries. I think a lot of the horribleness of this beating was also the extreme of the psychological abuse and the humiliation and degradation that went along with that, so that the thing that made it a severe beating was not just physical violence.

Q. Well, would you say after that she decided it would be better for somebody else to die other than her?

A. No; I don't think she decided that.

Q. Well, she did decide that at some point, didn't she?

A. I think that she did not decide.

The witness was cross-examined as to whether she volunteered to come to Alabama and testify for the defense.

Q. Let's put it this way. You came over to support the theories espoused by the defendant.

A. I came over to evaluate whether or not this individual woman fit the battered women's syndrome, and if she did, to then testify at this hearing to that effect and to then educate the community and the court about the battered women's syndrome.

Q. That's what you came here to do, was it not, to educate us and educate the court?

A. Yes.

Q. How many times did you say you've testified before in court?

A. Six.

Q. At each time on behalf of the defendant?

A. Yes. There had been about three or four other times when I had done an evaluation for a defendant and at the end of that evaluation told the defense attorney that I did not feel that the woman fit the battered women's syndrome and that I could not testify to that in that case, and if he wanted me to get on the stand and say that I could not testify that she was a battered woman, that was fine. Needless to say, he didn't put me on the stand.

Q. Certainly. How much time -- You say you spent in excess of three hours with the defendant. How much time was Mr. French in sketching to you about what happened?

A. About a half-hour.

Q. Who was present during the interview with Mrs. Neelley?

A. Nobody, Mrs. Neelley and I. That was all.

Dr. Nichols could not say whether or not she was for the death penalty with a simple yes or no. She did not believe the Judith Neelley was a sociopath. She was asked if the defendant knew what she was doing and that it was wrong when she killed Lisa Millican.

A. I think that she knew what she was doing. I think that she was so completely immersed in Alvin Neelley's mind and ideas and under his influence that I don't think that she thought about whether or not it was right or wrong. I don't think that even occurred to her.

Q. Are you saying that she did not know that it was wrong?

A. I'm saying that she did not think about that.

Q. If there was evidence that she hesitated before she pulled the trigger, what would that tell you?

A. That she certainly didn't want to do it.

Q. But what if she did then do it?

A. That she was doing what she was told to do.

Q. Without thought that it was wrong?

A. I'm saying that I don't think that that determination was made by her.

Q. No. I'm saying did she do that without thought that it was wrong?

A. I think that that's possible.

Q. Then what was the hesitation based upon? Why did she not want to do it?

A. She wasn't sure abut what this -- All she knew that this was something that he was telling her to do, and I would venture to guess that it didn't -- and this is purely speculation -- it didn't feel right.

Q. As a matter of fact, your whole testimony today had been purely speculation, had it not?

A. It had been my considered opinion.

The district attorney continued on the fact that Judy hesitated before shooting Lisa Ann Millican. Alvin had to yell at her to do it. Dr. Nichols said that the hesitation was probably based on fear.

A. She was scared.

Q. Of what?

A. I don't know.

Q. Why would being scared have caused her to hesitate?

A. Frequently when people are afraid they do hesitate. That's one of the primary functions of fear.

On re-direct, Dr. Nichols said that she had not discussed a question or her testimony before court. When she was given the thumbnail sketch of the facts of the case she was taken to the circuit clerk's office where she reviewed all the exhibits. This search of the file was done in the presence of the deputy clerk.

Q. And I believe late in the evening last night you mentioned to me, "Are you going to ask me anything about my testimony."

A. Yes; I did.

Q. And what did I say to you?

A. You said, "No; I am not."

Q. And I didn't, did I?

A. No; you did not.

Q. So, there was no way of my knowing what you were going to say this morning, was there?

A. Correct.

Q. Because you did not tell me what opinion you had formulated of Mrs. Neelley, did you?

A. Correct.

Dr. Nichols said that her testimony was not the defense version of what happened, nor was her testimony Mrs. Neelley's version of what happened. Her testimony was her considered opinion.

She then discussed physical injuries as opposed to mental trauma. Injuries happening to the body heal and are forgotten.

A.The psychic abuses go right into a person's sense of themselves. They wonder whether the world is a place to be trusted and whether or not they are the kind of people who can cope with the world. Humiliation and degradation are much more profound, long-lasting, and debilitating than any broken bones. These injuries alter the person's aspect of reality. When a person's aspect of reality is altered, it induces a reaction which may not be consistent with the rules of society.

Dr. Nichols had never heard of a battered wife case as serious as Neelley's. Judy's case was the outer limits of the battered woman syndrome.

The State moved to strike the entire testimony of Dr. Margaret Nichols on the grounds that she did not present newly discovered evidence, and there was no showing that she could not have been available at the trial. "Overruled." Defense given 15 days to submit a brief, and the proceedings were concluded.

CHAPTER FIFTEEN

PROBLEMS CONTINUE

———◆——

July 1, 1983, returning to my diary entries, I thought that the hearing had gone well. I began to believe that Judy had a good chance of getting a new trial.

Steve had changed. His attitude was different. I felt like during the motion he was afraid to go forward with the evidence because he was concerned that he might harm Charles McGee. Something wasn't right.

I looked at the firm's books, and we were hurting. If we didn't take in some money quick, we were going under.

July 2, 1983, a sunny beautiful Saturday. With every mail run, I received a tirade from some fool. I received one from Italy, written in Italian. I let my mother-in-law decipher enough of it to know I didn't want to hear the rest of it.

I sent Margaret Nichols copies of the clippings about her in the *Fort Payne-Times Journal* and the *Birmingham Post-Herald*. I never heard from Dr. Nichols again.

July 4, 1983 - TNT's birthdays. We survived, just barely. They received a computer game, "Pitfall Harry". It seemed to be taken from the Indiana Jones Movies. Harry gets into a world of trouble.

Most of my time was spent - when I wasn't saving ol' Pitfall Harry - on the phone trying to close the deal in Maggie Valley for Paul and Virginia Hyde.

The Nigerian oil deal was still alive. I had located a South American buyer who was willing to play the game with Lagos. Elijah said they were drowning in their own oil. He had obtained a 100,000-barrel-a-day allocation for Edgar. Maybe it would work. Edgar was putting a full-court press on it.

July 6, 1983, Steve was of the opinion Judge Cole would deny the new trial and try to poison the well on appeal.

"Poison the well," meant that he would write his order in such a manner that the appellate court would feel constrained to go along with him. The appellate courts posture in favor of the trial judge. They didn't see, observe, examine, and consider the witnesses, and other evidence. So the trial judge should be affirmed if at all possible.

If our motion was denied, I hoped that they would consider this case so serious that they would search the record on their own to determine if they could find errors in it.

Sometimes it was good for a case to be notorious. I thought of the headlines when Jeff the rapist came into Judy's cell that night in the DeKalb County Jail. I could see, "Convicted Rapist Rapes Murderess," or, "Convicted Murderess Murders Rapist." If I had known it in advance, I would have told Judy to just relax and enjoy it. She was a silly girl to protect her virtue when that might be the only sex she might get in 30 years.

FINANCIAL PROBLEMS

The bank was pursuing me relentlessly. When you are down, everybody kicks you. They were holding up my deposits, and causing my checks to bounce. They were calling my loans - showing no mercy.

The banker chose to ignore the fact that they got me into this mess. Their vice president did not keep up with the notes of Randall Bolton. I had guaranteed $25,000 for Randall Bolton against receivables of Sequoyah Structural Steel. He paid that note. Later a VP allowed Bolton to bring new notes to me for my signature. Instead of bringing notes, that he knew I would not sign, Bolton forged my signature. I had a balance due of more than $139,000.

I had owed them $74,000 for additional financing of the Neelley Case. They put the forged Bolton note with that balance. Bolton had paid $120,000 on his notes leaving A $65,000 forged signature note. My bank, since 1965, relentlessly pursued me for money. They embarrassed me when any opportunity came along. Apparently, they never bothered Bolton.

The bank president called me in and wanted security for the notes. He wanted me to put a second mortgage on my home. He said that this would solve my problems for a year. By then, I would be out of the Neelley mess and back to making money.

I was not willing to mortgage my home. The VP, who had allowed Bolton to forge my signature, had his wife call Celeste with a woebegone tale that he was going to lose his job, etc. For a year's relief, Celeste agreed to a second mortgage. We signed the documents believing I would be given a year before any payment would be due and, "the bank would work with me then." After the recording of the documents, the bank deemed itself insecure, and foreclosed on our home in a matter of days. We owed very little on our home so they felt safe in paying off the first mortgage, and foreclosing on the second. I knew that the Neelley case had a lot to do with the way I was being treated. The bankers didn't believe I could recover and pay them.

CHANGES

Steve chose that time to come in and say that he was not being paid enough. That was his excuse for leaving the firm. He knew I could not pay him any more money. I was barely making payroll.

Now it appeared he had a job with Charles McGee. I really liked Steve. I hoped he would survive McGee. It wouldn't be easy. McGee was different.

I received a letter from Judith Neelley wherein she admitted that she cheated when I took her on trust walks. She didn't fool me. She fooled herself. If Judith had told Steve and me the gory details of the beatings, and the mess that she was in, we could have built a better defense. We knew that she had lied at Bryce Hospital, and now she had lied about the trust walk.

The Alabama Court of Criminal Appeals handed down decisions that helped the Neelley position. In one, the Court held that leaving an alternate juror in the jury room during deliberations was reversible error. I thought that if he didn't grant a new trial, Judge Cole would be reversed due to this line of cases. The Alabama Court System would not give Judith any relief, but the Federal proceedings might eventually reverse the thing flat out.

I went back to running at least three miles a day. I had to do something to get healthy. My eyes were beginning to bulge out of their sockets, and I had to lean my head back to see clearly. I thought running might help get my blood pumping better.

I ran into Jeff Cook of the Alabama Band on the way back. He lived on my route and was down checking his pond. I told him hello and reminded him that he was Fort Payne's good boy, and I was Fort Payne's bad boy. He got a kick out of that.

July 7, 1983 was a busy morning. Michael decided to go to work for Bill Scruggs. The parting was going to be friendly. I guessed that I'd keep both Cindy and Anita. I could solve many of my problems with the expenses of two lawyers gone. I could understand the guys leaving. The Neelley Case had been more than most folks could handle.

July 8, 1983, the Democrats changed their rumor. "Both Michael and Steve had left the law firm because they could not stand by while Bob French was having an affair with Judy Neelley."

I was happy to be alone again. Scruggs had Michael, who would not take a chance on anything. Mike needed to be a judge.

McGee was also in for a surprise. Steve was a natural competitor, but he had trouble channeling his competition in a rational manner. McGee played what I call cutie-pie tricks, i.e., what he did with O'Dell to influence Hargis. Steve would do an electric chair act for Judy, complete with spastic jerks and the eventual death. He thought it was a riot.

I wrote these diary entries back in the '80's. Here's a postscript: After a couple of years, Scruggs fired Mike; and he became an Administrative Law Judge with the Social Security Administration

After McGee was disbarred, Steve went out on his own. He did well, and became the Democrat Party political boss of the county.

He went out to Seattle and helped me fly a plane back that I bought out there. Then I went out to Las Vegas, and flew a plane back that he had bought there. In the interim we owned an airplane together. I believe Steve and I will always be friends.

HAMMERING ON

July 8, 1983, a ruling now came in from the Alabama Supreme Court. They reversed my Danny O'Leary Case that I had tried down on the coast in Baldwin County. On *voire dire* one of the jurors said he had never served on a jury before. He had served as foreman of one. Surely the Hargis dissemble would result in a Neelley reversal.

The Alabama Bar asked Richard and me to discuss the trial at its convention.

Several hate letters came in. One said I should be shot. Another said I was going to be shot. Another said that I was going straight to hell for defending Judy Neelley. What about Cole who made me do it? Oh, he gets a pass; he sent her to the electric chair. Plus, he was a Democrat.

Judge Cole's secretary Joyce Daus, called, "I hear you are losing your help, what's going on with you?"

I told her that Mike wanted an office practice, and Steve wanted to make more money.

She said, "What are Bob's true feelings about the situation?"

I laughed, and she laughed. "You old dog," she hung up laughing.

I was happy for Billy Scruggs, Charles McGee, and me. "Them that don't believe can leave."

It was Friday afternoon. I needed to spend the weekend writing the brief for the Motion for New Trial as though it was an appellate brief. If Judge Cole did not grant a new trial, I would be ready for the appeal.

July 9, 1983, Saturday, Judy's aunt, grandmother, and great-grandmother visited me about Joe's case. Ron Adams did not send down the information he promised. So we were still talking in the blind so far as Hoover's liability was concerned.

Nita came by with the Saturday mail. More hate letters, unsigned. It seemed like the writers were simply saying what they wanted to get off their chests. They just wanted to participate a little. Short on courage, I felt sorry for them.

One said that she could not believe that I taught Sunday School and defended people such as Judith Ann Neelley. The writer stated that I was certainly going to be with the devil when I died.

Another one asked me numerous questions about my representation of Judith Ann Neelley and my relationship with my wife and family. I couldn't answer the questions because there was neither name nor address.

I have lost seven pounds this week. Maybe I was going back to what I weighed when I graduated from high school during the Middle Ages. There was something physically wrong with me, but I didn't know what it was. I liked being cold. I had trouble sleeping. I was losing weight, my eyes were bulging out, I was very nervous, and I was tried all the time. I needed to see a doctor.

July 10, 1983, Sunday, all day. After church, I worked on the brief for 10 hours.

July 11, 1983, I tried to make a living. It was a fast 24 hours.

A LONE WOLF AGAIN

July 12, 1983, working hard - just me - the lone wolf. I was glad I was able to part friends with the boys.

On my first day to work alone, I took in $550. The next day I took in $2,100. In the past I made a fortune practicing law, and though I was broke, I knew I could do it again. It was more difficult this time with Neelley draped around my neck. One day the hatred and malice will turn around. It didn't look promising, but I am a patient man.

The latest rumor flying around town was that I had been kicked out of the First Baptist Church. When the rumor was denied by church members, who were my friends, the speaker said, "Well he should be kicked out for what he did."

The rumormonger then went forward to tell what I did. I wished I could have lived up to the stories. As long as they said, my name right, I didn't care what they said. Attention is attention is attention.

My weight was 179 this morning.

I talked with Judge Cole today while waiting for Clyde Traylor, my old law partner, to arrive for a hearing.

My comfortable, well-defined world, had been turned upside down by Neelley. There I was, rocking along, be-bopping through life, watching out for number one, and here comes Neelley. If it weren't for the experience of being broke and hated, I might be in danger of getting fat.

July 13, 1983, Sandra Cason, Judy's aunt, came by to see me. She was Joe's mother. She had a beautiful little boy with her. He was obviously the son of a black father. He was a very well-behaved and well-mannered child. I wished him well.

Steve told me that he did not want to work on the Neelley appeal if I was involved. He had not helped with the Motion for New Trial other than appear at the hearing. I didn't understand his problem, but the case was going straight ahead.

July 14, 1983, I had worked on the Neelley brief all day. At 4:45 p.m. I asked the Court for 10 more days. I thought Judge Cole would grant the motion, especially since Mike and Steve had moved out. It was due July 15th, but there was no way.

All day, all night, I just kept writing the brief. I had to do without dinner; the brief was more important. I was broke. My life was at a standstill. The only thing happening was the brief.

July 15, 1983, out the door and on my way to St. Clair Correctional Facility to visit Darrell Gene McKnight. The night before I had pounded away on the brief into the wee hours. Today, when I returned I would have to pound away again.

Darrell Gene, a skilled carpenter, was the crew chief of the group of prisoners who built the warden's home. He was now building homes for the assistant warden, captain of the guards, and several other staff members.

I had filed a request that he be given work release. They gave me a bone by bringing him to North Alabama. They probably really did it because he was a skilled carpenter and could build the houses for pennies a day. He put in 10 hours, 6 days a week for 30 cents an hour. Who says slave labor does not exist?

Still, it beat staying behind that razor wire. Outside he saw people. He drove a truck downtown. He ate McDonald's hamburgers, etc. Behind the bars, he had nothing but supervision, guards that handed out disciplines for untied shoes or unbuttoned shirts, and other inmates trying to cause trouble. There were 25 lifers without parole there. It seemed that Warden Murphy had his hands full.

I told Darrell Gene that I would try again to have him moved to work release using the excuse that he could work on other state projects. I greased the skids for him to be placed on work release in two weeks. Darrel Gene walked away from a project, and they had put him back into the population. He had walked around Birmingham for two days. Can't help some folks.

INTERESTING ENCOUNTER

From St. Clair I drove to Birmingham and Samford University. We had to attend 12 hours of continuing legal education each year. I had been attending the National College of Criminal Defense programs.

I liked the National College programs because they featured people like Gerry Spense, Jim Shellow, Albert Krieger, or other trial lawyers who could put the corn down where the hogs could find it. I liked to hear trial lawyers tell about how it felt when certain things happened in the courtroom, and what they did to respond to their own feelings. I was not interested in war stories or cutie-pie tricks.

At Cumberland School of Law at Samford University, the first person I ran into was Herbert Stone.

Ed Nelson and I had represented Dr. Gus Prosch, who was tried for having the largest weapons cache owned by a single individual in U.S. History. Anticipating the revolution, Gus had trailers full of every kind of weapon, explosive and bullets imaginable. The government proved that if the cache had exploded, it would have leveled nine city blocks in Bessemer, Alabama.

After Gus was convicted, he wanted to keep his medical license. Nelson and I could not work that out for him. He hired Herbert Stone; and after working for Prosch for years, Stone finally obtained a medical license for Gus after he had served his time in the federal joint.

We sat together on the third row in the seminar. And who do you think came in and sat down to my right? Mel Alexander, the Assistant U.S. Attorney who had prosecuted Gus Prosch. He had retired as Assistant U.S. Attorney and was practicing law with another old buddy of mine, Don Collins. Mel had a fine gray mustache and looked good. We had opposed each other in a lot of cases and he was always a gentleman. Courthouse jokers said he would cry telling you "no deal" for your client.

Mel Alexander prosecuted Prosch, French defended Prosch, and Stone rehabilitated Prosch. Small world, huh? Super Doc kept us from being bored to death by guys lecturing about Hague Accords and the Treaty establishing the European Economic Community.

So there I sat listening to people with heavy German accents talk about commercial partnerships and international corporations. The speaker was discussing German Check Law. I wouldn't take a check from a German. A German shot my uncle off the ladder of a destroyer from a submarine near Greenland during World War II. I was there when they brought him back to Huntsville on a stretcher. He has a purple heart on his tombstone. Ah, I have to admit the Germans are okay. Just don't let them get around any loudmouthed paperhanger from Austria. Next thing you'll know, they'll be goose-stepping all over Europe.

The little Porsche was running good. Its favorite speeds were 80 and 105. I called the office. They told me the Court had granted my motion, and the brief was not due until July 25. Now I could relax and get the thing written.

BIKES AND AIRPLANES

July 16, 1983, Celeste had gone to get the mail and buy a bike pedal for my bike. The kids wanted me to go biking with them later that day. I had to have my bike fixed where Tommy had broken it. TNT each had 10 speeds. I had an old Western Flyer I bought from

Ed Nelson in Tuscaloosa in 1964. Darrell Martin borrowed the old bike when he was a child and broke two spokes out of it in 1970. I kept it oiled and aired and hanging in the garage. I would ride it with TNT.

Paul Hyde called. They wanted to sell him the hotel for a dollar and him pay the balance as he pleased. I guessed I'd pack a typewriter and drive over to Maggie Valley Sunday or Monday. Maybe this time I could close the deal.

I didn't intend to put this in the book, but it seems to be interesting. I must sell the Baron. I had specked it out at the factory in 1977. When Edgar found out I was selling it for $75,000, he offered to buy it and let me keep it. The offer was tempting, but I didn't want to become a private pilot, even for a friend. The prop-jet had gone early as had the Cessna 310. So now, for the first time in many years, I became a Kiwi, a bird that can't fly.

Eddie Brown called me and told me that he had hit a lick on some land and wanted me to pick out a Mooney Aircraft. He had $10,000 I could use as a down payment. I had more than 1,200 hours as a Mooney pilot. It was my favorite aircraft.

The Mooney is a single engine, retractable, land aircraft. Edgar and I were vectored into a thunderstorm by ATC one night coming out of New Orleans, and went through two oscillations over Meridian, Mississippi, and the Mooney held together. It cried with metal fatigue, but it held. Most other aircraft would have broken up. We went to 17,500 feet in a matter of seconds and then fell to the altitude of 900 feet before we bottomed out. The updraft caught us, and we went right back to 20,000 feet, lightening, thunder, St. Elmo's fire on the prop, hail, and all that goes with it. This time she bottomed out at 1,500 feet. I thought surely the wings would come off, she hit so hard. It was a wild ride, but the Mooney held together. Meridian was obscure and closed. I landed anyway, without ever seeing the runway. We had to sit in the storm on the runway 40 minutes before we could see to taxi off the main. I thanked God for old Art Mooney and his brother Al when that sucker held together at the bottom of those thunder bumpers. Another Mooney would be nice. I love to fly. But I was not counting on it.

BACK TO WORK

It was getting late. I had been in motion most of the day. I went by the office and took the typewriter home to work on the brief Sunday. I set up on the dining room table. I had an office downstairs in the rec room, but Celeste wanted me to work upstairs to be with the family.

Celeste came home, and we had a fantastic meal. Celeste was one of the world's great cooks. I had never seen a woman who could whip up a gourmet meal like she could. She brought in the mail. I had two letters from Judith Neelley.

Neelley wanted to know if Bronco Billy ever got down. Well, he might sometimes, but he recovered quickly. He always rode a white horse and looked so good up there you would just give him anything to ride off into the sunset with him. He just never stayed down in the dumps - too much trouble.

July 19, 1983, I had just tried a Social Security Disability case in Gadsden that morning. We won.

As I was leaving the hearing room in the federal courthouse, I ran into Clarence Rhea, one of the more respected members of the Etowah County Bar Association. He shook my hand and said, "I don't know whether any other lawyer had said this to you before, but I just want you to know that I appreciate the way you upheld the integrity of our profession in the Neelley Trial."

I really appreciated him saying that.

It had been a tough fight, a disappointment, and an overwhelming burden. But I was glad it was me. Otherwise, I would not have had the experience of defending the integrity of the profession. And, when it came to that fight, any lawyer should meet the challenge. The courage came from that spark that was ignited in the lawyer when he attended law school. Down and dirty, almost any lawyer will stand his ground and fight. Otherwise, he could not have paid the price of graduating from a law school and struggling with the law and facts in every possible theorized situation.

I couldn't remember the weekend - too many activities and too many miles. Oh yeah, I went bike riding with TNT on Saturday. So it was fast. I was on a radio talk show Sunday morning, talking about Judith Ann Neelley, of course. I went to church, then to lunch at home, and back to North Carolina.

I knew I had to start pounding out that brief again.

I had picked up a local paper, and the *Times Journal* had almost a headline front-page story, *"Extension granted in Neelley appeal case."*

July 20, 1983, I went to the office extra early hoping to get something done. I was convinced that if I arrived there at 5:00 a.m. the phone would be ringing. It rang that morning at 6:50 a.m. I could not believe someone would think I was in my office that early.

July 21, 1983, I was still working on that cursed brief. I was on page 883 of the transcript of the trial. It went on for more than 2,800 pages.

The brief was on my butt while my banker was trying to catch me. The judge called to tell me he was going on vacation so I had one more week on the brief.

ALABAMA STATE BAR ASSOCIATION CONVENTION

July 22, 1983, I had just finished outlining my remarks to the Bar Association. Although I was going to Birmingham to talk to the Convention about the Neelley case, I desperately needed to be working on the brief.

July 23, 1983, it was a beautiful day outside. For most folks I guess it was too hot. I liked hot weather. My nose was frostbitten while I was in the service during the Korean Conflict. The bridge of my nose had never been the same. It stayed red and the skin was wrinkled. My glasses sat on it, so it was rarely noticed.

The Bar meeting went over well. Neelley was the star of our part of the show. A reporter interviewed me for an hour and a half. He told me I should write a book.

It was hard for Richard to say anything bad about Judy, except that she had a choice to do what Alvin told her to do. He said she could have easily taken herself out of the situation. Therefore, the crimes Neelley committed were of her own free will and accord. He complimented me, and I complimented him.

It was great seeing Jerry Barksdale there. He told me this part of the program was all he came for. Mike Brownfield showed up for the presentation. He was still a great little guy.

As usual, Judith Ann Neelley created controversy at the Alabama Bar Association. The program indicated the Neelley case would be discussed at 3:30 p.m. I went down early just to get the feel of the place. I was lucky I did. Richard was there early also. David Johnson, Chairman of the Criminal Law Section, came in and started the program at 2:00 p.m. Jerry and Mike almost missed the entire program.

In our section, we had about 40 lawyers for the program. Richard and I sat in two chairs in the middle of a large circle, and the lawyers interrogated us. I did not know the press was in the room. So we shelled down the corn.

B.J. McPherson, an old buddy of mine from Oneonta, acted like he did not know me and threw me a few accolades while asking tough questions.

He said, " When your trial was going on, I went to the drug store every morning to hear the latest in the saga of Judith Ann Neelley. The old men and coffee drinkers said, `B.J., ain't that feller French going too far in his relationship with that woman?' And, I would have to agree. Hadn't you gone too far? Weren't you setting a new standard for appointed lawyers in this state?"

I said, "If a lawyer does not want to feel for his client, then he should represent South Central Bell, I.B.M., or some other non-breather. Who can get happy representing non-breathers? Victory or loss, it's a ledger entry. When I was trying the Neelley case I listened to a Gerry Spence tape where Spence said, 'If you can't love your client, send him to a golfer who represents banks and insurance companies.' So I had to put aside my hatred for what Neelley did and try to care for her individually; otherwise I would not care what happened to her."

One lawyer asked if I had not gone over the line? I told him that I would pay the price for victory. What was the price of victory? It was the price of never giving up!

B.J. asked, "Bob, what are you going to do when they ride you out of town on a rail?"

"Who cares?" I responded. "I'm leading the parade?" The group liked that.

July 24, 1983, Sunday, 5:45 p.m. I'd been writing the brief all weekend. I was finally over to the Jo Ann Browning testimony.

The first person to have possession of the facts was the court reporter, Lisa Hall. I told her to get the copies out to me as fast as possible. I was writing a long discussion of the facts to make the Alabama Court of Criminal Appeals read it without being bored.

July 25, 1983, Monday I was featured in the *Birmingham Post-Herald*. I didn't mention it earlier, but Richard and I were sorta the starring attraction at the Bar Convention. The *Post* gave us press by the yard. I knew I should not have given that interview. Oh well, was only the second largest paper in the state.

The *Post* article was one of the best I had seen from a lawyer's point of view. There was a good picture with the story.

I was almost through with the statement of the facts. That was the longest job in the brief, summarizing 2,800 pages of testimony accurately. You goof up, and the State jumps on you like a duck on a June bug. The legal research was already done for the argument. Thanks to the law students at the U of A.

NEW EXPERIENCES

I wondered what makes men enjoy beating women? All women are beautiful. They are the mother and mistress of the universe. Hitting a woman has to be a sickness.

July 26, 1983, I was taking a break and thinking about friendship. Roland Oliver and I have been buddies since we were 12 or 13 years old. I am lucky to have Jerry Barksdale as one of my dearest friends. Our backgrounds paralleled unbelievably. We are aces back to back. It is a mutual admiration society, and Jerry is a true friend.

July 27, 1983, shortly after dawn, I took the time for a deep meditation and heard the sound of the universe! It was the sound of time cutting through space. If one listens in the silence strong enough, and long enough, it is there. It was unbelievable! Once you hear it, you always want to hear it again. No, I'm not crazy - a little weird perhaps – just tuned in and turned on.

The Baraca Class was a tough class to teach as almost every one there was a Bible Scholar. I wrote my own lessons and did my own research. I tried to bring them a new thought every Sunday. My class ended at 10:30 a.m. We attended church until 12:00 Noon. Then the family went out to eat, or we ate something special at home. Ninety per cent of the time we would go out to eat so Celeste could have a day off. Afterward, I took a nap. I usually slept until 4:00 p.m. Then I got up and went to work until at least 10:30 p.m.

Saturday was the day I guarded for TNT. We biked, went swimming, played on the trampoline, or whatever they wanted to do. Sometimes we went fishing. Whatever we did, it was quality time.

Everyone should have a spot where they are perfectly happy and content. Mine is down below the house on the side of the mountain in the deep woods. There is a nice big rock down there that I sat on in the shade. I called it, "La Sitio" the spot. I took TNT down there and they loved it.

I spent most of the day out of the office trying to make a living. Eddie and I called on several of my clients and collected some fees.

Plea day was coming up; and if I was going to appear, I was going to have to be paid. I collected a little over $2,000.

July 28, 1983, Thursday, I had finished more than 400 pages of the brief.

A Letter came from Judy asking if Richard Igou hated her. I told her, Richard Igou did not hate anyone. He makes the Defense fight the system. All he ever wanted was justice. If he did not think he could convict, he did not go to trial. There was no smoke screen when Richard came to court. When the case was over, and he failed to convict, it was over. The citizens had spoken.

August 2, 1983, I was so bogged down in the Neelley brief.

I believed the brief would win the case. I lived by the motto that you aren't beaten until you quit. When they have you surrounded, all of them can't get away. Even if they kill you, make it tough for them to eat you. Never quit!

A California TV movie company called wanting to talk about the Neelley story. I told them to send me material about themselves. I never heard from them again.

Celeste was the person I counted on. She was one of the few people God blessed with a truly loving heart. She took a while to get it in gear; but once it was in place, Celeste would perform miracles for you. She was a fantastic woman. I think her attitude lay in the fact she was a first-generation Italian-American. Most Italians I had met trusted no one. Celeste was different. She would trust, but it would take time.

August 4, 1983, I had until 8:00 a.m. Monday morning to have this brief on the Judge's desk. It was almost there.

August 8, 1983, Monday. I had just returned from speaking with Judge Cole. He gave me until Friday to file the brief.

TOUGH FINANCIAL TIMES

Within days after the bank president had promised to give me a year to buy time if I would second mortgage my home, I picked up the paper and the bank was foreclosing. There was nothing I could do, other than file for bankruptcy protection under Chapter 11 of the Bankruptcy Act.

I owed about $565,000 on several million dollars in assets. I planned to drive to bankruptcy court in my Porsche, and I was not selling one inch of real estate.

I had thought that when I had practiced in his court the Bankruptcy Judge liked me. I had forgotten that he was appointed as a Democrat. The judge had no sympathy for me whatsoever. For example, he would give me 30 days to come up with $55,000 or he was going to sell my office building. I came up with it.

Then he did it again. After 31 months, I had paid my debts down to $219,000 and had kept all my hard assets.

Edgar's son, David, loaned me the money to get out of bankruptcy. I made two payments on the debt and conveyed my interest in Allen Switch, a 13- acre double switch 56-car industrial rail siding, to him for the balance. The property I deeded to him was worth more than twice what I used to clear myself of debt.

Now I was out of the merciless clutches of that little judge. I felt like I was once more agile, mobile, and hostile. I still had my assets, and I didn't owe a dime. I had paid everyone in full. I even paid a $65,000 debt to the bank that I didn't owe.

Now I just needed to go to a doctor and find out what was wrong with me.

FIRST JURY TRIAL AFTER NEELLEY

August 31, 1983, I had finished the brief. Now I had a jury trial facing me. Judith Ann Neelley passed her GED and was now a high school graduate! Mrs. Lobmiller had given her a mirror, a Bible, a robe, and an address book.

At 9:00 a.m., I began qualifying jurors as to their knowledge about my relationship with Judith Ann Neelley. Here is the way some of the *voir dire* examination was conducted:

"I was recently involved in a controversial trial here defending Judith Ann Neelley. Have any of you heard of that case? How many of you have heard about my defense of the case? How many of you have heard rumors, such as I am in love with Judith Ann Neelley and leaving my wife and family for Judy Neelley?"

Upon completion of each question, every member of the array raised their hand. There were giggles and smiles all over the courtroom. Steve had told me that I could not win a case again because of the Neelley case. I was determined to see what effect that mess had had on my future.

I explained to the jurors that I had been married to my wife, Celeste, for 28 years. And I really thought it was a put-down to say that the only woman I could find would be a jailbird on death row. Admitting I was out of practice, I did believe I could find some woman off the street who might be willing to involve herself in a relationship with me under proper conditions. Everyone was laughing. One male voice in the back, whom I could not identify, said, "I heard you could do more than that."

I told them that they could believe whatever they wished to believe. They could tell whatever they wanted to tell. "Let's hear what you have heard about me. Let's talk about it now before this trial begins."

The judge was letting me run a little, and the jury was eating it up. They were telling about how they heard I made love to her on the floor of the Sheriff's office; that I had promised to marry her as soon as I got her out of jail; that I was the father of her son who was born three months after she was arrested; and it went on and on. Finally, the jury realized how absolutely silly the entire matter was and began to laugh at the ridiculous rumors they had believed before coming to court.

I returned to my prepared questions:

> "12. Do any members of this venire feel that I should be punished for defending Judith Ann Neelley?"

Not one hand was raised.

> "13. Would any of you hold my defending Judith Ann Neelley against my client here, the defendant, Tom Crosley?"

All of the jurors said they would not. It was fun. I guess this was the beginning of the end of the lies and BS being told about me throughout the area.

I received a real ego boost as I was leaving the courthouse for lunch. The wife of the plaintiff was walking out with me. As we went down the steps she said, "You're good. You were really good, did you know that?"

I did my best foot shuffling bashful act, and said, "Naw."

Clyde Traylor, my former partner and law school classmate, who was on the other side said, "Donnie, you're with the wrong lawyer."

She caught herself and said, "Yeah, I didn't even realize it." Everyone laughed.

I thought it was cute, particularly since I had just cross-examined her and totally destroyed her without her ever knowing it.

A thousand times I have wondered why the Lord put me on a collision course with Judith Ann Neelley. I found it most exciting to watch the Father working this case into my life. Truly, God is so beautiful. We just have to place ourselves in His hands and watch Him take the ball and run with it.

The Court gave my case to the jury at 3:11 p.m. I needed to win that case to prove to the county that I was still a winner.

While the jury was out everyone was talking about the Russians shooting down the South Korean jumbo jet airliner.

4:59 p.m., the jury came back. We won! We won! I had won my first jury trial in DeKalb County since the Neelley case. I was happy.

Mrs. Appleton, the Jury Forewoman, told me that it was 11 to 1 when they went out. It took them almost two hours to convince one lone holdout to go with the others.

It was a sad construction case. To make it worse, Charles McGee had pulled one of his cutie-pie tricks. He manipulated his construction case, similar to mine, ahead of me. He had my early jury. He was able to persuade another lawyer to continue a case and give him the slot. His jury came in with a verdict of $50,000 against the defendant seller. I was representing a seller. I had to pull mine out of the hat, but it worked.

BACK INTO THE GRIND

Edgar was waiting when I got back to the office. We talked, and I drew up some quotes for Nigerian Oil.

September 2, 1983, Friday, Richard filed his brief, and I was anxious to look at it. Now that my brief was gone, I had to turn my attention to a U.S. Supreme Court brief that was driving me crazy.

I received notice that my Mobile 7 tons of pot case had been put off again.

September 6, 1983, the day after Labor Day. I rested so much that I was tired of resting. That day, the Court entered its order denying our Motion for New Trial. I am going to put a complete verbatim copy of it as **Appendix 6**.

I doubted he would really do it, but he did. Now his mistakes in judgment will be flashed around the world, and published in law books for all to see.

The Alabama Court of Criminal Appeals will back him up. The Alabama Supreme Court will back him up because they are the most political body in this state.

The U.S. Supreme Court will refuse to look at it until all of the state remedies are exhausted. So, the case will travel up and down several times before a conclusion.

The oil deal did not go through, the motel-restaurant was not bought, Arlene Crane would not take the $500,000, we resigned from her case, Eddie had been arrested, and would soon go to prison, Judge Cole denied the new trial, and I was broke. Just another beautiful day in paradise.

HOME AGAIN – WOW!

September 10, 1983, Saturday, 3:50 p.m. I was sitting at my breakfast room table on Lookout Mountain thinking that they had won the battle, but they would never win the war.

TNT were with a friend named Adam. They had gone down the street to Castle Rocks. These were huge stones grouped together in a formation which were probably 30 to 40 feet high. From a distance they looked like a giant castle; hence, the name of the subdivision where I live - Castle Rock Heights.

We called one of the rocks "Dinosaur Rock" because it looked like the sihouette of a Tyrannosaurus Rex. The kids had ridden their bicycles down there to look for treasure. Now and then some redneck came by and dumped his trash near the rocks. The kids found all kinds of great things in the junk - broken kitchen utensils, empty bottles, old tin cans - you name it. They did find one very old round Prince Albert tobacco can. I still use it to hold pens. One man's trash is another man's treasure.

Bulger, our pit bull, went with them to be sure everything was all right. Believe me, if it weren't all right, Bulger would see that it became that way in a hurry. That dog was tough, and he had a bad attitude.

As usual, Tammy was the first one to climb to the top of the rocks. The boys could not make it. They could make it to split rock, where one had to jump about four feet from one rock to another about 30 feet above the ground, and they did not quite have the determination to make the jump.

In desperation, Tommy came back to the house to see if I would come help him and Adam over the gap at Dinosaur Rock. I arrived in time to see Tammy preening herself as though she were alone in the world and had just climbed Mount Everest.

After all the "Hi, Daddy's!" from 200 feet away, and the waving, she settled back down to her play-like makeup and mirror.

I must admit it took a little courage to climb up the rocks, and jump that gap 30 feet above the blackness caused by the proximity of other rocks. However, I was never accused of being a sissy so up I went and pulled each boy over.

They oohed and aahed about the view, and how far they could see. They crawled around on the top of the rock and generally explored the area. Tommy spotted an old egg basket down in the garbage dump a short way from the rocks. He asked me to let him down; he wanted to get that basket.

I took a firm grip on his arm and let him jump the gap. Then, I allowed Adam to make the same move. Tammy said she would jump by herself. So with a lump in my throat I watched those skinny girlish legs run across the rock and jump the abyss. I made sure I had a firm grip on her when she landed on the second rock. I could just hear her mother on the way to the hospital if I had missed.

Adam and Tommy rescued the basket and took it home. It was an old hen house egg basket which had seen better days, but it was still in pretty good shape. Being the composite decorator, Celeste immediately saw a use for the antique basket in the house. She talked them out of their treasure. Tammy and Adam wanted to keep it for the three of them, but Tommy wanted his mother to have it. It's still in the hunt room holding out-of-date magazines and umbrellas.

Having had just about all the excitement I could stand, it was time to listen to the Tide demolish Georgia Tech in the 1983 game in Birmingham.

I couldn't help thinking that Judge Cole copped deuces on the Motion for New Trial. He must know he made error. He knew what McGee and O'Dell did, Hargis lied, and he knew Bill Burns erred in Rutherford County by denying Bill Burton the right to see his client.

I believed that if I had pulled the Charles McGee - Mike O'Dell trick, Cole would have moved my disbarment. I wondered how he would have defended Neelley .

I was saddened, but I was not disappointed – I smelled the faint odor of politics.

I was still struggling financially. The IRS had descended on the firm with an audit because our income had dropped over 80 percent triggering an audit. The agent came in and set up shop in my library. He stayed there three years. If you think the IRS going through your books for 3 years and are not going to find something, you are dreaming. This agent determined that I owed $28,000 due to mistakes in our books. It was mostly penalties and interest. However, if I didn't pay right away, they would begin seizing things, including my bank accounts.

It was time to sell the farm. I had lost all interest in the beautiful little place due to what happened in the Neelley case. I sold it to Randy Owen, the lead singer with the Alabama Band, for $44,000. A sad day indeed

CHAPTER SIXTEEN

THE YEARS ROLL ON

———◆———

The tide of time and events changes everything.

You have to have this flash back to get to the end of the story. The year was 1978, five years before I met Judith Ann Neelley. I was working away in my office when my secretary said that a Mr. Fob James was in the waiting room wishing to see me.

I was delighted to see him, and we renewed old times. I asked about Bobbie, and she had sent her regards. After preliminary pleasantry, he got down to business.

"I am going to run for Governor. I can't get elected as a Republican, and I am going to run as a Democrat. I need someone up here in the Northeast Alabama area to manage my campaign. I know that you can't do it, but do you have any idea who I might get?"

"My accountant, 'Buck' Borders, often talks about you. He says that you and he went to Auburn at the same time and he sounds as though you were fast friends. He brags that you were an All-American halfback. I think he would make a perfect representative for you up here. He is apolitical, part of the power structure, and a hard worker."

James liked the selection, and I pointed him toward Borders' office. "Go over there and greet him like a long lost buddy, and I think you'll have your local man."

Borders accepted and did a great job. Fob James was elected and was one of our better governors. Borders went on to manage the CMA winning Alabama Band.

Some 20 years later, Former Governor Fob James appeared in my waiting room once more. This time he was going to run for Governor as a Republican.

We visited, talked politics, families, and such. Then he digressed. "Tell me about that woman you represented. What's her name? Neelley? Bobbie has her in her prayer circle and is interested in her problems."

I had not heard from Judith Ann Neelley in at least six years. As with all capital cases, once the case was lost, the lawyer who originally represented the defendant is put on trial for the way he handled the case. Barry Ragsdale, a Birmingham lawyer, whom I had known several years, was appointed to represent Neelley. Rather than testing my competence, ineptitude, or other issues that I had preserved, he did little more than insult me in public.

I wanted Ragsdale to be successful but I could not understand why he never attacked Steve Bussman. Instead it was my love affair with Judith Neelley that intrigued him. He was wasting time with that one; however, that may have been all he could find. He should have tracked the numerous errors we preserved.

Now I had to respond to my old friend, the former governor, and the Future Governor. I thought about it for a moment, and then gave him an overview of the case. I hit pretty hard on the battered woman syndrome and the unspeakable cruelty of Alvin. I gave him a strong sales pitch on Judith Ann Neelley's behalf. I told him how hard we had worked on the case and praised Judy's attitude and Christianity. We talked about her for more than 30 minutes.

He was re-elected, and "Buck" was appointed to the board of the Tennessee-Tombigbee Waterway Authority. That was a political plum widely coveted. "Buck" had received his reward. He never knew that I had had a hand in it.

A year or so later, Fob's son, Tim, came by the office and casually mentioned that his mother, my old classmate and friend, had expressed an interest in the plight of Judith Ann Neelley. I had always known Bobbie to be a super Christian so I didn't think it out of the ordinary that she would take an interest in the beaten, battered, and damned life of Judith Ann Neelley.

Time passed, and there was never a week went by that someone didn't bring up Judith Ann Neelley. It got to where I would respond to inquiries and comments with, "So this week is your week to mention Judith Ann Neelley."

My life had gone back to as normal as possible. I had lost my darling Celeste to a brain tumor. My three children were successful. I had retired from teaching my Sunday School Class after 36 years, and I had begun composing my books on the four Gospels, and other works.

In 1998, Lowell Barron, a long time State Senator, ran against Judith Ann Neelley rather than mentioning his Republican opponent. To a degree, he was running against me because of my GOP background and my association with Neelley. So the Democrat rumor mill cranked up once more.

Then surprise, surprise! During his last hour in office before leaving for a hunting trip in Canada, Governor Fob James commuted the death sentence of Judith Ann Neelley!

He said that he had thought long and hard about the Neelley situation. He had studied a lot of documents; and, without going into detail, he felt the jury's verdict was appropriate and Neelley did not deserve to die at the hands of the trial judge.

The press somehow found out that I knew the governor's wife. The media immediately descended upon me and accused me of engineering the commutation of sentence. I could honestly say that I had never mentioned the name of Judith Ann Neelley to Bobbie Mae James. In fact, I had not spoken to Mrs. James since the senior class play in 1952.

I believe it was 2002. State Senator Barron immediately passed an *ex post facto* law barring Neelley from ever being released from Alabama Prison. Ragsdale attacked this Act and will no doubt be successful. It was a politically motivated stunt that was wholly unconstitutional. I think that Senator Barron, who was a member of my golfing foursome for several years, knew the "Judy Neelley Act" was illegal when it was passed. She was simply someone the entire Democrat Legislature of Alabama could pounce on with glee. As they chortled around the capitol patting themselves on the back, I thought, "Alvin Neelley in sear sucker suits." Although I thoroughly enjoyed the company of Senator Barron and our golf outings, we never mentioned Judith Ann Neelley.

Whether Judith Ann Neelley will ever see life outside prison is another matter. She has been in confinement, living in a structured environment, almost all of her life. I didn't know whether she can make it on the outside; however, I am sure Barry Ragsdale is going to try to make that happen.

When it was all said and done, I won the case! I had to have help from that cute little red-headed girl from the 4th grade. But then, what are friends for? I won the blooming case! Furthermore, Alabama was finally completely Republican.

CHAPTER SEVENTEEN

TO KILL A MOCKINGBIRD

———◆———

The year was 2014. I was standing across the street from the courthouse in Monroeville, Alabama. I was attending the annual Alabama Writers Symposium. The old courthouse was made famous by Harper Lee's book and Gregory Peck's performance as Atticus Finch. His defense of Tom Robinson, a black man accused of raping a white woman, caused Finch serious problems in Maycomb, which was fictitious Monroeville in Monroe County.

I was in the company of a very good friend of mine, the widow of a judge from Chattanooga. We had been enjoying the meetings and activities of the symposium. We were on a break at the time.

Monroeville was alive with Harper Lee and her work, *To Kill A Mockingbird*. There were numerous mentions of Ms. Lee and the book at the symposium.

As we looked at the famous white courthouse clock tower, my friend said, "Now, tell me again what you went through with that Neelley case."

"I was forced to take that horrible case at my own expense. I spent over $320,000 defending it out of my funds on hand and funds I could borrow. I used my liquidity - 401(k) and retirement. I was forced into Chapter 11 Bankruptcy for 31 months. I divested myself of Allen Switch. I had to sell my farm. My reputation was ruined. My family suffered greatly. I developed Graves' Disease due to stress which left me with atrial fibrillation that took my pilot's license. I sold my three airplanes. My law firm was decimated. I received death threats on a daily basis. My car was stolen and run into the ground. My office was picketed. My home was rocked. My old clients left me. My income dropped to one-tenth of what it was when I met Mrs. Neelley. As a consequence of that red flag, the IRS began a three-year audit of my firm that resulted in my owing the government $28,000. My law firm never recovered. And my name is forever associated with perhaps the most horrible case in Alabama history and a woman I never wanted to meet. That's most of it."

She looked away from studying the clock tower and looked directly at me. "You are the real life Atticus Finch."

"No, the last names – French and Finch - just sound alike. Atticus Finch was a Democrat."

APPENDIX 1

Court's Ruling on Defense Motion to Suppress Confession of Judith Ann Neelley:

When court re-convened, the following findings were announced by the Court:

The defendant was properly advised of her Constitutional rights as enumerated in Miranda. The defendant made a voluntary and understanding waiver of those rights.

The defendant made a knowing and voluntary waiver of her right to have counsel present during the interview.

Defendant was advised on numerous occasions during her interview of her rights and that the interview could be terminated upon her request, and she voluntarily elected to continue the interview.

The defendant's statement was a product of rational intellect and a free will.

> Attorney Bill Burton did not represent defendant in connection with the criminal offense being investigated by Burns and other officers conducting the interview, and defendant did not request to have an attorney present. The refusal to admit attorney was not an interference with the attorney-client relationship.

Mr. Burton was representing her in regard to charges pending in Murfreesboro, Tennessee.

As to the statement taken on October 15, 1982, by Investigator Smith in Fort Payne, the Court found the following:

> Defendant was properly advised of her Constitutional rights as enumerated in Miranda. Defendant made a voluntary and understanding waiver of those rights.

> The remark made by Smith that the information would be relayed to the Judge for consideration in setting bail did not constitute a promise or inducement for the defendant to make the statement.

> The remark by Smith about "maybe working out something" whereby defendant could see her husband was inconclusive and did not constitute a promise or inducement for the defendant making the statement. Defendant's statement was a product of a rational intellect and a free will.

> Recognizing that a confession is presumed to be involuntary, the Court, however, finds that there is sufficient evidence to rebut that presumption as to each confession, and the motion to suppress is denied. The state may offer the statements as evidence for the jury to consider, with the exception of any matter relating to the offense charged in Murfreesboro, Tennessee.

APPENDIX 2

Defense motion to excuse Juror Hargis:

1. She has not listened to the evidence since the opening statements.

2. During the first week of trial, she smiled and looked at the Defense. Defense observed her looking at the audience and singing while the State put on the most gruesome part of the case.

3. Once the Defense began its case, she constantly looked at the State and tried to smile and give them various and sundry glances and non-verbal communications. The State has not rejoined in these things, just as the Defense did not during the first week.

4. During the questioning of the psychiatrist, she looked at the State, where she could be observed by anyone, and told them to make an objection. She did that on more than one occasion. On the last occasion, she was blatant in mouthing, "Object, object," and looked directly at the State's table.

5. She glared at defense counsel when he looked at her after her mouthing "object" to the State and she glared at Counsel for 20 to 30 seconds.

6. This juror has not participated in the trial in the spirit in which a juror should participate. Based on its research into her family, Defense was convinced the juror would take a minority position in the jury room, no matter which side was favored by the majority.

7. The Defense was firmly convinced that she would attempt to manipulate the jury from her minority position. She would cause a hung jury from her minority position.

APPENDIX 3

Sentencing order that is conclusive as to the Court's rationale:

SENTENCING ORDER

The defendant was charged by indictment with the murder of Lisa Ann Millican during a kidnapping in the first degree, a capital offense. A jury returned a verdict on March 22, 1983, finding the defendant guilty of the capital offense, whereupon, the court adjudged the defendant guilty in accordance with the jury's verdict.

Following the adjudication of guilt, a separate sentence hearing was conducted before the same jury, and the jury returned a recommendation that the defendant be sentenced to life without parole.

The court has ordered and received a written pre-sentence investigation report and has conducted an additional sentence hearing pursuant to Section 13A-5-47, Code of Alabama (Recomp. 1975). At the sentence hearing, the state, through its district attorney, urged that the court fix the defendant's punishment at death. The defendant, through her counsel, argued that the court should fix her punishment, in accordance with the jury's recommendation, at life in prison without parole.

FINDING OF FACTS SUMMARIZING THE CRIME AND THE DEFENDANT'S PARTICIPATION IN IT

The body of Lisa Ann Millican, age 13, was found in a gorge known as Little River Canyon near Fort Payne on September 29, 1982. Lisa was a resident of the Ethel Harpst Home, a Methodist home for neglected children located in Cedartown, Georgia.

Lisa and five other girls from the home were taken by a house parent on an outing to Riverbend Mall in Rome, Georgia, on September 25, 1982. While at the mall, Lisa became separated from the others. During this separation, she was abducted by the defendant, who asked Lisa to go "riding around." Lisa hesitated at first, but then agreed. The events which followed the abduction led to the death of Lisa when the defendant shot her in the back on September 28, 1982, and threw her body into the canyon.

The abduction of Lisa Ann Millican was part of a bizarre scheme whereby the defendant attempted to lure girls and young women into the car with her for ultimate purpose of making them available to her husband, Alvin Neelley, for sex with him. For several days immediately prior to Lisa's abduction, the defendant and Alvin drove up and down Rome streets in separate automobiles looking for girls who would be suitable. When Alvin would see one who appealed to him, he would communicate with the defendant by CB radio, and the defendant would invite the girl to go riding around with her.

Numerous girls refused the defendant's invitation; her first successful pick-up was Lisa Ann Millican.

The defendant took Lisa to a motel in Franklin, Georgia, where she tried to persuade Lisa to submit to sex with Alvin, but Lisa resisted. Finally, Alvin told Lisa that if she did not submit to sex, the defendant would kill her. Following this threat, Alvin engaged in sex with Lisa, and later that night, Lisa was hand-cuffed to the bed to prevent her escape. The next day, the defendant and Alvin, traveling in two cars, took Lisa with them to Cleveland, Tennessee, where they picked up their two-year-old twins who were being cared for by Alvin's mother. Later that day, they traveled to Scottsboro, Alabama, where they rented a motel room. Shortly after their arrival at the motel, the defendant hit Lisa in the head several times with a slap jack in an attempt to render her unconscious, but she was unsuccessful in achieving that result. Alvin then had sex with Lisa, and afterward Lisa slept overnight on the floor, unclothed, and hand-cuffed to the bed.

The following day, Alvin had sex with Lisa twice more despite her cries and pleas that he stop. The defendant was present during these sexual encounters and at one point during the day, she handcuffed Lisa to the plumbing in the bathroom and interrogated her about a man she had appeared to know at a dairy bar near the motel.

The next morning, Lisa was taken to Little River Canyon by the defendant where the defendant instructed Lisa to lie face down and place her hands around a tree. The defendant then handcuffed Lisa's hands. She explained to Lisa that she was going to give her a shot that would make her fall asleep and that when she waked up, Lisa would be free to go. Using a needle and syringe, the defendant injected Lisa in the neck with liquid drain cleaner. When Lisa did not die in five minutes, the defendant injected her again in the neck. She injected Lisa four additional times, twice in the arms and twice in the buttocks, waiting about five minutes after each injection for Lisa to die. Twice during the infliction of these injections, Lisa requested to get up and "use the bathroom" in the woods. She was allowed to do so, and each time she returned and resumed her position on the ground with her hands around the tree.

Following the last injection, the defendant instructed Lisa to walk around for awhile to hasten the work of the poison in her body. When it finally appeared that Lisa was not going to die from the drain cleaner, the defendant marched Lisa to the rim of the canyon to shoot her in the back in a manner that would cause her body to fall into the canyon. Lisa begged to go back to the Harpst Home and promised not to tell what had happened. The defendant told Lisa to be quiet and then shot her in the back. Lisa fell backward toward the defendant instead of falling into the canyon. The defendant picked up the body and, using her knee, propelled it into the canyon.

During the defendant's trial testimony, she testified that Alvin was present at the canyon directing her every action. However, in an out-of-court statement made shortly after arrest, the defendant stated that Alvin was not present at the canyon.

Five days after the death of Lisa Ann Millican, the defendant picked up a young woman named

Janice Chapman and her common law husband, John Hancock, from a street in Rome. Later that night, the defendant shot John Hancock in the back and left him for dead. He survived, however, and was present at the trial to testify to the incident.

The defendant and Alvin took Janice Chapman to a motel in Rome where Alvin engaged in sex with Janice. The next day, the defendant killed Janice Chapman, shooting her once in the back and twice in the chest. During the defendant's trial testimony, she testified that Alvin was present during the shooting of John Hancock and Janice Chapman and that he directed her to shoot them; however, in her out-of-court statement given shortly after her arrest, she stated that Alvin was present when she shot John Hancock but that he was not present when she killed Janice Chapman.

On October 9, 1982, the day before the defendant's arrest, she picked up another young woman in Nashville, Tennessee, who was present with the defendant and Alvin in a motel room in Murfreesboro, Tennessee, on October 10, 1982, when the defendant was arrested on a bad check charge. Later, this woman was released by Alvin unharmed.

Alvin was arrested in Murfreesboro on October 13, 1982, also on a bad check charge. While the defendant and Alvin were in custody on the bad check charges, additional charges were placed against them arising from the murders of Lisa Ann Millican and Janice Chapman, and the shooting of John Hancock.

Robert B. French, Jr.

FINDINGS CONCERNING THE EXISTENCE OR NON-EXISTENCE OF AGGRAVATING CIRCUMSTANCES

In compliance with the requirements of the law that the trial court shall enter specific findings concerning the existence or non-existence of each aggravating circumstance enumerated by statute, the court finds that none of the aggravating circumstances enumerated by statute were proved beyond a reasonable doubt in the proceedings before this court except the following, which the court finds were proved beyond a reasonable doubt:

The capital offense was committed while the defendant was engaged in kidnaping. The jury's verdict establishes the existence of this aggravating circumstance, and the verdict is supported by the evidence.

The capital offense was especially heinous, atrocious and cruel compared to other capital offenses. The court reaches the conclusion that this aggravating circumstance exists based upon uncontroverted evidence of the following:

a. The victim of the crime was a child, age 13.

b. Repeatedly, the child was abused and violated sexually causing her enormous fright and pain. While the evidence is insufficient to establish that the defendant participated in sex acts upon the child, she was an accomplice to the sexual abuse perpetrated upon the child by Alvin Neelley.

c. The defendant inflicted pain and suffering upon the child by hitting her on the head

with a slap jack in an attempt to knock
her unconscious.

d. The defendant physically restrained the
child much of the time following her abduction by the use of handcuffs.

e. The defendant made the child lie on the
ground with her hands handcuffed around
a tree while the defendant injected her six
times with liquid drain cleaner.

f. The defendant marched the child to the rim
of the deep canyon, with the child begging
to be released, where the defendant shot her
in the back.

By any standard acceptable to civilized society, this crime was
extremely wicked and shockingly evil. It was perpetrated with a
design to inflict a high degree of pain with utter indifference to the
suffering of the victim. The court recognizes that all capital offenses
are heinous, atrocious and cruel to some extent, but the degree to
heinousness, atrociousness, and cruelty which characterizes this
offense exceeds that which is common to all capital offenses.

FINDINGS CONCERNING THE EXISTENCE OR NON-
EXISTENCE OF MITIGATING CIRCUMSTANCES

In compliance with the statutory requirement
that the trial court enter specific findings concerning the existence or non-existence of each mitigating
circumstance enumerated by statute, the court finds
that none of the following mitigating circumstances
exist in this case:

1. That the defendant has no significant history
of prior criminal activity. The defendant testified to

a significant history of criminal conduct. When she was 16 years of age, she robbed a woman of her purse at gunpoint. As a result of this offense, she was committed to the Georgia Youth Development Center, and her husband, Alvin, who was an accomplice to the robbery, was sentenced to a term in the Georgia State Penitentiary.

The defendant was released from the Georgia Youth Development Center in December, 1981 and Alvin was released from the penitentiary several months later. The defendant testified that upon Alvin's release, he was obsessed with the notion that she had been sexually abused by employees at the Youth Development Centers in Rome and Macon. To avenge the alleged wrong, Alvin and the defendant set out to kill or terrorize employees of the YDC. Pursuant to this objective, they shot into the house of one employee and attempted to fire bomb the automobile of another in Rome. In Macon, the defendant attempted to lure YDC employees to a motel room where Alvin was prepared to kill them. The defendant was unsuccessful in luring any employees to the motel, and none were harmed.

Additional criminal activity by the defendant, according to her own testimony, includes writing bad checks, raising the amounts on money orders, stealing checks from post office boxes and cashing them with false identification, and stealing from convenience stores where Alvin was employed.

2. That the capital offense was committed while the defendant was under the influence of extreme mental or emotional disturbance. When the defendant was arraigned on December 17, 1982, her

counsel requested that the defendant be committed to Bryce Hospital for psychiatric examination and evaluation. The court granted the request, and the defendant thereafter underwent psychiatric examination and evaluation at Bryce Hospital. Dr. Alexander Salillas, a staff psychiatrist at Taylor Hardin Secure Medical Facility and a consultant at Bryce, testified that as a result of his examination of the defendant, he found no mental disease or defect and that, in his opinion, she knew right from wrong at the time of the offense and that she acted with deliberation and premeditation.

While the court recognizes that this mitigating circumstance contemplates a disturbance of the mind which might exist separate and apart from a mental disease or defect, and that the testimony of the psychiatrist is, by no means, conclusive, the court finds from a consideration of all the evidence that the defendant was not under the influence of extreme mental or emotional disturbance.

3. That the victim was a participant in the defendant's conduct or consented to it. There is no support for this mitigating circumstance. Although Lisa Ann Millican initially agreed to go with the defendant when the defendant picked her up at the mall in Rome, the fact that Lisa was less than 16 years old and that the Harpst Home, which had legal custody of her, had not acquiesced to her being taken by the defendant, makes any consent given by Lisa legally ineffectual. Any consent given by the child to the acts of violence and abuse committed upon her was the result of threats or false promises and provides no support for this mitigating circumstance.

4. That the defendant was an accomplice in the capital offense committed bv another person and her participation was relatively minor. The evidence is uncontroverted that the defendant abducted Lisa Ann Millican, that the defendant injected her six times with liquid drain cleaners, and that the defendant shot her in the back and threw her body into the canyon. Although there is evidence that the defendant's husband, Alvin, was also involved in this criminal conduct, there is no support for a finding that the defendant's participation was relatively minor.

5. That the defendant acted under extreme duress or under the substantial influence of another person. The defendant's primary contention throughout the trial and the sentence hearings was that she had become completely submissive to the will of her husband, Alvin, and that he exercised total control over her. Perhaps the strongest support for this contention is found in the following:

a. testimony by Alvin's former wife that Alvin dominated their relationship and imposed his will upon her;

b. evidence including pictures of the defendant's bruised body, that Alvin beat the defendant frequently;

c. letters written by Alvin while he was incarcerated in the penitentiary which portray him as a vile and dominant husband; and

d. the fact that the defendant had no record of criminal activity prior to her association with Alvin Neelley.

The evidence cited above, together with the defendant's testimony, convinces the court that the defendant was substantially influenced by her husband, but the court concludes that the husband's influence did not constitute extreme duress or substantial domination.

The defendant is an intelligent person capable of making independent choices. The evidence is substantial that she made a willing choice to follow her husband's influence rather than to depart from it. There were numerous opportunities for the defendant to break with her husband and seek help had she felt the need or been so inclined. These opportunities were enhanced by the fact that the defendant was armed and traveling in a separate vehicle during most of their exploits. Ultimately, the defendant chose, rather than to make the break or turn on her husband, to brutally murder Lisa Ann Millican.

The court finds that the defendant was not brainwashed and that she retained her will and her capacity to make independent choices.

<u>6. That the capacity of the defendant to appreciate the criminality of her conduct or to conform her conduct to the requirements of law was substantially impaired</u>. The defendant entered a plea of not guilty by reason of mental disease or defect. With regard to this defense, the court instructed the jury that a person is not responsible for criminal conduct if at the time of such conduct, as a result of mental disease or defect, such person lacks substantial capacity to appreciate the criminality of his conduct or to conform his conduct to the requirements of law. By its verdict of guilt, the jury found the evidence

insufficient to support the plea of insanity, and the jury's finding is supported by the evidence. While the court recognizes that this mitigating circumstance contemplates impaired capacity which might exist separate and apart from a mental disease or defect, the court finds from a consideration of Dr. Salillas' testimony and the evidence as a whole that this mitigating circumstance does not exist.

The court finds that the following mitigating circumstance enumerated by statute does exist in this case:

1. The age of the defendant at the time of the crime. The defendant was 18 years of age at the time she committed the capital offense of which she is convicted. While the court finds the defendant's age to be a mitigating circumstance, the court considers the weight to be given this circumstance lessened by the fact that the defendant, since a much earlier age, had adopted the lifestyle of an adult. She commenced a marital relationship with Alvin Neelley when she was age 15, and gave birth to twins when she was age 16. The criminal activity in which the defendant engaged was less akin to the behavior of a teenager and more akin to the conduct of a seasoned criminal.

The court finds two additional mitigating circumstances not enumerated by the statute:

The defendant was substantially influenced by her husband. Although the court has heretofore found that the husband's influence did not constitute extreme duress or substantial domination, it seems appropriate that such influence should be given weight as a mitigating circumstance.

The defendant voluntarily and intentionally set in motion the events which led to her arrest and the arrest of her husband, thus ending the reign of terror which they had perpetrated throughout three states. The defendant did this while at her mother's house in Murfreesboro by instructing her mother to notify the police that she was in the area and could be arrested on bad check charges pending against her. In the defendant's testimony, she could not explain what prompted her to give her mother these instructions, but it is fair to infer that conscience had a hand in it.

CONCLUSION

The court has carefully weighed the aggravating and mitigating circumstances which it finds to exist in this case, and has given consideration to the recommendation of the jury contained in its advisory verdict. While the mitigating circumstances and the jury's recommendation of life without parole have weighed heavy in the court's consideration, it is the judgment of this court that they are outweighed by the aggravating circumstances of this horrible crime.

Accordingly, IT IS ORDERED, ADJUDGED, AND DECREED that the defendant shall be punished by death.

A formal sentencing entry shall be made by separate order.

Dated April 18, 1983, and signed by Randall L. Cole, Circuit Judge.

Robert B. French, Jr.

SENTENCE ORDER

This day came the State by its district attorney and also the defendant in her own proper person and by her attorneys, Honorable Robert B. French, Jr. and Honorable Stephen P. Bussman, and the defendant having heretofore been duly convicted in this court of murder during a kidnapping in the first degree, a capital offense, and the defendant being asked by the court if she had anything to say why the sentence of the law should not now be pronounced upon her, says nothing in bar or preclusion of sentence.

It is the judgment of the court that the defendant, Judith Ann Nelley, shall be punished by a sentence of death.

Accordingly, IT IS ADJUDGED by the court that the Sheriff of DeKalb County, Alabama, shall remove the defendant to the Julia Tutwiler unit of the prison system of this state from which the defendant shall thereafter be removed to the William C. Holman unit of the prison system at Atmore, Alabama, and on May 25, 1983, in strict accordance with law the warden of Holman unit shall put the defendant to death by causing to pass through the body of the defendant a current of electricity of sufficient intensity to cause the death of Judith Ann Neelley, and that the application and continuance of such current through the body of such defendant shall continue until such defendant is dead.

IT IS FURTHER ORDERED by the court that the clerk of this court shall issue the necessary warrant for the execution of the defendant as required by law.

The judgment of conviction being subject to automatic review by the Alabama Court of Criminal Appeals, IT IS ADJUDGED that the sentence in this cause be and the same is suspended pending such appeal.

Dated April 18, 1983,
Randall L. Cole, Circuit Judge.

APPENDIX 4

Defendant's Motion for New Trial

Motion for New Trial

Comes now the defendant, Judith Ann Neelley, by her attorneys, and moves the court for a new trial and as grounds for this motion, cites the following:

1. The alleged confession of the defendant, introduced at the trial over defendant's objection, was legally inadmissible. It is uncontroverted that while law enforcement personnel from Alabama, Georgia, and the Federal Bureau of Investigation were interrogating defendant and extracting the alleged confession, defendant's attorney was in the hallway of the Rutherford County Jail, in Murfreesboro, Tennessee, just outside the door of the interrogation room attempting to see his client, the defendant. Danny Smith, the chief prosecuting witness for the State of Alabama, and Investigator for the district attorney's Office admitted barring the path of defendant's attorney and advising him that he could not see his client unless she asked to see him. The defendant's attorney of record in Rutherford County, Tennessee, advised Investigator Smith that he was there to see his client, the defendant, and the denial of access to his client by law enforcement personnel was a denial of her constitutional rights and endangered any case the law enforcement officers intended to bring against the defendant. FBI Agent, Bill O. Burns, called an Assistant U.S. Attorney to determine whether the defendant's attorney should

be allowed into the room where the defendant was being interrogated. Apparently, he was advised that unless the defendant specifically requested an attorney the interrogation should continue. Defendant was asked on several occasions whether she wished to have an attorney. She replied in the negative according to the FBI typed confession. Defendant states that she wanted to talk with her attorney. This testimony is borne out by the FBI report wherein she is alleged to have stated:

". . . that she did not want to talk about traveling through those states to pass money orders or checks without her attorney present. She states that Bill Burton was her attorney and that the reason she did not want to discuss this issue was because some people would think that a person who traveled around without having a steady job was not a good person.

She did state that she was willing to talk about any other matter. She was told, at that time, that if she wanted to terminate the interview, that she could, and that she could return to her cell without further questioning. She insisted that she did not want to leave the interview, and she wanted to continue talking at that time."

According to testimony at the trial, this interview took place on October 14, 1982, at approximately 10:55 p.m. The attorney, Bill Burton, was present at the jail for the express purpose of protecting the defendant. He had been the family attorney for a number of years, having represented the defendant's mother, her sister, her uncle, her husband, and the defendant herself. Mr. Burton was the attorney of record for the defendant in Rutherford County, Tennessee. He has represented her in court in Rutherford County a few days before she was being interrogated for the extraction of the alleged confessions introduced by the state.

It would have been a simple matter for the FBI, or one of the other officers, to advise the defendant her attorney, Bill Burton, was in the hallway wishing to speak to her. Did she wish to speak to him? This was not done. Defendant was asked on more than one occasion if she desired an attorney. She was never given her full option for counsel by being advised that her attorney was just outside the door asking for her. Her interrogators knew who her attorney was, and they knew that he was present outside the door. Defendant could not make a valid waiver of her right to counsel unless the law enforcement officer informed her of the presence of her attorney.

Bill Burton, attorney for defendant, presented himself at the interrogation site, he had a bona fide right within the ambit and limitations of the Code of Professional Responsibility to hold himself out as the defendant's attorney, and he had a duty to protect his client to the best of his ability under the circumstances. He was physically prohibited from talking with the defendant, his client. He had been retained to come to the jail and protect the defendant by her husband. Thus, Bill Burton, the attorney for the defendant, appeared at the Rutherford County Jail, late at night, for the express purpose of protecting the rights of the defendant. Only after being fully informed of the attorney's presence could the defendant have knowingly and intelligently waived her right to counsel.

2. There was misconduct in this case on the part of the jury and the court committed error in refusing defense motions to excuse the juror, Eileen Hargis, when there were alternate jurors available to replace Juror Hargis. The misconduct of this juror, who later became foreman of the jury, was as follows:

a. The juror did not pay attention during the trial of the issues of this case. This juror constantly looked out into the courtroom audience and mouthed words to members of the audience observing the case. When evidence was passed to her as a member of the jury, she simply glanced at it and passed it on. One morning this juror spent the entire session of court singing silently while gazing out into the audience. It was apparent to the defense that this juror was not involved in the case and this lack of interest was pointed out to the court.

b. Toward the end of this case, this juror glared at the defense counsel on several occasions. She repeatedly smiled at the prosecution,

particularly Danny Smith and Michael O'Dell, while indicating con-
tempt for the defense. This activity was also pointed out to the court
by the defense.

c. During the examination of the state's rebuttal witness by the
defense, this juror mouthed to the prosecution, "Object, object."
This demonstration was witnessed by almost the entire press corps
in attendance at the trial. Subsequent to this activity on the part of
this juror, the defense moved that she be replaced by an alternate.

d. When the jurors went into the jury room to elect a foreman and
begin their deliberations, this juror took upon herself the role as
foreman of the jury. She was not elected to this position. This juror
just simply took the position as foreman of the jury and began to
function as foreman. The other jurors did not oppose her usurpation
of the position as foreman and allowed her to serve during the deliberations, without benefit of an election.

e. At the time, this juror was qualified to take her position on the
jury she was asked about bias and prejudice and interest in the case.
Unknown to the defense, charges were pending against the juror
through the Office of the District Attorney who was prosecuting the
defendant. The state was aware of these pending charges; the juror
was aware of the pending charges for passing worthless checks. The
defense was unaware of these charges and the charges were not disclosed to the defense by the juror nor by the state.

f. The defense asked questions on voir dire designed to elicit from
prospective jurors their bias or interest in this case. This juror was
asked if she could consider all the evidence in the case before making
up her mind as to the guilt or innocence of the defendant; could she
consider only the evidence that came from the witness stand before
reaching a verdict in this case; could the juror assure the defense
that she would not be swayed by anything other than evidence given
to her, under oath, from the witness stand; she was asked if she had
any feelings which might affect her verdict which counsel for defendant did not mention specifically, answers to questions missed by the

defense; things which the juror had not spoken out on; and she was asked if she knew Richard Igou or Michael O'Dell, the prosecutors in this case. If she did know them, how did she know them? She was asked if she would feel uncomfortable if she felt she must bring a verdict for the defense. The juror always came up with answers satisfactory to the defense. She did not disclose her relationship with the Office of the District Attorney. She did not tell the defense she knew the prosecutors; she did not tell the defense she was in trouble with the state of Alabama and was trying to keep from going to jail herself. Certainly, she knew the district attorney as she had been arrested and made bond. She had paid off some cases and had others pending against her.

g. Juror Hargis had a personal interest in the outcome of this case as the charges pending against her were being pressed by the state at the time of this jury selection. She could anticipate that a verdict in favor of the defense would increase the tempo of the prosecution against her. Whereas, a verdict in favor of the state would tend to alleviate the pressure of the charges against her.

3. The court erred in allowing into evidence facts concerning the shooting of John Hancock in Georgia, the murder of Janice Chapman in Georgia, all subsequent to the murder of Lisa Ann Millican. The court allowed this testimony for the purpose of showing habit or motive. This testimony was so devastating to the defense that there was no way to overcome the prejudice and ill will these crimes created in the minds of the jurors. The court required the defense to actually defend three to seven cases rather than the case charged in the indictment. The cumulative effect of the presentation of these other crimes in this case made it impossible for the defendant to receive a fair trial for the murder of Lisa Ann Millican. The other crimes were unrelated to the murder of Lisa Ann Millican other than to show habit. Such a showing of habit was far outweighed by the necessity for the defendant to receive a fair trial in facing the charges of murdering Lisa Ann Millican.

4. The court erred in allowing the state to introduce evidence illegally seized from the home of the mother of the defendant in Murfreesboro, Tennessee, and from the office of the attorney for the defendant in Fort Payne, Alabama. This information, which should have been suppressed, was used by the state in its case-in-chief and such evidence substantially contributed to defendant's conviction and subsequent sentence to death in the electric chair.

5. Error was committed in this case when the state, knowing its relationship with Eileen Hargis, failed to disclose to the defense that charges were pending against Mrs. Hargis. The state had a duty to disclose this information to the defense and willfully failed to do so. The state explicitly denied that Mrs. Hargis was biased or prejudiced when the defense moved to have her excused and allow the alternate to take her place. This representation was made to the court, on the record. There was an explicit duty to disclose to the court that charges were pending against her at that time, and the state willfully failed to disclose this information to the court. The withholding of this information by the state clearly prejudicial to the administration of the justice.

6. Since the completion of the trial in this case, the attorneys for the defendant have discovered the defendant was unable to cooperate with her attorneys in the preparation of her defense in this case due to the influence on her by her husband, Alvin Neelley. Until Jo Ann Browning testified as to her life with Alvin Neelley, the defendant remained under his influence. The defendant would not admit to her attorneys the truth of the facts in this case until she testified under oath from a witness stand. Thus, the attorneys for the defendant heard the truth as to the facts in this case at the same time the court and jury heard said facts. Although the attorneys for the defendant believed they knew the facts of this case, a comparison of the opening statement of the attorneys for the defense is at variance with the defendant's testimony in a number of important different aspects of the case. Subsequent to the trial of this case and the sentence of the Court entered thereon, attorneys for the defendant were contacted

by experts who had heard about this case in other states. Said experts in the field of persuasive coercion and learned helplessness, wife battering, and domestic violence volunteered their services as witnesses on behalf of the defendant should the defendant be granted a new trial. These witnesses are recognized experts in their fields of expertise. Attorneys for defendant did not have the means nor the knowledge to make these witnesses available to the Court and jury at the trial of this case.

Attorneys for defendant can now prove the Dependent Personality Disorder of the defendant in conjunction with the total domination of Alvin Neelley over the person of Judith Ann Neelley deprived defendant of the requisite intent to kill Lisa Ann Millican. Such witnesses were not discovered by defense attorneys prior to the trial of this case and the sentence entered thereon.

7. The court erred in denying defense motions for a verdict by acquittal made at the conclusion of the state's case, the case of the defendant, and renewed at the conclusion of the trial of this case.

8. By allowing the alleged confessions of the defendant to be admitted over the objection of the defendant and by allowing illegally seized evidence to be admitted against the defendant, the defendant was forced to take the stand and testify in her own behalf. As a result, she was deprived of her right against self incrimination and she was deprived of her right to remain silent rather than testify against herself.

9. The verdict of the jury and the sentence of the court are contrary to the law and the evidence in this case.

10. The court committed error in overruling the recommendation of the jury and entering a death penalty in the sentence in this case.

11. The Alabama Law relating to capital punishment is unconstitutional.

12. The court committed error in failing to sustain each and every motion made by the defendant during the course of the trial of this case.

13. The court erred in failing to sustain defendant's objections in each and every instance where and when such objections were overruled during the course of the trial.

14. The court erred in failing to sustain defendant's motion to exclude the evidence made at the end of the state's case.

15. The court erred in failing to overrule each and every objection made and offered by the state in regard to evidence and testimony offered by the defense during the trial.

16. The court erred in denying the pre-trial motions of the defendant.

17. The court erred in failing to grant to the defendant youthful offender status.

18. The court erred in failing to find that the defendant was insane at the time of the commission of the act charged against her by the State of Alabama.

19. The death penalty, as administered by the State of Alabama, is cruel and unusual punishment, illegal and unconstitutional.

20. The electric chair used by the State of Alabama for the purpose of executions is antiquated and in disrepair. This instrument of death is not suitable for killing dogs. It was constructed by an Alabama prison inmate in the early 1930's and has not been renovated since its construction.

21. The sentence of the defendant by the court is unconstitutional and continues cruel and unusual punishment.

22. A new trial should be granted to the defendant because of the prejudicial impact of emotional outbursts in the courtroom by members of the audience hostile to the defendant, Time and again the court was forced to call down the audience because of its conduct toward

the defendant in the presence of the jury. Members of the audience talked loud enough to be heard by the jury in an effort to influence the jury against the defendant. One courtroom audience member stated in a voice loud enough to be heard all over the courtroom, "I'll pay the electric bill if they'll pull the switch." Another said, "I think I'll have a barbecue for lunch. The jury should barbecue her for lunch." Another said, "Frying her is too good. She should be taken to the canyon and injected with Drano, shot in the back, and thrown in the canyon." A woman was heard to say, "They ought to kill her and her lawyer both." One spectator held up a newspaper for the jury to see the headline which was derogatory to the defendant. Many female spectators commented in stage whispers, overheard by the jury, that the defendant did not shed a tear on the stand, she was not sorry for what she did, and she was only saying what Bob French told her to say. Another spectator held up an "Alabama" LP record jacket. Apparently, this was done to attract the attention of Eileen Hargis, who had recently been employed by the Alabama Band and was wearing an Alabama Band jacket in the jury box each day.

The courtroom spectators clapped and cheered on one occasion when the prosecution witness made a point against the cross_examiner for the defendant. The spectators made the trial have the atmosphere of an athletic contest where the prosecutors were the home team and the defense were the bad guys. Time and again the jury could hear the approval of the audience with the manner in which the trial was progressing. Members of the audience clearly let the jury know that they wanted the defendant not only convicted, but also electrocuted. The hatred of the audience for the defendant was so apparent it could be felt in the courtroom by the defense. Certainly this attitude by the spectators was recognized by the jury, and the jurors were influenced by the same. Thus, the defendant did not receive a fair trial.

There were members of the audience who sat near the west wall of the courtroom where they might stage whisper to their neighbor and be overheard by some of the jurors and the defense. These spectators, both men and women, made comments throughout the trial which were loud enough to be heard by some of the jurors and the Defense. The whispers were not loud enough for the court or state to hear. All of these whispers were derogatory toward the defendant. These whispers consisted of statements about the defendant's demeanor, her clothing, her attorneys, and the crimes of the defendant. Many times these persons were heard to whisper in voices loud enough to be heard by the jury, "Al made me do it." They made these statements before the defendant could answer questions being propounded to her on the stand. These statements were made by one particular woman who assumed the role of a folk hero by entertaining her section of the courtroom with this phrase each time a question was asked the defendant. Members of the jury heard this woman make these comments and some of them found her quite amusing. These statements denied the impact of the defendant's answers to the jury and turned her testimony into a comedy before the jury.

Although the court warned the audience time and again to refrain from commenting on the evidence in this case, the spectators on the west wall, nearest the jury, constantly attempted to influence the jury with their comments and statements regarding the case. As a result, the defendant did not receive a fair trial.

23. The age of the defendant, 18, renders the death penalty in this case as cruel and unusual punishment.

Respectfully submitted,
Robert B. French, Jr.,
Attorney for the Defendant.

Amendment To Motion For New Trial

Comes the Defendant, Judith Ann Neelley, by her attorneys, and amends her original Motion for New Trial to move the court for a reconsideration of the sentence imposed as grounds for this motion cite in addition to the grounds specifically enumerated in the Motion for New Trial the following grounds, to-wit:

1. The findings of fact, the sentencing order, the findings concerning the existence or nonexistence of aggravating circumstances, the findings concerning the existence or nonexistence of mitigating circumstances, and the sentence imposed by the court are contrary to the law.

2. The findings of fact, the sentencing order, the findings concerning the existence or nonexistence of aggravating circumstances, the findings concerning the existence or nonexistence of mitigating circumstances, and the sentence imposed by the court are contrary to the evidence in this case.

Respectfully submitted,
Robert B. French, Jr.,
Attorney for the Defendant.

Second Amendment To Motion For New Trial

Comes the Defendant, Judith Ann Neelley, by her attorneys, and amends her original Motion for New Trial and her first Amendment to Motion for New Trial to include the additional grounds, to-wit:

3. The Alabama Law relating to capital punishment is unconstitutional in that it imposes upon the one convicted of a capital offense the burden of proof in the sentencing phase.

Respectfully submitted,
Robert B. French, Jr.,
Attorney for the Defendant.

Third Amendment To Motion For New Trial

Comes now the Defendant, Judith Ann Neelley, by her attorneys, and amends her original Motion for new Trial and her first and second amendments to Motion for New Trial to include the additional ground to_wit:

4. The court committed error in granting the state's strikes for cause of prospective jurors who professed the belief that under no circumstances would they impose the death penalty when such a response would have no bearing in the guilt phase of the trial and only at best a limited bearing in the sentence recommendations phase of the trial.

5. The verdict was based on the misconduct of one of the trial jurors, Eileen Hargis, and said misconduct was not known to the defendant before she went to trial, or could not have been known in the course of exercising due diligence. It is shown unto the court that attorneys for the defendant conducted extensive research into the backgrounds of each prospective juror and said research determined the following in regard to Eileen Hargis; She had lived on Lookout Mountain near the Chief of Police, Bob Parker, and that she had just moved here. She worked for the Alabama Band where she was on the road for a while and later worked in the warehouse. She subsequently was fired. Her husband, James, still worked for Wild Stallions, the people who sell souvenirs for the Alabama Band. Apparently, she and her husband had no marital problems. They have had four or five children, some grown and others young. She was bossy and strong_willed, and didn't take anything off anyone. She was not very religious, but was gossipy and talked too much and could talk for hours. She didn't care what others thought of her, and she was kind of odd. At least one individual stated that they would not want her on a jury if that person were being tried. In exercising due diligence in determining the qualifications of the juror, the attorneys for the defendant talked to neighbors, friends, and former fellow workers with Eileen Hargis.

During voir dire examination, the attorneys for the defendant propounded questions to prospective jurors in panels of 20 persons each. Eileen Hargis was a prospective juror in the second panel questioned. She and her panel were questioned as to their interest in the case and other matters tending to show bias or prejudice. On one occasion the attorney for the defendant asked the following question:

"I talked with you earlier about non-violent crimes and violet crimes that had perhaps affected you. I want to ask you, just in case I missed it--I'm not even going to talk about crime. I'm just going to talk about criminal acts, something nobody was prosecuted for. Have any of you or any of your close relatives or close friends ever been involved in a criminal act, and I'll exclude Terry on this. I'm talking about a criminal act that has affected your life." (No response).

At another point in the voir dire examination the attorney for the defendant asked:

"Mr. Igou asked you if you knew myself and the others as part of the Defense team. Let me just ask you if you know Richard and Michael, other than Mr. Dilbeck? Richard Igou and Michael O'Dell, do any of you know them?"

At the time, the foregoing questions were propounded to Juror Hargis and others of her panel. She knew that charges were pending against her for passing bad checks. She had recently settled one of the cases with representatives of the state. She had other charges still pending in the District Court of DeKalb County, Alabama. Yet, she did not respond truthfully to the questions propounded by the Defense.

The Defense had a right to have the questions propounded answered fully and truthfully. The response of the prospective juror would have affected her qualifications to serve on this jury so far as the Defense was concerned. The correct answers to the two questions quoted herein would have resulted in her being struck by the Defense. Contrarily, by failing to fully and accurately answer the questions, the juror was selected to serve on the jury and was the foreman of the jury.

The information concerning this juror was withheld from the Defense by the juror and by the state. This information was not known to the defendant nor her attorneys prior to the trial; and the defendant, nor her attorneys, could have discovered this information through the exercise of due diligence.

This case involves capital murder. The attorneys for the defendant investigated each potential juror individually by interviewing neighbors, friends, acquaintances, and community leaders. Since the attorneys for the defendant anticipated honest and complete answers from the prospective jurors on the voir dire, they did not check the court records of all the courts in Dekalb County, Alabama, to determine if any of the prospective jurors had charges pending against them. Such action on the part of the attorneys would have been beyond the exercise of diligence and would have required the attorneys appointed to represent the defendant and devote full time to the case of the defendant.

There are other allegations in this motion for new trial involving this juror. Certainly, this juror would have been struck by the Defense had it been made known to the Defense that the juror had cases pending against her and she was working out a settlement of those cases with the state.

Respectfully submitted,
Robert B. French, Jr.,
Attorney for Defendant.

APPENDIX 5

Testimony of Robert B. French, Jr. - trial preparation

Q. "Well, from our initial interviews with her, we went forward and attempted to marshal the facts. We had difficulty in marshaling the facts because of our initial interviews with her. Subsequent interviews were more fruitful but not necessarily truthful. We marshaled the facts and researched the law and generally wrote memorandums which we placed in the file to as to trial strategy and how this case should be presented before the jury and as to what kind of jurors we needed. We did a profile on the jurors that we felt would be most suitable for this case, and then we commenced - when the jury list was published and after the pre_trial activities were completed - when we received the jury list - then we began our investigation of the potential jurors.

Q. What did those steps consist of?

A. From the time we received the jury list -- We had in our office eleven file drawers of juror cards. We maintain a card on every client. We maintain a card on every defendant in our cases. We maintain cards on almost every person that ever served on one of our juries. We maintain cards and we apply information to those cards as to -- for example all members of the First Baptist Church. Due to my political affiliation, I keep up with all people I know who are Republicans. We keep up with members of the Junior Chamber of Commerce, the Jaycees, the Rotary Club. If we can find out a person is a member of a garden club, we put that on the card. We had as much information as possible on the cards, and as I said, there are eleven boxes of them, and I'm sure each box contains several hundred cards. Once we receive a venire list, one of the secretaries is assigned the job of pulling cards that we had on each member of the venire. From that information, we get a small card like I'm holding right here on, for example, Brenda Chapman. This came directly from our card file, and this shows where she lives, what her phone number is, who her sister is, that she's related to the Blevins', that she is a housewife, what her birthday is, that she's related to Bernard and Gerald, who her husband is and what he does for a living, and what we feel about her. She was part of this venire. We had a card on each juror like that. This information is then transported to a larger card at the time we strike the jury, and this card is made specifically for this case, and we take all of this information and then we go into the communities where these people live and we talk to people who we know who know them and we reduce that information to this card. When we come to trial for the venire we had these five by seven cards on each member of the venire. We know all of our information about them and we had talked with their neighbors. We had tried to view where they live and we had talked with their friends and community leaders, anybody who might know them, and we run them down until we know a juror - until we had a profile, and in this case we, then, had a juror profile information sheet in which we put profile information. This one happens to be Sandra Bain who was on this jury. We make a profile of the juror, and all of that is in preparation for the voir dire examination, so that when a juror actually walks into the courtroom we know that juror, and we did that here, and then we prepared an exhaustive, I thought, voir dire examination to find out opinions, to find out bias, prejudices, and to comply with our ideas, put into our original memorandums the type juror we needed in this case. There were some definite jurors that we were not going to had, and we had them listed on this sheet, and after the voir dire examination is over, as to how the juror responded, then we take this main card on the juror, in conjunction with what we got from the juror on voir dire, and at that point in time we make a decision as to whom we would strike off.

Q. What did you learn about Mrs. Hargis?

A. She lived right near myself and Chief of Police of Fort Payne, Bob Parker. We live almost across the street from each other. She had lived in that community, but I could not find out anything about her in the neighborhood because she had been traveling on the road with the -- I believe it's the Wild Stallion group – with the road crew. They sell the souvenirs for the Alabama Band. She and her husband were both employed by that group. In other words, they would go with the Alabama Band and they would sell T-shirts and buttons and whatever they sell. So, our card reflects that she had just moved here, she had worked for the Alabama Band, she was on the road for quite some time, and her husband stayed on the road while she came into the warehouse. I think the warehouse is down here on the south end of town. After she came into the warehouse, from that point on we were able to find out information about her from her fellow work-ers. We interviewed various and sundry fellow workers with the Alabama group, and we found that she had been fired from the group, that her husband's name was James, that he still worked for the Wild Stallions, that they were the people who were in charge of selling souvenirs. She was a very difficult - a very dili-gent worker. She worked very hard. So far as we could determine she had been in no trouble. She had no trouble with her husband. She had been married before, she had four or five children, she had some grown children and some young children. The peo-ple who worked with her felt that she was bossy, strong-willed, doesn't take anything off of anyone, she is not very religious, she gossips, talks too much, she can talk for hours, she generally is her own person, she does not care what others think of her. One person told us she was kind of odd. One person told us that if she were being tried she would not want her on her jury. That was the information we had when we waited for her to walk in the door, and based upon the profile, when she walked in the door over there I knew exactly who she was.

APPENDIX 6

The Court's final order denying the Motion for New Trial

ORDER

The defendant filed a motion for new trial, and evidence was presented on the motion at hearings before the court on June 21, 1983 and July 1, 1983. The motion is submitted to the court on the evidence, a brief filed by the defendant on August 8, 1983, and the district attorney's response thereto.

I.

The first issue raised by the defendant's motion for new trial is whether the court erred by admitting into evidence two out-of-court confessions made by the defendant to law enforcement officers while she was in custody.

The first confession was made by the defendant while she was incarcerated at the Rutherford County jail in Murfreesboro, Tennessee, on forged money order charges. Upon learning that the defendant was incarcerated, an FBI agent from Rome, Georgia, and other law enforcement officers investigating the murder of Lisa Ann Millican went to Murfreesboro and interviewed the defendant on October 14, 1982. During the interview, the defendant confessed to the murder of Lisa Millican and related other incriminating information about events leading up to the murder and events which followed.

A Murfreesboro attorney, Bill Burton, had been retained by the defendant's husband to represent the defendant on the forged money order charges, and the attorney had accompanied the defendant to a preliminary hearing on such charges a day or two before October 14. While law enforcement officers were interviewing the defendant, attorney Burton appeared in the hallway outside the interview room and requested that he be allowed to enter the room where the interview was being conducted, but his request was denied.

The defendant contends that this denial, coupled with the fact that she was not told of the attorney's availability, made the defendant's waiver of her right to counsel involuntary and her confession inadmissible.

The court makes the following findings of fact regarding the defendant's statement of October 14, 1982:

a. Prior to making the statement, the defendant was properly advised of her constitutional rights as enumerated in Miranda.

b. The defendant made a voluntary and understanding waiver of her constitutional rights including her right to have counsel present during the interview. c. The defendant was advised on numerous occasions during the interview of her constitutional rights and that the interview would be terminated upon her request, and she voluntarily elected to continue the interview.

d. The defendant's statements during the interview were the product of a rational intellect and a free will.

e. Attorney Bill Burton did not represent the defendant in connection with the murder of Lisa Millican, the offense about which the defendant was being interviewed, and the refusal to admit him into the interview room was not an interference with the attorney-client relationship.

f. The defendant did not request to have attorney Burton or any other attorney present during the interview.

g. There were no threats, trickery, or cajolery practiced by law enforcement officers during the course of the interview, and there was no improper influence, intimidation, coercion or other inducement made to obtain the statement.

h. Considering the totality of the circumstances, the confession was voluntarily made. The defendant made an additional statement to Investigator Danny Smith on October

15, 1982, after being charged with the murder of Lisa Millican and returned to Fort Payne, Alabama. This statement repeated much of the information related by the defendant in the earlier interview but added some details not furnished earlier.

The defendant contends that this statement was a continuation of the interview which had been conducted the night before in Murfreesboro, and that if the first confession was involuntary, then the second one fails as well.

The court makes the following findings of fact regarding the defendant's statement of October 15, 1982:

a. Prior to making the statement, the defendant was advised of her constitutional rights as enumerated in Miranda.

b. The defendant made a voluntary and understanding waiver of her constitutional rights.

c. There were no threats, trickery or cajolery practiced by law enforcement officers during the course of the interview, and there was no improper influence, intimidation, coercion or other inducement made to obtain the statement.

d. The defendant's confession was the product of a rational intellect and a free would.

e. Considering the totality of the circumstances, the defendant's confession was voluntarily made.

The defendant took the witness stand at her trial and admitted that she killed Lisa Millican. The primary difference between her trial testimony and her out-of-court confessions was the motivation she expressed for the killing. In both her trial testimony and her out-of-court confessions, however, she admitted that she shot Lisa Millican and threw her body into a deep canyon after efforts to kill her by injections of liquid drain cleaner failed.

If a defendant takes the stand and admits facts essentially the same as those contained in an out-of-court confession, the defendant cannot complain that the confession was illegally obtained and erroneously admitted into evidence. Thomas v. State, 373 So.2d 1149 (Ala. Cr. App. 1979). It is the judgment of this court that even if the confessions were involuntarily made as contended by the defendant, the error of their admission into evidence was cured by the defendant's taking the witness stand and admitting facts essentially the same as those contained in the out-of-court confessions.

II.

The court finds that the juror, Eileen Hargis, was not bias and was not guilty of misconduct prejudicial to the defendant. The court is convinced from the evidence presented at the hearing on defendant's motion for new trial and its own knowledge of events occurring in the courtroom during the trial that the juror did not mouth the words "object, object" to the prosecution during defense counsel's cross-examination of a state's witness. The court finds that the incident on which this allegation is based was, in fact, an effort on the part of the juror to get the attention of the bailiff, Martha McPherson, who was seated near the district attorney.

This allegation of misconduct by the juror was first made by defense counsel at the conclusion of testimony on the day of the alleged incident, at which time, counsel requested that the juror be replaced by an alternate. Before ruling on the request, the court offered defense counsel an opportunity to present evidence in support of the allegation but the offer was declined. The court did not observe the alleged misconduct charged by defense counsel and, therefore, there was absolutely no evidence before the court which would justify removal of the juror; nevertheless, the court reserved a ruling on the request until immediately before submission of the case to the jury so that the court might direct its attention to the juror's demeanor and conduct during that portion of the trial remaining prior to submission.

Immediately prior to submission of the case to the jury, the court denied the request that Mrs. Hargis be replaced. The denial was accompanied by the following statement by the court:

I have observed her very carefully today during the course of these arguments, and I have found her, for the most part, to be very attentive to both your argument (defense counsel's) as well as the state's argument. There were times when she looked away and didn't keep her eyes on either of you, but I think for the most part, I was convinced from her demeanor today that she was appropriately attentive.

The court observed no communication, verbal or non-verbal, between the juror and prosecutors or between the juror and courtroom spectators. The court observed nothing during this lengthy trial which would necessitate or support a finding of misconduct or bias on the part of the juror or that would require her replacement by an alternate juror.

The defendant's allegation that the juror Hargis inappropriately usurped the position of jury foreman is without merit. The allegation is unsupported by the evidence, but even if the evidence supported the allegation, such conduct would not be an indication of bias or corruption in performance of the juror's duty, nor would it indicate that the jury's verdict was wrongfully influenced. See Carr v. Irons, 288 Ala. 211, 259 So.2d 240 (1972). Also, it is a settled principle of law that conduct and remarks of jurors during deliberation were not such "extraneous facts" as would be permitted to impeach a jury's verdict.

The defendant contends that the juror Hargis improperly responded to two *voir dire* questions propounded by defense counsel, the first of the two questions being as follows:

Attorney French :I talked with you earlier about non-violent crimes and about violent crimes that have perhaps affected you. I want to ask you, just in case I missed it -- Was going to talk about criminal acts, something nobody was prosecuted for. Have any of you or any of your close relatives or close friends ever been involved in a criminal act, and I'll exclude Terry on this. Was talking about criminal acts that have affected your life.

The juror Hargis did not offer any response to this question. At the hearing on motion for new trial, it was established that Mrs. Hargis had been charged in the District Court of DeKalb County with five cases of worthless checks, all of which were pending at the time of the *voir dire* examination. Mrs. Hargis testified at the hearing on motion for new trial that although these charges were placed against her, she never believed she had committed a criminal act and that her attorney had advised her that writing the checks was not a criminal act because she lacked criminal intent.

Mrs. Hargis' attorney testified that prior to Mrs. Hargis' involvement in the Neelley trial, he had negotiated a dismissal of the cases against Mrs. Hargis whereby she would pay restitution and court cost, and that the cases remained pending at the time of the Neelley trial solely for payment by Mrs. Hargis of the sums due.

Without regard to Mrs. Hargis' belief about whether she had committed a criminal act by writing worthless checks, a response to defense counsel's question which would reveal the pending charges was not required by Mrs. Hargis because of the context in which the question was asked. The question was prefaced by a reference to an earlier series of questions which sought to elicit if any of the venire had been the victim of criminal activity. In this context, the question set forth above appeared to be calling for responses from any member of the venire who had been <u>the victim of unprosecuted criminal activity</u>. Evidence that this was the intent of the question is found in the fact that defense counsel excluded a member of the venire named "Terry" from the question. In the earlier series of questions, this venireman had revealed that his father was killed by a drunken driver.

Even if the question is construed to call for responses from members of the venire about criminal acts in which they have engaged, it is clear that the question had reference only to criminal acts for which nobody was prosecuted. Because Mrs. Hargis' writing of worthless checks was conducted for which she was prosecuted, such conduct and the resultant charges were not within the scope of the question. The court concludes that the question set forth above did not reasonably seek to elicit the information which defendant now contends was improperly withheld by the juror Hargis.

The second question which the defendant contends was answered improperly by juror Hargis is as follows:

Attorney French:Mr. Igou, (the district attorney), asked you if you knew of myself and the others as part of the defense team. Let me just ask you if you know Richard and Michael, other than Mr. Dilbeck? Richard Igou and Michael O'Dell (the deputy district attorney), do any of you know them?

Mrs. Hargis gave no response to this question. The defendant contends that Mrs. Hargis knew the state's prosecutors as a result of the worthless check charges pending against her and the negotiations which occurred in connection with the disposition of those charges. The evidence, however, does not support this contention. Mrs. Hargis' attorney testified that he handled the negotiations with the district attorney's office and that Mrs. Hargis was not present at the time and had no personal contact with either of the prosecutors. Mrs. Hargis testified that she was not acquainted with either of the prosecutors prior to the commencement of the Neelley trial, and there is no evidence to the contrary. The court finds that Mrs. Hargis was not acquainted with the prosecutors before the trial and that her lack of response to defense counsel's question was not improper.

The court finds no probable prejudice resulted to the defendant from the responses or lack of responses by juror Hargis during the voir dire examination by counsel.

Further, the defendant alleges that the prosecutors wrongfully withheld from defense counsel their knowledge of Mrs. Hargis' pending cases. Assuming arguendo that the prosecutors had a duty to make such disclosure, the court finds that there was no breach of that duty because the information was not brought to their attention until after the jury was struck and impaneled. This finding is based on the testimony of Deputy District Attorney Michael O'Dell that he did not connect juror Hargis with the worthless check charges until it was called to his attention by an employee of the clerk's office after the jury was struck.

III

The defendant contends that it was error for the court to allow evidence of the following events which occurred subsequent to the killing of Lisa Ann Millican: (a) that the defendant shot John Hancock, (b) that the defendant shot and killed Janice Chapman, and (c) that the defendant attempted to lure other potential victims.

The evidence in this case established that the abduction of Lisa Ann Millican was part of a bizarre scheme whereby the defendant attempted to lure girls and young women into the car with her for the ultimate purpose of making them available to her husband for sex. For several days immediately prior to Lisa Millican's abduction, the defendant and her husband drove up and down the streets of Rome, Georgia, in separate automobiles looking for girls who would be suitable. When the defendant's husband would see a suitable girl, he would communicate with the defendant by CB radio, and the defendant would invite the girt to go riding around with her. Numerous girls refused the defendant's invitation; her first successful pick-up was Lisa Millican. After Lisa Millican was killed, the defendant and her husband went back to Rome and continued to look for girls. Five days after the death of Lisa Millican, the defendant picked up a young woman named Janice Chapman and her common-law husband, John Hancock, from a street in Rome. Later that night, the defendant shot Hancock in the back and left him for dead - although he survived. The defendant and her husband took Janice Chapman to a motel where the husband engaged in sex with Janice. The next day, the defendant killed Janice, shooting her once in the back and twice in the chest. Less than a week thereafter, the defendant picked up yet another young woman who also became a sexual companion for her husband.

It is settled law that evidence of the accused's commission of another crime is admissible if it tends to prove that the crime presently charged was committed pursuant to a single plan, design, scheme or system. The evidence of which the defendant complains was admitted for that purpose and its admissibility clearly is within the scope of the stated rule.

IV.

An additional ground of the defendant's motion is her assertion that there were emotional outbursts in the courtroom during the trial which, along with comments from spectators, prejudiced jurors against the defendant. An emotional outburst from spectators occurred on one occasion but the jury was not in the courtroom at that time. The outburst was in the form of applause from certain members of the audience during a suppression hearing from which the jurors had been excluded. The court finds that no prejudice to the defendant resulted from this occurrence.

Two media representatives who covered the trial and three other spectators testified at the hearing on motion for new trial that they overheard prejudicial remarks made by individual courtroom spectators at various times during the trial which were loud enough for jurors to hear. The court did not hear the remarks and concludes that any such remarks were not heard by the jury. This conclusion is based upon the court's observations during the trial of which it takes judicial notice, the testimony of jurors who testified at the hearing on motion for new trial that they did not hear the remarks and, further, upon the fact that spectator comments were less likely to be heard by the jury than by media representatives and other spectators because of the physical layout of the courtroom.

Because public interest in this trial was high and spectator seats were filled every day with additional spectators waiting outside the courtroom to enter, the court employed procedures designed to prevent spectator interference with the fair and orderly conduct of the trial. The following were some of the special procedures:

a. Spectators were allowed in the courtroom only to the extent that there were seats to accommodate them.

b. Law enforcement personnel provided security at the door of the courtroom to regulate the entrance by spectators.

c. The court routinely instructed spectators that they should not talk aloud or whisper while the jury was in the courtroom.

d. Law enforcement personnel were stationed in the spectator section, with orders from the court to remove spectators who did not comply with the court's instructions.

e. A row of seats across the front of the spectator section was reserved for news media representatives; thus the media representatives sat between the jury and the spectators.

The court adopted early in the trial a firm approach to spectator behavior, and gave close attention to the spectator section during much of the trial when other matters did not require the court's attention. On one occasion, the court privately reprimanded a spectator who sat near the back of the courtroom for making facial expressions in response to the testimony of a witness. This incident was not observed by the jury and at no time during the trial did the court see or hear any misconduct from a spectator which appeared to have been observed by a juror. The spectator section was orderly at all times, with the exception of the one emotional outburst mentioned above which occurred when the jury was not in the courtroom, and the court finds that the defendant was not prejudiced by spectator conduct.

In support of her motion for new trial, the defendant offered the testimony of Dr. Margaret Nichols, a clinical psychologist, experienced in counseling battered women. The essence of Dr. Nichols' testimony was that the defendant's behavior pattern fits the battered woman syndrome, and that the defendant was, in Dr. Nichols' judgment, totally under the control of her husband at the time she killed Lisa Millican. These conclusions were based upon an interview with the defendant conducted by Dr. Nichols on the day before the hearing and upon relevant information supplied by the defendant's counsel.

For the court to grant a new trial on the basis of newly discovered evidence, the defendant must meet the following requirements: (1) that the evidence is such as would probably change the result if a new trial is granted, (2) that the evidence have been discovered since the trial, (3) that it could not have been discovered before trial by the exercise of due diligence, (4) that it is material to the issues, and (5) that it is not merely cumulative or impeaching. The court finds that Dr. Nichols' testimony is not such evidence as would probably change the result in a new trial, and further finds that evidence from an expert witness in the same field as Dr. Nichols could have been discovered before trial by the exercise of due diligence. It follows that Dr. Nichols' testimony is insufficient evidence on which to grant a new trial.

VI.

The court has examined all the grounds asserted by the defendant in her motion and finds that none of them merits the granting of a new trial. It is the judgment of the court that the defendant received a fair trial free from error prejudicial to her rights and, accordingly,

IT IS ADJUDGED AND DECREED that the motion for new trial, as amended, is denied.

DATED SEPTEMBER 6, 1983
Randall L. Cole, Circuit Judge.
Copy of this order to Honorable A. Richard Igou,
Honorable Robert B. French, Jr., and
Honorable Stephen P. Bussman.

AFTERWARD

The years have passed, and times have changed. Although she is not on death row, Judith Ann Neelley has been in Tutwiler Prison for Women for more than 32 years. Her present attorney is attempting to have her released to Georgia. If Ragsdale is successful in transferring her to Georgia, more than likely Georgia will parole her for time served. I believe she pled guilty in Georgia and received a life sentence. For the record, she is eligible for parole in Alabama at this time.

Looking back on the case, there are a number of things that still baffle me: Judge Cole's rulings - his sentencing, and his denial of the Motion for New Trial. The affirmation of his rulings by the Alabama Court of Criminal Appeals, the Alabama Supreme Court, and the U.S. Supreme Court are a puzzlement. I can only conclude that the Neelley crimes were so heinous that the judges could not get past the criminal acts perpetrated on the victims to the legal issues involved.

Succinctly stated, look at the legal issues they successfully explained away, or danced around, with adroit legal gymnastics:

1. **Does a citizen accused have to ask for his or her lawyer by name before being interrogated?**

   Bill Burton, Neelley's duly retained attorney, went to the jail at night to protect his client. He was denied access to her until her confession was extracted. The excuse was that she did not ask for an attorney or she was not being questioned about what he had been retained to defend. She testified that she did not know Burton was there, and had asked to see him before she was questioned, as he was her attorney.

2. **Where an attorney has been duly retained to protect his client, can that attorney be prohibited from protecting his client based upon the fact his client is being questioned about something he has not been specifically retained to defend?**

The ruling on this issue defies logic. It took some real legal gymnastics to sustain the questioning of Neelley while Burton had her retainer in his pocket and was denied access to his client until she confessed to kidnapping and murder.

Confessions are never considered to be voluntarily. The courts had to conjure up magic to find Neelley's confession voluntary. I have been involved with a lot of confessions, and I have never had an officer of the law testify it was not voluntary. According to officers, the citizen accused always wants to keep talking and to confess. The citizen denies the confession was freely given, but the courts usually believe the officers.

Once the Court allowed the confessions, Neelley had to testify. Then, the Court said that she admitted to murder on the stand and was precluded from saying the original confession was not voluntary. This is a legal conundrum.

3. **Can the prosecution of a citizen accused willfully hide evidence that might contribute toward his or her exoneration?**

I didn't discuss this issue earlier as we learned about the evidence late in the trial. The Chattooga County Georgia Sheriff's Department admitted that it had intentionally hidden more than 200 pieces of evidence that would have gone a long way toward exonerating Judith Ann Neelley. The Court said that this evidence was simply cumulative. How did the Court know what was there? We were given a few innocuous letters and papers. The officers were never required to explain what they had, where it was found, nor what it was. The Court sustained police misconduct at its highest level.

4. **Can a potential juror willfully lie to the attorney conducting *voir dire* examination testing the qualifications of the jurors?**

The very meaning of *Voir Dire* is to speak the truth. Eileen Hargis did not answer truthfully during *Voir Dire* examination as a potential juror. During Neelley, the Supreme Court reversed a case that I had tried in Baldwin County where a juror did not answer that he had served on a jury in the past. Hargis had charges pending against her. She knew the questions and her responsibility was to answer truthfully. Yet, the Hargis violation of the Alabama Law was legally ignored. Not only that, she seized the foremanship of the jury because she thought it was to her advantage due to the charges pending and represented the position of the State asking for the death penalty.

5. **Can a criminal defense attorney, who knows his client has charges pending and is on the jury, come to the State's table and influence his client-juror in the State's favor?**

Eileen Hargis' Attorney, Charles McGee, came to the courtroom for the express purpose of swaying her to the State. ADA Mike O'Dell went along with it. Both of them knew what they were doing. I knew that something was happening that was wrong, but I didn't know what it was until after the trial. DA Richard Igou did not know of their chicanery. However, once this jury tampering was made known to him, he did nothing about it and defended the outcome of the case.

———

At some point, perhaps the late '80's or early '90's, Judith Ann Neelley began writing to a battered woman in Gadsden - Alisha Diane Wall. I know very little about their relationship, other than Wall had visited Judy at Tutwiler on several occasions. According to Wall's father, Judy called him and asked if he minded that she and Alisha had fallen in love. This has been contested by Neelley's Lawyer, Barry Ragsdale.

Judith Ann Neelley, having given up all hope of ever escaping death by electrocution, and Alisha Wall, having nothing to live for, over time devised a pact to commit joint suicide. They chose a day and an hour when they would carry out their pact. The 26-year-old Wall took a shotgun, pointed it at her throat, and pulled the trigger. At that same time, I believe 10:00 p.m., May 19, 1994, Judith Ann Neelley slashed both of her wrists with disposable razor blades.

Wall was found; and authorities discovered her pictures, tape recordings, and letters involving Neelley. They immediately called Tutwiler Prison. Staff found Neelley bleeding to death in her cell and rushed her to the hospital saving her life.

Sadly, Judith Ann Neelley had participated in the deaths of three women and the shooting of John Hancock.

Although he died in prison, I cannot imagine a more terrible case than the one perpetrated by Alvin Howard Neelley. His life demonstrates what a maniac can accomplish over time.

Alvin Howard Neelley & Judith Ann Neelley

Lisa Ann Millican

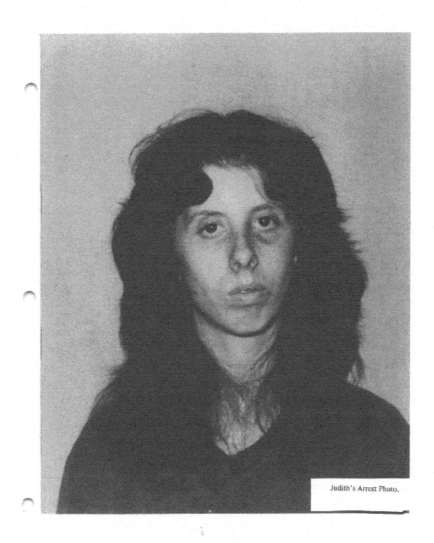

Judith's Arrest Photo.

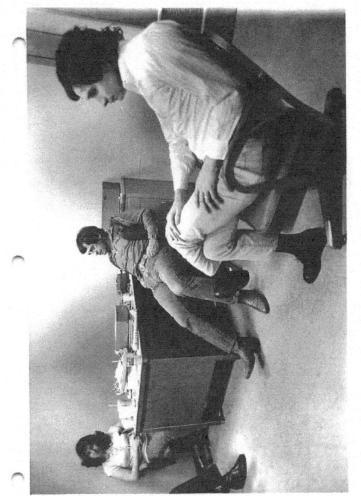

Judith Ann Neelley, Bob French, and Steve Bussman - Preparing for Trial

DAVE DIETER PHOTO

Judith Neelley at trial

DAVE DIETR PHOTO

Investigator James, Sheriff Taylor, Chief Deputy Reed, Judith Ann Neelley and Bob French being escorted to court.

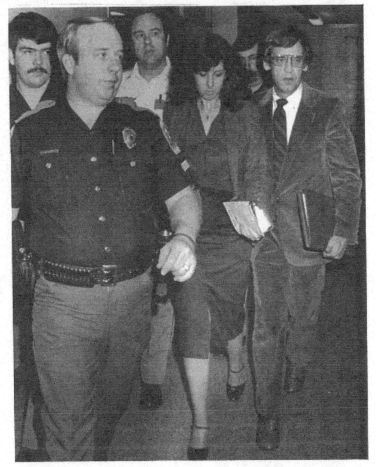

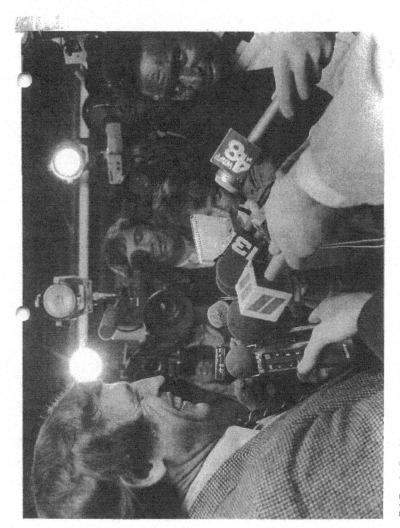

Bob French talks with reporters after the judge had charged the jury.

Dr. Patrick Ewing, author of "Women Who Kill", and Bob French talking to reporters. French stressed after trial.